Accounting Problems of Multinational Enterprises

Accounting Problems of Multinational Enterprises

Elwood L. Miller
Saint Louis University

Lexington Books
D.C. Heath and Company
Lexington, Massachusetts
Toronto

Library of Congress Cataloging in Publication Data

Miller, Elwood L.
    Accounting problems of multinational enterprises.

    Bibliography: p.
    Includes index.
    1. International business enterprises—Accounting. I. Title.
HF5686.I56M54   657'.95   78-20273
ISBN 0-669-02712-X

Second printing, March 1980

Published simultaneously in Canada

Printed in the United States of America

International Standard Book Number: 0-669-02712-X

Library of Congress Catalog Card Number: 78-20273

To my teammate,
Virginia

Contents

List of Figures and Tables

Figures

Tables

Acknowledgments

Few books, if any, are merely written. They are built, literally and figuratively.

Cutting, pasting, and revising manuscripts are necessary but not necessarily interesting chores.

All works are constructed upon the ideas and teachings of others. Copyright regulations require that the words of others be paraphrased when used in quantity or, where paraphrasing would lose the meaning, be reproduced with permission. Such contributions to this book have been appropriately acknowledged. However, the seeds of ideas implanted over time by countless teachers, friends, and associates—many whose names have been forgotten—are woven throughout this work, unacknowledged but not unappreciated.

This work was begun over three years ago out of desperation. A text was required as the foundation for a new course in the area of international accounting, but there were no such books in print. As a result, this book benefits from the refinements of three years of classroom testing.

Particular gratitude is owed to many: to my wife Virginia, for typing every word many times; to Dr. Charles E. Wuller, for his criticism and support; to my son Scott, for his help with the edited manuscript. Special appreciation is due the editors and publishers of *Harvard Business Review* for their permission to use portions of my article, which appeared in the November-December 1978 issue. Special thanks also must go to the editors and publishers at Lexington Books for their interest and efficiency.

Errors of omission or commission are mine.

Suggestions and comments are invited and would be appreciated.

**Part I
The Multinational
Enterprise**

1 Background and Evolution

The multinational enterprise (MNE) is an enigma in many respects. Only a few other topics, such as religion or politics, will divide the discussants into two camps with such opposite viewpoints so stubbornly defended. Individuals, firms, and nations tend to be either for or against the MNE, much as if the subject were a coin having only two sides rather than an "inside" or middle ground. Such is the nature of the multinational enterprise.

As a foundation for examining some of the major accounting problems confronting the MNE today, this chapter will attempt to assess what a multinational enterprise is, some idea of its significance, how it evolved, what caused the expansion, the types and characteristics of MNEs, and some of the challenges confronting the MNE today.

Definitions

A multinational enterprise may be defined in several ways. Traditionally, a firm's "nationality" has been derived from the location of either its ownership or its control. From this standpoint there are no more than a handful of MNEs, since virtually all parent firms are domiciled in a single country, which also is generally the locus of control. Exceptions that come to mind are the Arabian-American Oil Company (Saudi Arabia and the United States), the Royal Dutch/Shell Group, and Unilever (both British and Dutch).

Perhaps the simplest definition is that which considers the MNE a business organization operating in more than one country. Prior to World War II, this description may have been adequate for most purposes. Today, however, such a definition would commingle relatively small corporations having limited overseas operations with industrial giants of mind-boggling proportions. Consequently, the description constructed by Professor Raymond Vernon of Harvard University is widely used today, particularly for statistical purposes. It depicts an MNE as a "parent" or dominant enterprise controlling the operations of a network of foreign corporations and furnishing them with "common" objectives, strategies, and resources. Statistical modifiers specify annual sales above $100 million, operations in at least six countries, and at least 20 percent of total assets represented by overseas subsidiaries.[1]

Using these criteria, more than 4,000 firms worldwide can be classified as MNEs, with the number increasing each year.

The need for quantitative cutoff criteria, such as those mentioned, is understandable but unfortunate. Since the United Nations publishes data only on MNEs that generate sales of more than $100 million, an estimated 44 percent of corporations with international activities do not meet the sales criterion and are excluded. Also, other quantitative measures, such as percentages of assets or sales overseas, are simply statistical devices, and, while necessary, their use does necessarily reduce the total magnitude of international data in published reports.

The multinational enterprise has been described in other ways, such as in the form of models, but these concepts will be examined in the sections that follow concerning attributes of the MNE.

Present Magnitudes

Multinational enterprises overwhelm! The economic activities (sales or gross national products) of the world's 100 largest entities in 1974 are listed in table 1-1. The summary of this listing, provided in table 1-2, indicates that *50 of the largest entities are nations and 50 are multinational enterprises*! Admittedly, sales of corporations are not identical to the gross national products of countries, yet the yardsticks are representative of the relative scope of economic activities.

The world's largest industrial firm (Exxon) posted sales in 1974 larger than the individual GNP of 87 percent of the nations of the free world for which data are available (106 out of a total of 122 nations) and larger than the GNP of the smallest 54 nations combined.

The smallest of the 50 industrial firms (Petrobas) reported 1974 sales larger than the GNP of 72 individual nations (those with a GNP less than $5 billion, as shown in table 1-3) and larger than the GNP of the smallest 18 nations combined.

Another interpretation of magnitude presents itself in the realization that no industrial firm and only 16 free-world nations produced and marketed more in 1974 than Exxon Corporation, the world's largest multinational corporation (MNC).

Estimated sales of goods and services by multinational corporations in 1974 exceeded $650 billion, an amount roughly equal to one-fifth of the gross world product. Given the magnitude of MNEs in the world economy today, it is not at all unusual for an MNE to have annual sales greater than the gross national product of many of the nations in which it operates. The sheer size of most multinational enterprises casts them into roles of desirable yet fearsome partners for developing countries.[2]

Early Predecessors

Trading companies were the earliest ancestors of the multinational enterprise. The colonies of the early empires and the traders of the Middle Ages had one primary purpose in dealings with other countries—to accumulate wealth in the form of gold. Either by necessity or design (or both), some of these early mercantilists diversified their activities until they became importers, exporters, retailers, commercial agents, and small-scale manufacturers with branches in many countries. Typical examples are represented by the families of Dantini of Florence (1335-1410) and the Fuggers of Austria (beginning in the early 1400s, with branches of the family still existing). The international banks quite naturally followed the wake of trade. Among the well-known houses were the Medici and the Fuggers.

Developers (or exploiters) of resources represented the third phase in the evolution of the modern-day MNE. While several resources could be selected, the most notable is oil. The invention of the internal combustion engine initiated an exploration for "black gold" that encompassed most areas of the world. This stage not only ushered in the age of industrialization but also changed the concept of wealth defined as gold to one with an emphasis upon productive capital and useful goods.

The fourth phase in the international development pattern is represented by the transportation industries. Resource exploitation and development could not have proceeded very far without the means to move the materials from the places of extraction to the locations of conversion or use.

The pursuit of markets marks the fifth and present stage of development. Today, international production exceeds international trade. The first European firms developed international operations for two primary reasons: the perishable nature of the product itself (such as margarine in the case of Unilever, and chocolate in Nestle's case) and to overcome the wave of protectionism that followed World War II (Royal Dutch Shell and Philips N.V. of the Netherlands are examples). Early U.S. multinationals also were anxious to offset the effects of protectionism; however, most were concerned with another, possibly more important motivation—to protect their inventions covered by U.S. patents. Singer, Bell Telephone, Otis, Kodak, and National Cash Register are some early cases in point.[3]

For the United States, the MNE is by and large a post-World War II phenomenon. American direct investments in foreign countries were roughly $7 billion in 1940 and primarily represented operations of the oil industry. As of 1975, the book value of U.S. private direct investments overseas was approximately $115 billion—and our share of the world's total was reportedly declining![4]

Based upon the data in table 1-1, although European multinationals may be older, those headquartered in the United States are larger.

Causes of Expansion

International trade paved the way for the free movement of capital to many areas of the world. The United States, for example, became the world's first

Table 1-1
World's 100 Largest Nations and Industrial Firms Ranked by 1974 GNP or Sales
(data in billions of dollars)

Rank	Nation or Firm	GNP or Sales	Hqs. of Firm	Rank	Nation or Firm	GNP or Sales	Hqs. of Firm
1	United States	$1294.9		51	U.S. Steel	$ 9.2	USA
2	Japan	413.1		52	Thailand	9.2	
3	West Germany	348.2		53	Egypt	9.1	
4	France	255.1		54	Standard Oil-Ind.	9.1	USA
5	United Kingdom	174.8		55	Peru	9.1	
6	Italy	138.3		56	Israel	8.9	
7	Canada	118.9		57	Cie Française des Petroles	8.9	France
8	Brazil	77.2		58	Nippon Steel	8.8	Japan
9	India	71.0		59	Thyssen-Hutte	8.7	W.Germ.
10	Argentina	61.4		60	BASF	8.5	W.Germ.
11	Spain	60.2		61	Pakistan	8.3	
12	Netherlands	59.7		62	Hoechst	7.8	W.Germ.
13	Australia	52.2		63	Algeria	7.8	
14	Sweden	50.1		64	Bangladesh	7.7	
15	Mexico	48.6		65	Chile	7.7	
16	Belgium	45.7		66	Shell Oil	7.6	USA
17	Exxon	42.1	USA	67	Saudi Arabia	7.6	
18	Switzerland	40.9		68	Western Electric	7.5	USA
19	Royal Dutch Shell	33.0	UK/Neth.	69	ENI (Oil)	7.4	Italy
20	General Motors	31.5	USA	70	Kuwait	7.2	
21	Austria	27.9		71	Continental Oil	7.2	USA
22	Denmark	27.3		72	Imperial Chem.	7.0	UK
23	South Africa	26.1		73	E.I. duPont	6.9	USA
24	Iran	25.6		74	Atlantic Richfield	6.9	USA
25	Ford Motor	23.6	USA	75	Siemens	6.7	W.Germ.
26	Texaco	23.2	USA	76	Iraq	6.7	
27	Turkey	22.0		77	Volkswagen	6.6	W.Germ.
28	Mobil Oil	18.9	USA				

29	Norway	18.7		
30	*British Petroleum*	18.3	*UK*	
31	*Standard Oil-Calif.*	17.2	*USA*	
32	Finland	17.1		
33	*National Iranian Oil*	16.8	*Iran*	
34	*Gulf Oil*	16.5	*USA*	
35	Greece	16.3		
36	Venezuela	16.1		
37	Indonesia	15.4		
38	Nigeria	14.8		
39	*Unilever*	13.7	*UK*	
40	*General Electric*	13.4	*USA*	
41	*IBM*	12.7	*USA*	
42	South Korea	12.4		
43	New Zealand	11.7		
44	Portugal	11.2		
45	*ITT*	11.1	*USA*	
46	*Chrysler Corp.*	11.0	*USA*	
47	Philippines	10.3		
48	Taiwan	10.2		
49	Colombia	10.0		
50	*Philips NV*	9.4	*Neth.*	
78	Malaysia	6.6		
79	Ireland	6.6		
80	*Westinghouse*	6.5	*USA*	
81	*Bayer*	6.3	*W.Germ.*	
82	*Daimler-Benz*	6.3	*W.Germ.*	
83	Libya	6.2		
84	*Montedison*	6.2	*Italy*	
85	*Hitachi*	6.2	*Japan*	
86	Hong Kong	6.0		
87	*Toyota Motor*	5.9	*Japan*	
88	*ELF Group*	5.9	*France*	
89	*Occidental Petrol.*	5.7	*USA*	
90	*Mitsubishi (Indust.)*	5.7	*Japan*	
91	*Nestle*	5.6	*Swtzland.*	
92	*Bethlehem Steel*	5.4	*USA*	
93	*Renault*	5.3	*France*	
94	*British Steel*	5.3	*UK*	
95	*Union Carbide*	5.3	*USA*	
96	*Goodyear Tire*	5.2	*USA*	
97	*Brit.-Amer.Tobacco*	5.2	*UK*	
98	Morocco	5.0		
99	*Tenneco*	5.0	*USA*	
100	*Petrobas*	5.0	*Brazil*	

Sources: Compiled by the author from: GNP of nations at 1974 current market prices from Agency for International Development, *1974 Yearbook*, pp. 681-682; Sales of industrial firms from *Fortune*, August 1975, p. 63.

Notes: While GNP and sales data are not directly comparable, they are indicators of relative economic proportions. Of the economic entities listed, 50 are nations and 50 are industrial firms (see table 1-2). Names of firms are in italics.

Table 1-2
World's 100 Largest Nations and Firms Ranked by GNP or Sales Ranges, 1974

Range of GNP or Sales	Number	
	Nations	Firms
More than $1 trillion	1	—
$100 to $500 billion	6	—
$50 to $99 billion	7	—
$25 to $49 billion	7	3
$10 to $24 billion	13	12
$5 to $9 billion	16	35
Totals	50	50

Source: Summary of table 1-1.

common market. European capital represented the "seed money" needed for development of American industry. The corporation flourished in the environment existing in the United States during the last quarter of the nineteenth century. The relatively free enterprise system, or laissez-faire relationship between government and business (however it might be described), nurtured the business unit, and it grew in both size and complexity. Then, as now, many of the giant corporations espoused free competition up to a point—that point usually being the maturity of the firm. Thereafter, competition between two or more behemoths for the same market was generally considered to be detrimental to the interests of the firms involved. The attitude that competition was fine, but for someone else, ushered in the era of cooperation between and among large corporations, followed shortly by the Sherman Anti-Trust Act. Several of the large U.S. corporations began to seek the greener pastures of foreign locations, where the Sherman Act did not directly apply. They joined the ranks of the single-resource firms, which were required to go where the material resources existed, and formed the second layer of firms with international operations. The seed capital that originally came from Europe began to find its way back.

A third layer of foreign investment by U.S. firms was encouraged by the income tax laws. Prior to 1962, earnings of U.S. corporations that were generated by wholly owned subsidiaries outside the United States were not subject to federal income taxes until such earnings were received by the U.S. parent as dividends. Consequently, if host countries levied no similar tax, the earnings of subsidiaries were tax-free. In the majority of instances, the environments of these so-called tax haven countries were not conducive to large-scale manufacturing operations. As a result, the base companies set up in tax havens were primarily designed to avoid income tax levies, and operations of significant size rarely existed.

Table 1-3
Number of Nations with Less than $5 Billion GNP, 1974
(data in billions of dollars)

GNP Range	Number of Nations	GNP for Group	
		Total	Average
$3.0 to $4.3	2	$ 7.4	$3.7
$2.0 to $2.9	18	43.3	2.4
$1.0 to $1.9	16	21.1	1.3
Less than $1.0	36	16.0	.4
Totals	72	$87.8	—

Source: Developed from data compiled by Agency for International Development, *1974 Yearbook*, pp. 681-682.

The real metamorphosis of the U.S. multinational corporation occurred following World War II.[5] The United States needed additional markets for its goods. The $10 billion of Marshall Plan aid, together with other assistance, supplied the wherewithal for Europe and Japan to acquire the machinery and equipment to rebuild their production facilities. As the recovery proceeded, it was accompanied by a surge of demand for consumer and other finished goods. The recovery also witnessed the beginnings of the economic integration of Europe and of protectionism for developing industries. During this same period, there were increasing numbers of invitations for foreign capital and technology from many of the "emerging" nations in other parts of the world. The structure of overseas investments by United States MNCs changed from the previous branch concept to on-site manufacture and competition. The era of the full-fledged MNE had arrived.

For the United States, the coming of the MNE reflected the realization that America was no longer the single source for many items. For many industrial firms this signaled the need for a revision of the scope of operations from a basically national orientation to at least a regional or, in many cases, a global perspective.

The change in the character of U.S. activities overseas from international trade to on-site manufacturing significantly increased the complexities of communicating, reporting, and controlling. The patterns of growth within the MNEs themselves added to the problems. According to reports of studies of the MNE by the Committee on International Accounting of the American Accounting Association,[6] the surge of growth in MNE volumes was more the result of the spawning of affiliates than an increase in the number of MNEs. In 1957 there were some 2,800 U.S.-parent multinationals; this number increased to 3,500 in 1971 and is estimated at slightly over 4,000 today. However, the growth in the number of foreign affiliates has been much more rapid: from 7,000 in 1950, to

10,000 in 1957, to 23,000 in 1966, and to some 25,000 by 1972. Today, overseas operations are estimated to account for more than 25 percent of the total volume of more than 200 U.S. corporations. Thus, while the trend toward direct foreign investments by large corporations increased problems of communication and control, jet aircraft together with the virtual revolution in telecommunications made worldwide operations feasible. In fact, a strong argument could be made in support of the premise that, without the revolution in communications technologies, the expansion of the MNEs would not have been possible, in either extent or structure.

The United States is by no means alone in these adventures. All the major industrial nations of the free world are similarly increasing their excursions into other countries, including into the United States. Today there are cross-flows of funds, as we have become more of a world partner as well as a competitor.

Prior to the skepticism and inflation resulting from the actions of the Organization of Petroleum Exporting Countries (OPEC), the growth rate of MNEs worldwide was roughly twice that of the world economy as a whole. This growth resulted from efficiencies afforded by economies of scale and the growing recognition of interdependency among the industrial nations of the world. As an example of the latter point, the United States must depend upon imports of certain raw materials. Consequently, for its international balance-of-payments needs, the United States must look to increases in exports if imports cannot feasibly be reduced. MNEs provide the solution for our nation; other countries have recognized this fact as well, or are beginning to appreciate its significance. This feature of MNEs, among others, is covered in the chapter that follows. However, one statistic is worth mentioning at this point: exports by U.S. multinational corporations to their overseas subsidiaries alone are estimated to account for one-fourth of total current U.S. exports. The Tariff Committee of the U.S. Department of Commerce reported in recent hearings regarding MNEs that, during the period from 1966 to 1971, the exports of U.S. MNEs increased by more than $3 billion and resulted in an estimated increase of 500,000 to 600,000 jobs in the United States.

In the last decade, growth of multinational enterprises has been further assisted by a general improvement in the business environments of most countries. In the main, most of the aids to further growth represented actions that reduced the risks of foreign investment. However, both internal and external factors were involved. Internal factors included:

1. Obtain essential raw materials from abroad.
2. Acquire exports to assist in balance-of-payments problems.
3. Escape local regulations and restrictions on capital flows.
4. Accommodate the inherent nature of the product manufactured.
5. Escape local competition and/or protect or increase the share of the total market.

6. Increase overall adaptability and flexibility and thus reduce risks.
7. Achieve or make fullest use of economies of scale.
8. Increase total profitability.

External factors included:

1. Overcome protectionism.
2. Protect inventions or technologies.
3. Pursue new or expanding markets.
4. Reduce total costs by means of less expensive labor.
5. Capitalize on tax havens, reciprocal tax agreements, and other host-country inducements.
6. Reduce risks provided by administered exchange rates.
7. Capitalize on the availability of local and/or Eurocurrency financing.

This listing identifies the most important issues but certainly is not all-inclusive. Furthermore, some of the motivations, such as the tax havens and the administered exchange rates, have been either removed or reduced. Nonetheless, each had or has a role to play in the expansion of the MNE.

In 1973, the American Institute of Certified Public Accountant's (AICPA) Conference Board prepared a study for the Department of Commerce to determine why MNEs invested in overseas facilities. As would be expected, the 76 firms surveyed cited more than one reason, but the 10 reasons most often mentioned are shown in table 1-4.

The motivations shown for overseas investments support the general oligopoly theories, in which growth is depicted as vital for the survival of the

Table 1-4
Reasons for Overseas Investment

Rank Order of Reason for Investment	Companies Citing
1. Maintain or increase market share	33
2. Overcome protectionism or shipping costs	25
3. Meet competition	20
4. Host-country pressures/requirements	18
5. Greater sales prospects	15
6. Availability of materials or components	13
7. Reduce wage costs	13
8. Better profit prospects	11
9. Follow important customers	10
10. Host-country inducements	8

Source: Adapted from "Tax Reform—Foreign Income," *The Journal of Accountancy*, November 1975, exhibit I, p. 40. Adapted with permission. Copyright © 1975 by the American Institute of Certified Public Accountants, Inc.

large oligopolies. Growth in this context is defined as an increasing share of the total potential market, foreign as well as domestic. Support is also evident for Professor Vernon's concept of the "product cycle model."[7] According to Vernon, technology is paramount during the introduction and maturing phases of a product's life cycle, and it is advantageous to produce at home. When a product reaches the phase of standardization, the emphasis switches to low-cost labor and the advantages inherent in the use of cheaper labor within an overseas market area or adjacent to it. Other advantages accrue from such direct foreign investments, Vernon contends; principally, that the parent corporation often is in position to control the release of its technology, thereby preempting foreign competition while increasing its market area and profits. In effect, another product life cycle is begun in a new environment.

These conjectures regarding the expansion of the multinational enterprise focus primarily on economic and technological factors that Gilpin[8] considers to be "sufficient conditions" only. According to Gilpin, power represents the "necessary condition" for expansion. He argues that today's world economy developed along with the successive emergences of the "great national economies"—Britain in the nineteenth century, the United States in the twentieth century. Gilpin believes that these dominant nations nurtured and cultivated environments that were conducive to the expansions of MNEs. Insofar as the United States is concerned, Gilpin argues that American MNEs flourished because of the political influence and "power" of the U.S. government as well as from the belief that such expansion served the government's perceived best interests, politically and economically.[9]

The foregoing observations indicate the complexity of the phenomenon called the multinational enterprise or corporation. It is a part of the total international business environment and, as a consequence, is affected by a multitude of interacting economic, legal, social, and political factors. All factors in the environment are important, although the relative significance of one or more may vary with the time and locale. Consequently, attempting to classify the factors into categories such as "necessary" and "sufficient" makes no more sense than applying the same exercise to the ingredients of a ham-and-egg sandwich.

It should be apparent, then, that most differences of opinion regarding MNEs result from the different perspectives from which they are examined.

Types of Multinationals

It seems that few phenomena exist very long before someone attempts to classify them, and the multinational enterprise is no exception. Classification systems have taken as many forms as there were perspectives or purposes for such classification—ownership, control, strategy, policy, and organization, among others.

For assistance in relating accounting systems, the method of classification suggested by Howard Perlmutter[10] is perhaps the most useful and certainly the most widely referenced. He proposed that MNEs be segregated into three classes or groups based upon the frame of reference or attitude of the parent corporation:

1. Home-country oriented (ethnocentric)
2. Host-country oriented (polycentric)
3. World-oriented (geocentric).

To this listing a fourth category or operating scheme might well be added today—call it duocentric for conformity—to encompass the joint-venture mode of operation, which is becoming more prevalent and which does not fit exactly into any of the three categories developed by Perlmutter.

A multinational enterprise that is *home-country oriented* is virtually dominated by the parent company. The parent's concept of doing business, its attitudes, methods, norms, and standards are employed throughout the system wherever possible. Each branch and/or subsidiary is perceived as a small-scale replica of the parent. Overseas operating units are treated as mere extensions of the parent rather than as "foreign" operations. Each overseas unit is tightly controlled; very little independence of action is considered to be desirable or necessary.

Accounting systems and reports would be specified by the parent, except in those countries where regulations dictate that the "official" records conform with criteria prescribed by the country of domicile. In the latter case, two sets of records usually would be maintained—the official set to satisfy the host country and the set prescribed and used by the parent. Often, two or more sets of records are necessary regardless of the orientation of the parent; for example, some countries still require cumbersome manual postings to the official records, which, if adhered to solely, would preclude any form of timely reporting useful to anyone. Most often, host-country requirements that certain official records be posted manually reflect make-work legislation by nations having many more people than jobs. Consequently, this sort of requirement is usually limited to underdeveloped or developing countries.

The set of records following procedures specified by the parent company also enhances the process of consolidation, since a minimum of adjustments are necessary to bring the subsidiary reports in line with the accounting principles of the parent's country, followed by translation of the foreign currency. In some instances, the translation process, or part of it, is performed on an ongoing basis by the subsidiary if the second set of records is also maintained in the parent's currency.

It should be apparent that a home-country orientation is a highly centralized concept of international operations that, except for the nuisance caused by foreign currencies, treats subsidiaries in Spain or Brazil as if they were located in Illinois or California.

Some useful conjectures can be made concerning home-country orientation by the MNE. This approach will tend to be that usually *attempted* by a highly centralized parent in the establishment of its initial overseas subsidiary or affiliate—and possibly with the first several such foreign adventures. It seems logical that attitudes and practices that have been proved successful in the parent's domain should be transplanted overseas as well. This strategy is beneficial only in the very short run, if at all. Few successful international operations are conducted with only the best interests of the parent's country in mind; a foreign subsidiary must learn to be a good citizen in the host country as well. Social responsibilities aside, problems of time, distance, size, and lost opportunity would eventually require a change of attitude.

Host-country orientation is the most common frame of reference for multinationals today. Of course, no multinational enterprise that operates for profit can function with total emphasis upon one or more host countries in which it operates. The primary purpose of the MNE is to earn a return on its investment, and, in that context, all MNEs possess a basic home-country orientation. However, recognition of the fact that plant and equipment investments are long-term in nature, as are, in most instances, the profits to be derived therefrom, causes all but the most stubborn managements to recognize that the best interests of the parent require more than a passive concern for the host environment.

Few business methods or attitudes can be universally employed with success. Rather, most parent companies usually find that their affiliates must adapt in many ways to local conditions and markets. In addition, the problems of size, distance, communication, and compliance with local law soon require that the MNE loosen the extent of structure and control, thereby providing a degree of independence for its subsidiaries. This decentralization of certain aspects of operating controls characterizes the host-country orientation. Other side benefits can also accompany the relative independence of affiliates, an important one being the image of a local rather than foreign company in the host country. For example, in only a very few oil-producing states, such as Oklahoma, is Shell Oil considered a foreign company within the United States. Thus, it is evident why a host-country orientation would be the prevalent form of MNE operation.

Accounting systems would also follow a host-country orientation. That is, accounting within the foreign affiliate would be designed to serve several purposes: compliance with the laws and regulations of the host country; management orientation, to provide the information needed by local managers to compete and adapt to changes in the local environs; and financial orientation, to enable the parent company to monitor and respond to those variables critical to the well-being of the entire MNE as well as to expedite preparation of consolidated statements and other external reports. In a sense, the accounting and reporting system would tend to be an amalgam of many subsystems, some similar in many respects, others unique.

A *world or global orientation* may be characterized as the penultimate category or phase of the multinational enterprise. Few, if any, exist today or will evolve in the near future simply because, given the present state of international law, parent companies are subject to the laws and regulations of the country of domicile. Majority ownership and control also now tend to rest within a single country of origin. In addition, no matter how loosely structured or decentralized an MNE might be, or might want to be, it still is a single economic entity, and, as such, it seems plausible that certain decisions affecting the entity as a whole will continue to vest in a central point.

An entity with a global orientation would be faced with such decisions as what accounting standards to follow, what currency to reflect in financial statements, and what language to use in published reports. Without an international accounting framework, currency, or language, the only reasonable option would be to employ several, each geared to the country to which the reports were addressed. While the adjustments necessary would be formidable, they would certainly not be impossible. Given a sufficient number of such global entities and their collective influence, it also seems plausible that pressures for international standards would eventually bring them about. For accounting, in particular, this change would represent a natural phase in its metamorphosis, since the language of business has evolved by changing with the needs and demands of business.

Some trade-offs would be involved, of course, since no one country can attest to the "best" accounting framework; however, time and perceived need would surely prevail. The real constraints would likely relate to political, legal, and tax matters, and these would require much greater soul-searching and a wider recognition and appreciation of the interdependencies of the world economy, regardless of ideologies.

The fourth category or class of MNE suggested—that of *joint venture*—would seem to preclude the adoption of a home-country, host-country, or worldwide orientation by the parent company, since each venture would represent a unique contractual agreement. A joint venture is, for all intents and purposes, a partnership and, as such, presents all the disadvantages peculiar to a partnership; that is, the sharing of ownership, management, profit, and risk. Consequently, the joint venture has long been considered to be an impractical and undesirable mode of operation for the multinational enterprise.

The negative aspects of joint ventures primarily relate to the sharing of management and control and only secondarily to the sharing of profits. Since an MNE is considered to be a single economic entity, the sharing of control over its pool of resources has been frowned upon. This lack of total control has generally been crucial wherever commands over monopolistic advantages, such as technology or market dominance, were concerned. Joint management further requires a continuous interaction with individuals and/or governments having purposes and goals not necessarily in line with those of the MNE. Concerning profits, more often than not the major problem was not their sharing, which is often done in arrangements other than joint ventures, but rather limitations on the repatriation of the profits.

In recent years, however, circumstances and events have greatly increased the attractiveness and use of joint ventures. In many controlled economies, collaboration with the host government in the form of a joint venture is the only avenue available that will permit access to a highly desirable market area. In other instances, such as in Mexico, company laws require 51 percent local ownership, with almost the same net effect as a joint venture. (It is recognized that equity forms of ownership, such as cited in Mexico, are subject to company laws rather than contract law, which governs joint ventures. However, other than the difference of legal domain, the effective results are similar.) The 1962 Revenue Act also furnished a U.S. tax incentive for joint ventures and similar arrangements in which the U.S. parent held 50 percent or less ownership by deferring U.S. taxes on foreign earnings until such time as they were repatriated. Various forms of joint-venture agreements have increasingly been used by U.S. oil companies as a deliberate method of spreading the risk and thereby reducing the loss that would be sustained upon nationalization or expropriation. A final example, and one increasingly being employed by developing countries, is the emphasis upon the joint venture as a practical means of assuring local participation in management and profits as well as of providing some control over balance-of-payments and exploitation concerns.

As may be surmised, most multinational enterprises of any size would probably not fit neatly or completely into any one of the three conceptual classifications suggested by Perlmutter. Instead, the MNE will usually employ a home, host, or global orientation, or enter into a joint-venture arrangement, dependent upon the perspective and circumstance.

Professor Perlmutter has recently added a fourth category to his "social-architectural" approach of classifying multinational corporations—that of a "transnational network (TNN)." He emphasizes that the transnational network does not exist as yet but represents the logical choice between two alternatives open to MNCs today, paraphrased as follows:

1. Continue premises based upon control of ownership and operations, which can only lead to divestitures and a contraction of operations and markets, or
2. Evolve into a transnational network (TNN) having affiliations with a wide variety of firms, consortia, and operating concessions in all sectors of the globe.[11]

The evolving transnational network will not merely have stockholders, as they are known today, but other influential interests as well, such as trade unions and governments, which Perlmutter collectively terms "stakeholders." These stakeholders will, as insiders, have the opportunity to influence the operations and policies of the transnational enterprise; management will necessarily become more difficult. Decisions will be the result of compromise more than fiat.

Insofar as accounting is concerned, it is difficult to imagine how such a transnational network or linkage could function without a network of compatible reporting systems. Consequently, the TNN envisioned by Perlmutter would either be made possible as the result of harmonization of accounting systems in the various environments, or, more likely, would serve as the forerunner or the agent of harmonization. The latter conjecture is more plausible since, historically, accounting has responded to needs rather than creating them.

The preceding comments pertained to conceptual classifications of multinational enterprises in accordance with attitude or orientation. Prior to examining the general characteristics of MNEs in the next section, a brief mention of efforts to classify MNEs according to organizational structure and financial control should be made here. Unfortunately, most empirical studies of MNEs suffer from the disadvantages inherent in social research, primarily their temporal nature and limited scope. Also, study results tend to support logical conclusions regarding operations of MNEs and present few surprises. It seems reasonable to assume, therefore, that problems inherent in the operation and organization of MNEs, and their solutions, are neither unique nor characterized by different approaches between and among nations.

Two studies for the National Industrial Conference Board serve as examples. In his examination of the organization structures of 42 prominent multinationals, including 10 U.S. firms, Stieglitz reported the use of the traditional forms with variations—functional, product, and regional.[12] Use of standard approaches to financial control was also found by Meister in her examination of 300 international firms—centralized control at either corporate or regional headquarters plus some form of combination of the two.[13]

A final dampening of efforts to isolate some significant and different operational characteristic of the multinational enterprise, and hence its "magic," should be clear from an observation by Pieter Kuin, a retired director of Unilever N.V., a highly respected MNE. According to Mr. Kuin, the "magic" associated with the management of the MNC appears to be elusive:

It lies not so much in perfection of methods or excellence of men as in developing respect for other nationalities and cultures.[14]

Last but not least, the abilities to adapt and innovate are paramount. These characteristics alone act to defy attempts to classify MNEs into any system of neat categories. The attitudinal and organizational classification schemes that were examined are helpful from certain general perspectives only.

Characteristics

Virtually all the characteristics of a multinational enterprise are a *function of its enormous size*.

Few, if any, of its most vocal opponents would deny that the multinational enterprise is *efficient.* In fact, the very efficiency of the MNE is the source of some of the concerns voiced by its local competitors. The magnitude of the resources available to the MNE enables it to distribute these resources where it desires throughout much of the world. These pools of men, money, machines, materials, and methodology are managed from a global, rather than a national, perspective. This attitude of globalism in management thinking usually prevails to the extent that all decisions that are beyond the scope of any single affiliate are reserved for determination by headquarters. From this vantage point, the MNE is capable of tapping and manipulating its resources on a worldwide basis, using them in the locations considered to offer the best opportunities and/or the lowest risks. In other words, the MNE can generally obtain financing and produce its products at the lowest possible total costs worldwide, as well as select the most promising available markets in which to sell. This is efficiency from all but the narrowest economic veiwpoint.

The *power* attributed to the multinational enterprise is a result of its size and scope of operations. As mentioned previously, it is not at all unusual today for an MNE to record annual sales greater than some of the countries in which it operates. Consequently, as a giant among local firms, the MNE generally has the power, in an economic sense at least, to dominate and control the local markets. Direct investments in foreign affiliates, sometimes in more than 100 countries, enhance and regenerate the economic power of MNCs, since such investments tend to assure a permanent source of supply and/or earnings. Economic power is a prerequisite for most multinationals, since, lacking the protection of international law, the MNE has to rely upon itself to compete and win. In many respects the multinational firm transcends national boundaries and controls, making many of the traditional macroeconomic and microeconomic concepts inappropriate for application to the MNE as a total entity.

The characteristic *stability* of the multinational is also clearly a function of size. Given its relatively vast resources, an MNE can absorb losses from unforeseen operating constraints that render an investment unprofitable, or from expropriation, or from other externalities without threatening its continued existence. Its relative strength also enables it to sustain losses in the short run until an efficient economy of scale is achieved. An affiliate of an MNE also can absorb losses resulting from undercutting competitors in a new market area, if such a practice is chosen to be employed. This latter facet of its stability is one that causes concern to host governments. Ironically, however, the very stability inherent in an MNE can also be transmitted to the host economy, thereby reducing the frequency as well as the amplitude of its business cycles.

Multinational enterprises are usually *oligopolies* and consequently are the by-products of developed countries. In order to acquire the growth vital for their existence, these oligopolies attempt to capitalize on their technology and access to capital and other resource markets. All other conditions being equal, the MNE will choose an environment in which continued growth is further assured by its ability to regulate competition through controlled release of its technology. However, other conditions are rarely equal, and, in order to capitalize on technological and other competitive advantages, an oligopolistic firm requires an environment of relatively free enterprise. This latter point is crucial. It accounts for the otherwise paradoxical fact that the majority of investments by all MNEs, regardless of the parent country, occurs between and among the leading industrial nations rather than within the developing nations. Logic should dictate that the MNC would elect to establish its affiliates in countries having little or no technology and therefore little or no competition.

Yet in many developing countries the oligopolistic multinational often encounters two formidable barriers. First, it is not at all uncommon to find an intense spirit of nationalism pervading the young emerging nations. This condition, whetted by fears of external dominance or exploitation, usually manifests itself in conditions or controls that destroy the free-enterprise environment essential for the MNE. Second, very few emerging nations offer prospects of stability in government, economy, or exchange rate. These constraints, either real or potential, often make investments in emerging nations too risky for even the goliath MNEs, since their primary objective is the production of local earnings in local currency over the long run; improvement in the economic well-being of the host country is an ancillary motive.

As a result, multinational enterprises often ascribe less risk to an investment in the more stable and predictable environment of an industrialized nation, even though it involves competition from established local firms or fellow MNEs, than to one with all the uncertainties common to a developing country. This is unfortunate, because it adversely affects the world economy as a whole and the betterment of the "have-not" nations in particular.

As a side comment, yet a potentially significant one, it is interesting to note that a substantial yet unknown amount of assistance, both economic and technological, is being furnished the have-not nations by the controlled economies, China in particular and the USSR to a lesser extent. The best example that comes to mind is the trans-African railway, nearing completion as the result of the human labor, technology, and other resources furnished by China. The feat represents a visible monument to the interests of China in helping the less fortunate. Since such government-to-people adventures have other than profit motives, a plausible conjecture would stipulate that, due to the uncertainties involved, profit-oriented efforts to assist developing nations are less practicable than direct assistance of other governments—*direct assistance* meaning the actual performance, such as construction of the railroad by the Chinese, rather than monetary aid, since this form of assistance rarely filters down through the echelons of the elite to benefit the people as a whole.

A multinational enterprise certainly is *dynamic* in every sense of the term. It must grow in order to survive, particularly where advanced technologies are involved. An MNE is frequently described as a key innovator in that it creates markets as well as the products related to them. By means of its integrated planning techniques, an MNE can convert conflicting forces and apparent problems into opportunities. It assimilates, adapts, and reconciles external threats into beneficial strategies. As an innovator, the multinational not only adapts to change but, more often than not, anticipates or initiates change.

Given its size and scope, an MNE is certainly the most *flexible* of economic institutions. Excellent communication systems enable widely decentralized operations to serve local needs yet permit centralized direction to assure goal congruence. Thus, the headquarters can manipulate the mobile resources of the MNE on a global basis as deemed in its best overall interests. It can produce, assemble, and market in those locations offering the best total opportunity. This sort of flexibility often enables the multinational to offset or escape restrictive regulations or controls in certain sections of the world. Transfer prices, credit terms, intraunit loans, and multiple assembly points are examples of devices available to the multinational.

The foregoing represent rather superficial summaries of the major attributes of a relatively new phenomenon—the multinational enterprise—and, in a sense, are one-dimensional snapshots of a dynamic economic entity that continues to evolve. As with any business enterprise, confidence and sophistication come with time and experience. Even a relatively large national corporation recognizes the greater risks involved as it takes its first steps in the international arena. Before long the neophyte MNE learns how to exist and prosper in multiple environments and how to benefit from the mistakes, as well as the successes, in dealing with legal, political, cultural, and economic problems of every description. Confidence and sophistication come when there are no longer "foreign" markets, simply markets; when ownership and earnings are shared by persons in many countries; when management personnel are selected for their respective abilities rather than national origins. At this stage, to consider a multinational enterprise as being American, or British, or Dutch is rather sophomoric since the location of the parent company is little more than circumstantial.

Since the MNE transcends national boundaries and their related constraints, it holds an enormous promise for greater international understanding and world economic development. But the multinational enterprise cannot, and will not, function as a philanthropist. There must be mutual benefits involved in its ventures, and the promises of its rewards must be greater than the perceived risks. Under these conditions, as the multinational enterprise innovates, adapts, and changes, it also changes the environment by exerting pressures upon the existing social and economic institutions. In this respect, "MNC" represents *multinational change*—and change is uncomfortable for all participants because it involves uncertainties.

Challenges

The attributes of the multinational enterprise described in this chapter may seem to portray the MNE as a huge, powerful, monolithic structure subject to few real controls and, therefore, faced with few challenges of any consequence. This is not altogether true.

Governments of parent and host countries present the front-line challenge to the MNE. Lacking an international law, the MNE is not really controllable by any single external power. The managements of most multinationals recognize that all governments, parent as well as hosts, will be hostile at *some* time but rarely at the *same* time. Nonetheless, since multinationals operate within a variety of political environments, governments represent formidable adversaries.

The second challenge facing a multinational enterprise is competition from another MNE having similar strengths and options.

Other than unfriendly governments and competitive MNEs, other obstacles to the multinational firm actually represent problems waiting to be transformed into opportunities.

In the succeeding chapters of this part, the problems of host relationships, socioeconomic development, and ethics will be examined. Part II will delve into accounting and related problems of multinational enterprises; and the final chapter will consist of conjectures relating to the most interesting challenge of all—the future.

Notes

1. Raymond Vernon, *Sovereignty at Bay* (New York: Basic Books, Inc., 1971), pp. 4-11.

2. See Anant R. Negandhi and S. Benjamin Prasad, *The Frightening Angels: A Study of U.S. Multinationals in Developing Nations* (Kent, Ohio: Kent State University Press, 1975).

3. For the development of U.S. multinationals up to 1914, see Mira Wilkins, *The Emergence of Multinational Enterprise* (Cambridge, Mass.: Harvard University Press, 1970).

4. Address by Frederick T. Knickerbocker, Harvard University in "Proceedings: First Annual International Business Conference," Saint Louis University, December 1, 1975. Unpublished, © Saint Louis University School of Business and Administration.

5. The growth of the MNE depicted here was adapted from testimony by the Tax Division of the American Institute of Certified Public Accountants before the House Ways and Means Committee hearing on July 15, 1975. The

essentials of this testimony appeared in the *Journal of Accountancy*, November 1975, pp. 34, 36.

6. For examples, see *The Accounting Review, Supplement to Volume 48*, 1973, pp. 120-167, and *Supplement to Volume 49*, 1974, pp. 250-269. It is interesting to note that these cited reports represent the first major efforts by AAA committees on the topic of MNEs. The next earlier report by the Committee on International Accounting, published in the 1968 *Supplement*, consisted of a rather cursory review of the quality of international reporting.

7. Raymond Vernon, "International Investment and International Trade in the Product Cycle," *Quarterly Journal of Economics*, LXXX (May 1966), pp. 190-207.

8. Robert Gilpin, *U.S. Power and the Multinational Corporation* (New York: Basic Books, Inc., 1975), pp. 5-6.

9. Ibid., p. 41.

10. Howard V. Perlmutter, "The Tortuous Evolution of the Multinational Corporation," *Columbia Journal of World Business*, January-February 1969, pp. 9-18. Much of this section has been developed around the framework suggested by Perlmutter.

11. Howard V. Perlmutter, "Alternative Futures for the Multinational," in "Proceedings, Second Annual International Business Conference," Saint Louis University, December 16, 1976, p. 23. © Saint Louis University School of Business and Administration.

12. H. Stieglitz, *Organization Structures of International Companies* (New York: National Industrial Conference Board, 1965).

13. Irene W. Meister, *Managing the International Financial Function* (New York: National Industrial Conference Board, 1970).

14. Pieter Kuin, "The Magic of Multinational Management," *Harvard Business Review*, November-December 1972, p. 89. Reprinted with permission.

2 Host Relationships

At the outset, the reader should be forewarned that no magical solutions will be conjured in this chapter. Instead, the interests and concerns of two international participants—the multinational enterprise and the host government—will be examined, from a standpoint as neutral as possible, in order to enable the reader to become a more informed mediator.

Concerns of the Multinational Enterprise

The multinational enterprise has been depicted as a giant among economic entities and, primarily because of its immense size, as efficient, powerful, stable, dynamic, flexible and, quite often, a technological oligopoly. Its size limits the sources of real concern for an MNE to primarily two—a competitive MNE or a government. Competition, whether local or international, is certainly not a new phenomenon for most businesses; it is something that is expected at one time or another, even by an MNE. When the competition emanates from another MNE, various forms of cooperation are possible and have been employed. The only effective challenge to the multinational corporation is represented by government—in most instances, the host government.

Regardless of the concerns expressed by host governments, in the game of international business the host government holds "four aces," namely, the powers to legislate, to tax, to expropriate, and to use "immoral suasion," to coin a phrase.

The host's power to *legislate* is a key factor, since it can restrict or motivate. Initially, the host government can determine who will be permitted to enter its dominion and in what particular areas of the economy. Various forms of legislation can also be used by the host to control operations, foreign-exchange holdings, dividend remittances, interest rates, and other fees charged by the parent or other affiliated firm. In short, the host can essentially determine the rules under which the game is to be played. Of course, the rules can be drawn in such a manner as to totally exclude foreign participation—but such action would also exclude the opportunity for the economic benefits that the foreign firm might provide.

Various forms of *taxation* represent the most direct and visible sharing by the host government of the economic activity created by a foreign firm. The ability to tax is also one that can restrict or motivate and, like legislation, can be used to change the game rules if the host nation so desires. This is particularly true in those sectors in which different tax rates or schemes are applied to domestic and foreign firms. The most unfortunate aspect of taxation relates to its visibility. All too often it is the primary, if not the only economic benefit recognized by the host government, and, in most industrial activities, this is a myopic viewpoint at best. Compliance with local regulations and tax requirements often represents the initial function of the accounting system of the foreign firms, followed by the needs of management—both local and parent—with the external financial reporting function of the parent relegated to third priority. This structuring does not necessarily indicate importance or merit in the form of a pecking order, per se, but simply reflects the timing requirements of the data reported.

The ability of a host government to *expropriate* or take over a foreign firm operating in its dominion is not only an ace card but one in the trump suit as well. Whether conducted with or without eventual compensation, the act of expropriation puts an end to the game.[1]

Immoral suasion is a feature to which none of the players in the game will admit, and, much like the proverbial "little man who wasn't there," most of the participants wish it would go away. Pressures or coercion applied to cause certain actions to be taken or avoided can be effective in the short run, but they leave scars that are subsequently remembered when circumstances change.

Every multinational enterprise contemplating the establishment of a foreign subsidiary is aware of the foregoing four factors, which give the host government the ultimate ability to control the game or bring it to an abrupt halt. Thus, governments represent the source of most problems confronting the MNE. To use some of its prerogatives, the host government must either be willing to forgo the economic benefits offered by the MNE or be able to supplant the MNE as operator of the activity concerned. In the latter case, the MNE is analogous to the marketing concept of the "middleman"—he can be eliminated but his function cannot. The multinational enterprise, on the other hand, attempts to assess the probability of such actions, in conjunction with the other economic and environmental variables involved, in order to determine the degree of risk associated with the venture. Given the ultimate powers of host governments, their political roles are as significant as the economic and technical complexities affecting the risks of foreign ventures.

Concerns of Developing Countries

Most of the criticisms of multinational enterprises presented in this section are peculiar to the so-called Third World[2] or developing countries. The effects of the multinationals are also being critically examined by many industrialized nations, including the United States, but along somewhat different lines.

Where the developing nations are concerned, the giant multinationals certainly are capable of performing the disservices of which they have been accused. And just as certainly some MNEs have been, and possibly still are, poor citizens in other countries.

United Fruit Company's reputation as "the octopus" was well-earned in the 1950s as a result of its incursions into the political, governmental, and tax affairs of the Central American countries that the firm exploited in creating its banana empire. These ill-advised activities culminated in the divestiture of many of the firm's croplands in Central America, particularly in Guatemala.[3] With the suicide leap of its president, Eli M. Black, on February 3, 1975, United Fruit Company (now a division of United Brands) also acquired the dubious distinction of being the causative agent that provoked the continuing investigations into overseas bribes and payoffs by American corporations.

An earlier and often overlooked example concerns the meddling by American oil companies into the internal affairs and reforms of Mexico during the 1930s. These activities fostered the expropriation of the majority of American oil concessions in 1938.

In fairness, however, it should be recognized that neither of the preceding examples could or would have taken place without the express support of American politicians.

However, as in most controversies, the ill-advised acts of a few can be magnified to such an extent that the overall contributions of the many become overshadowed. Where host relationships of multinationals are concerned, the only equitable method of assessment requires a case-by-case examination; that is, a cost-benefit analysis of the operations of a specific MNE or groups of allied firms in a given national environment. Even then the task is not easy, since many variables are involved and some are intangible and therefore difficult, if at all possible, to quantify.

The most frequent charges levied against multinationals by developing nations are presented here. The list is certainly not all-inclusive, but it should serve to illustrate the common types of concerns expressed. Multinational corporations are charged with:

1. Being above any government.
2. Abrogating the sovereignty of the local government.
3. Evading taxes.
4. Competing unfairly.
5. Fostering technological dependence.
6. Lacking social responsibility.
7. Disrupting foreign exchange markets.
8. Destroying stability of labor markets.
9. Exploiting local resources and capital.

Being above Government

Multinationals are often characterized as beyond the control of any single government, home or host. Mobile resources permit worldwide operating flexibility for the MNE. The sheer size of the multinational relative to that of the host government and the seeming flexibility enjoyed by the MNE because of its many apparent options are often synonymous with power insofar as the host nation is concerned. Operating and financial results, when disclosed, are rarely in a form that facilitates control by any single governmental unit.

Since it functions as a supranational economic entity, it is true that the entire multinational enterprise is effectively beyond the legal control of any *single* government. However, where host nations are concerned, control of the entire MNE is not relevant. What is pertinent and what does exist is host control of the affiliate or subsidiary operating within its domain. There is no doubt that a subsidiary in Mexico is under the control of the Mexican government, and if the subsidiary violates Mexican laws or regulations, it will have to pay the penalties if it is caught. Most host governments have the ability to control entry and scope of operations by means of a multitude of licenses, permits, and authorizations. Thereafter, the governments normally require ongoing data and reports.

Usually, foreign-owned firms are required to file reports in addition to those levied on domestic firms. As is typical of most government bureaucracies, however, systems rarely exist for interchange of the information between and among the government offices. As a result, one or more bureaus will complain of the lack of information while the data needed will have been reported to other sister agencies. A second deficiency that is also systems-related is evidenced by the virtual absence of data interchange between and among nations having similar concerns and interests. Notable exceptions, of course, are represented by the OPEC cartel and, to a lesser extent, the European Common Market.

Abrogating Sovereignty

Many of the smaller developing nations allege that they are not the masters of their own fates. Such countries look upon the multinational enterprise as a monolithic structure, with all important decisions being reserved for and made by a foreign headquarters and little or no regard being given to the interests of host governments. These attitudes are much more prevalent where the host nations are primarily single-resource economies in which foreign firms represent the only or largest extractor or developer of that resource. Furthermore, if the subsidiary is a part of a giant MNE, such as Exxon, and the host nation is relatively small in an economic sense, it is understandable that the host government would tend to feel a loss of identity through virtual dependence upon the MNE. There is little question that it is imperative for an MNE to function as a good citizen in a nation in which it has acquired a dominant economic influence. Many small nations also charge that foreign political influence accompanies economic dominance by a foreign multinational.

Recently there has been evidence of instances in which U.S. multinationals have been charged with and have admitted to making political contributions and/or bribes to influence local politics. Where such practices are uncovered and proved, the host governments have the power and authority to impose appropriate penalties upon all participants in the illegal activity.

Host nations can also protect their sovereignty by excluding foreign firms from operating in areas that involve the national interest or defense. In the case of a single-resource country, which, of necessity, must permit a foreign firm to develop the resource, a joint-venture arrangement can be used in order to provide the nation with a voice in its economic destiny. Such arrangements, after all, although between nation and MNE, are simply business agreements that are subject to the usual negotiation and contractual process. Each participant has something to offer and something to gain; a meeting of the minds should not, and does not, necessarily abrogate a nation's sovereignty nor a multinational's rights and obligations of contract.

All too often, however, partners become adversaries in the future when terms originally negotiated and agreed upon lead one (or the other) to believe he is being shortchanged. While renegotiations are possible, they change the risk variables and may well render an operation undesirable. Multinational decisions to invest tend to be long-range actions based upon known or predictable risk and reward factors. Built-in renegotiation or scheduled reduction in foreign ownership (fade-out) provisions can adversely affect the interests of both participants: the risk factors of the MNE are subject to modification, and this may encourage a "skimming-of-the-cream" operation; the host country may have to be in position to contribute capital, technological, and managerial resources at specified future times. Again, any such conditions should be made known to, understood by, and agreed upon by all participants at the outset.

Evading Taxes

Tax evasion is a common accusation of the multinationals. Few firms, or people, like to pay taxes. Accounting and tax departments of multinational enterprises devote most of their resources to tax regulations, either in complying with them or in attempting to minimize their total bite of the revenue dollar.

Tax regulations in other countries, while not as complex as those in the United States, differ in one important respect—the *effective* tax rates themselves. Rates vary from zero to levies that Americans would consider to be confiscatory. In addition, many countries impose relatively high border taxes and tariffs to supplement normal income tax revenues. Naturally, since it usually can select the countries in which it wishes to operate (the exceptions would be certain natural-resource-oriented firms, such as the oil companies), the multinational will attempt to select the lowest total tax environment wherever otherwise practicable. Since it is common for intraunit transfers of materials and products to occur throughout the MNE network, the amounts at which these resources are transferred (transfer prices) have been used by MNEs to restructure incomes to those countries with the lowest tax rates. This sort of tax evasion is illegal in almost all countries, but it is difficult, if at all possible, to investigate, substantiate, or control. Companion methods of tax evasion involve charges by the parent firm to subsidiaries in selected countries of excessive or even fictitious fees for research and development or other services, as well as abnormal interest rates on financing.

Host nations can regulate interest rates and other fees charged simply by requiring their approval in advance; this is a growing practice. As mentioned, transfer pricing is extremely complicated and difficult to control. However, the host government can require, at least, that "arms-length" transfer prices be used wherever practicable (since such prices theoretically would be determined by the economics of the marketplace rather than motives of tax evasion) and thus place the burden of proof of compliance on the MNE. Bilateral tax agreements, including interchange of data, are effective only when a single home and host country are involved. Ultimately, host nations have two effective deterrents at their disposal—the imposition of stiff penalties on guilty firms and publicity by means of direct notification of the government of the parent firm.

Competing Unfairly

Multinationals are depicted as having an edge on local competitors, and this is generally true. The MNE is also accused of undercutting local competition where it exists, knowing that temporary losses can be sustained until such time as the local competition is disposed. The multinational enterprise generally does have this potential for dominance in most local market areas. Transfer prices have also allegedly been used unfairly in order to support local prices charged.

Competition to any meaningful degree is met by the MNE primarily in developed countries and, more often than not, originates from one or more fellow multinationals. In those arenas there are few holds barred, and the more efficient firms will prevail.

Real competition for a multinational is not often encountered in the developing countries. Usually an MNE will be authorized to enter an economic area of a developing country that simply is not tractable with local capital and technology. In these situations, competition is not direct but indirect, concerning primarily the importation of certain resources and secondarily the allocation of exported products. It is not unusual for the perceived best interests of the MNE and the host country to be divergent in some of these instances. The most appropriate solution is afforded by joint discussion and resolution of all forseen problems prior to inception of the investment by the MNE, augmented by joint consideration of unforeseen problems as they arise.

Price controls by host governments have not proved to be practicable, since the MNE has access to world markets and the ability to use transfer pricing to advantage.

Fostering Technological Dependence

Host nations naturally develop a feeling of technological dependence when their large, primary industries are controlled by foreign firms. This feeling is further aggravated when the foreign firms conduct little research and development locally or when the technologies developed are not appropriate for the host environments. Ill will of this sort is hardly excusable today and is the result of a mutual lack of understanding.

Host nations must recognize that, given the interdependencies in the international environment, no nation, including the United States, can consider itself independent—technologically or otherwise. If the developing countries have little or no technology, it must be imported in some fashion from somewhere. To acquire technology directly, separate from any related foreign investment, is a possible alternative that has been used, but it has proved to be relatively costly. If technology is imported along with investment, the necessary know-how that accompanies the package is often more important than the process or patent itself. Also, technology is not a static concept in most fields but rather tends to be a continuous process. To acquire the complete package also requires, at least in the short run, a certain degree of dependence on the part of the host. The trade-off need not be traumatic. Negotiation and reason can result in the establishment of local research and development facilities of the level and scope appropriate for the needs of the host environment. Such research and development would, of course, concern itself not with the more sophisticated problems normally reserved for investigation at the parent location but rather with local problems, processes, and adaptations. Agreements can be arranged whereby this same research and development facility can devote some of its talents to indigenous problems not necessarily related to the primary activities of the MNC.[4] Such facilities can also be used to absorb qualified local technicians as they become available rather than have them look to the greener pastures in other countries.

Lacking Social Responsibility

This is the broadest and most nebulous category of complaints registered against multinationals by lesser-developed countries.

The sheer size and scope of MNE operations within many developing nations often bring about significant social changes that disrupt or counteract social programs and goals of the host governments. In some nations, a new economic middle class is created where none previously existed. In others, the increased wages, which were first seen as an advantage, sometimes become the source of a real problem; for example, the higher wage levels and their perceived stability often change consumer tastes and result in increased levels of imported consumption goods and balance-of-payment problems. Foreign firms are also charged with the production of items that run counter to social goals and tastes of the populace. (However, social tastes can often be deceiving. For example, who ever would have imagined that the largest industry in the Israeli nation would be pig farming?)

Another often-heard lament is the excessive burden placed upon existing infrastructures by MNC operations. The criticism most often voiced in that multinational corporations are interested only in profits; they are accused of investing, producing, and divesting as they choose with little regard to the impacts upon host governments. This type of MNC investment has been called "FIFO—that is, 'fast in, fast out' " by Hans Thorelli.[5]

Many of the complaints relating to changes in the social structures of host societies represent the normal growing pains associated with agricultural nations that are groping with the adjustments accompanying the first stages of industrialization. Such changes, even where anticipated, are often traumatic experiences, particularly for the more conservative and rigid societies. With adequate planning, host governments can use the approach of regional development via permits and authorizations in order to localize the impacts of change within the most adaptable sectors of the country. Where possible, reasonable degrees of local economic participation can be negotiated along with agreements calling for the training and participation of indigenous people for technical and managerial positions.

Since the process of economic development causes greater stress on host societies than on the MNE, host nations should recognize that their best interests are served by working closely with foreign firms. An example would be requesting advance notice of and, if at all possible, participation in all major changes proposed by the MNE. Such cooperative approaches can minimize the effects of change on all parties concerned at little more than the cost of common courtesy.

Disrupting Foreign Exchange Markets

Problems relating to international balances of payments are usually complex. Yet many host countries base their allegations of the disruptions of foreign investment solely upon a myopic comparison of inflows of capital and outflows of earnings repatriations; that is, as if it were a portfolio investment. One probable cause is the ready availability of such data in financial reports. A second reason is that in many developing countries national income accounting is inadequate to disclose the effects of import substitutions and export increases brought about by foreign investment. Where the latter situation is suspected, the multinational can improve its image and posture by keeping the host government informed of these data and, more important, their trends. The effect of import substitution, for example, tends to have a long lead time and, while it develops slowly, it usually reflects a clearly favorable trend. Disclosure of such information helps the host government to examine the entire spectrum of balance-of-payments effects.

Currency restrictions, import and export levies, and other controls imposed by host nations tend to be ineffective because of the financial flexibilities, intergroup payments, and transfer prices enjoyed by multinational firms. Even in those instances where the MNE plays according to the rules, excessive controls only complicate matters and leave a residue of distrust rather than the goodwill that results from mutual consideration and cooperation.

Destroying Labor Stability

Developing countries are examining the impacts of multinationals on labor markets and tend to have dissimilar complaints. In the lesser-developed countries, foreign investment is criticized for introducing labor-saving technologies in labor-intensive markets. In other developing nations, the MNEs are charged with paying excessively high wage scales, thereby inducing workers to leave local employers and/or disrupting indigenous wage structures.

Multinational firms have the resources that enable them to pay top wages, and it is inconceivable to expect them to attempt to pay less than the prevailing rates of established firms and begin operations of any magnitude. Host governments should anticipate this behavior and discuss the gamut of industrial relations with the foreign firm. Such discussions could cover the local labor organizations, if any, prevailing or suggested minimum and maximum wage scales, the extent and nature of fringe benefits common to the region or country, and the available or needed skills. Negotiations with many of the lesser-developed countries often include advance agreements on ratios of indigenous to foreign personnel, particularly in supervisory and middle-management levels, together with opportunities for on-the-job training of local personnel.

Exploitation

Exploitation has long been a prominent complaint registered by developing countries. Most of the emphasis has centered around natural resources, and some of the complaints have been warranted. One common characteristic of all complaints is that they are ex post facto. It can be said that resources are not, but are becoming; that is, a natural resource deposit in a country lacking the technology, capital, infrastructure, or interest necessary to extract it is *not* a resource. It *becomes* a resource often due to foreign investment. During the initial negotiations, more often than not, local persons or firms with capital to invest simply do not wish to participate in such risky ventures. After the foreign seed money has been deployed, infrastructures or special forms of transportation have been provided, and the lag time required for the foreign firm to transform "red ink" into profits has passed, then local investors characteristically change their attitudes. So long as the royalty, tax, or fee paid the host government for the raw resource is fair insofar as market conditions are concerned, there is little to support a charge of exploitation.

Some host nations believe they are exploited because, even if they are given a fair price for their resources, their raw material exports are insufficient to cover the costs in foreign exchange of the manufactured goods that must be imported. In many cases, arrangements can be negotiated that are beneficial to both parties. For example, it may be practicable for some primary as well as intermediate processing to be done within the host country. Of course, such arrangements generally require the tapping of another resource—the human one. In this domain, adequate arrangements for skills transfers, supervisory or management training, and participation in the form of partial local ownership will tend to prevent afterthoughts of exploitation.

In some economies, the multinationals are accused of buying local firms, creating monopolies, and otherwise limiting competition. In still others, the MNEs are charged with discouraging the establishment and preventing the growth of locally owned firms. Undoubtedly there is some truth in both allegations. The purchase of a locally owned firm is, in some countries, the most feasible method of entering the market. Also, few countries have adequate antitrust legislation (or it simply is not enforced); cartels, associations, or monopolies have always existed; and the multinational firm simply becomes one of the prominent players in the game. Adequate legislation can prevent such associations but often not without some attendant costs. Host nations that wish to compete in the international marketplace must depend upon organizations that have the abilities and resources to compete successfully. If domestic firms cannot succeed, no matter how they may be allied, foreign investment may well be the only recourse.

Summary

The foregoing discussion has concerned conflicting wants. The multinational corporation wants stable and/or predictable rules with which to operate. Host countries want major shares of economic benefits as well as the power to assure that their best interests are protected. These desires traverse the economic, political, and social milieu. Without a common denominator, resolution seems impossible.

Some useful generalizations are possible, however. In his study for the United Nations, Raymond Vernon concluded that the bulk of the complaints registered by developing nations of economic exploitation by MNCs was a "charade." Vernon also stipulated that evidence indicated that the economic effects of such foreign operations were "generally benign."[6]

Lacking support for economic disruption, host-country complaints evidently focus upon the perceived diminution of their respective sovereignties and abilities to control their own destinies. Such political and social costs are not measurable and can only be diminished effectively by restricting or eliminating foreign investment.

The solution, like some medicine, is easy to prescribe but uncomfortable to take. All participants must accept the concept that international business and investment is a positive sum game. This recognition is the critical foundation for all negotiations, since both sides must recognize that each receives various economic benefits from the other. With the establishment of this basic framework, conflicts such as those cited and others that will certainly arise over time can be resolved by negotiation and some accommodation by both parties.[7] Such a process produces synergistic partnerships rather than adversary relationships.

Concerns of Developed Nations

The boom period of super growth for multinational corporations "topped out" in late 1972 or early 1973 for a multitude of reasons. Just prior to the downturn, the majority of the developing nations expressed their collective fears of the MNEs to the United Nations. A receptive ear was found; although the United Nations numbered 135 members—all but 10 nations of the world—some 98 of the member nations were classified as "developing countries." Groups affiliated with the United Nations initiated pronouncements and studies that generated further studies and investigations by the industrial nations as well, but for somewhat different reasons.

The United Nations Conference on Trade and Development (UNCTAD) began a review of restrictive business practices employed by MNEs in October 1972 and concurrently issued a resolution that affirmed that nation states had sovereign rights over their natural resources, could nationalize industries involved with these resources, could unilaterally fix compensation for nationalized foreign property, and could settle disputes over the adequacy of compensation in local courts. At about the same time, another United Nations affiliate, the

International Labor Organization (ILO), asked the United Nations to study the social impacts of multinationl enterprises and to issue guidelines for their control. The United Nations Economic and Security Council (ECOSOC) appointed a series of groups and commissions to study the roles and impacts of the MNEs.

Given the inherent bias toward and emphasis upon the developing countries in most of the U.N. pronouncements, the developed nations also began to study the effects of multinational corporations, but primarily as a defensive measure. The Organization for Economic Cooperation and Development (OECD) was a natural vehicle for such investigations. The OECD was composed of 24 member countries of Europe, America, and Asia: Australia, Austria, Belgium, Canada, Denmark, Finland, France, Germany, Greece, Iceland, Ireland, Italy, Japan, Luxembourg, Netherlands, New Zealand, Norway, Portugal, Spain, Sweden, Switzerland, Turkey, United Kingdom, and the United States.

The OECD group also hosted the headquarters of most of the world's multinational firms, accounted for some three-fourths of the world's trade, and produced two-thirds of the gross world product. A further narrowing of the OECD into the eight leading industrialized countries—France, Germany, Japan, Netherlands, Sweden, Switzerland, United Kingdom, and the United States—also produces some impressive statistics. This "big eight" represents home base for about 95 percent of the MNEs and accounts for approximately 75 percent of the annual volume and profits of the world's multinationals.

To insure that the views of the industrialized nations would be presented, the OECD began its own analyses of MNEs in late 1973 and early 1974. Member countries, including the United States, as well as regional groups (particularly the European Economic Community) also examined the effects of the multinational corporation. Thus, at the outset, the efforts of the United Nations and the OECD were studies in contrast: nationalism on the one hand in confrontation with internationalism on the other.

As studies of multinational enterprises proliferated, some chinks in the armor of the MNE were exposed. The industrialized nations, historically at least, were usually supportive of the multinationals, since the parent firms, for the most part, were located in the developed countries, which also perceived themselves to be net beneficiaries of multinational operations. Furthermore, the size of the MNE did not pose the same threats to the larger, developed nations as were felt by the lesser-developed countries. However, events in the 1970s, coupled with data furnished by some of the studies, disclosed some of the diseconomies associated with the multinational enterprise. The role of the MNE came under scrutiny by the industrial world. In the United States, familiar examples are represented by examinations of the following:

1. The continued desirability of the vertical oligopoly ruled by a handful of giant oil companies.

2. The effects of escalating overseas investments upon projected domestic capital needs.
3. The loss of tax revenues through loopholes enjoyed by U.S. multinationals.
4. The impact upon domestic unemployment of the exportation of jobs overseas.
5. The worsening international trade and payments balances.
6. The scourging of the environment by industries.
7. The exposures of bribes and political payoffs made by big business.
8. The potential for foreign takeovers of certain financial and industrial sectors.

One consequence of OPEC's declaration of economic warfare against the industrial world[8] was a resumption of the skirmishes between the U.S. government and "big oil," reminiscent of those in 1911 and the early 1940s. The primary focus was not industry concentration, but rather the *vertical integration* of the oil industry, which, according to government allegations, enabled some 20 firms to control 90 percent of the total oil production. This structure presumably had been tolerated in order to provide the large oil firms with sufficient power to deal effectively with the oil-exporting countries. Since OPEC succeeded in wresting control over the supply and price of oil from the big oil companies, the continued desirability of the integrated control of operations from wellhead to gas pump by a few large companies was challenged. The Federal Trade Commission filed suit in 1973 and Congress proposed legislation aimed at divesting the large oil firms of some of their functions and prohibiting them from engaging in other energy fields, such as coal and atomic or solar power. These actions are still open and will not be resolved quickly in spite of public pressure and frustration.[9] In its defense,[10] the oil oligopoly cited other industries (such as the chemical, food, auto, and steel operations) that functioned with higher percentages of concentration among the leaders. In retrospect, the oil companies called attention to potential problem concentrations in other industries. Reviews of the effects of multinational enterprises took on more of an *inward focus* in the United States.

The world's monetary system, often described as fickle, proved true to form, and normally strong currencies, such as the British pound and the U.S. dollar, were weakened. The declining value of the U.S. dollar increased the cost of doing business overseas by American firms. Also, tariffs walls were lowered further during this period and reduced some of the incentive as well as the need for MNEs to produce goods on site overseas. While these events caused most American multinationals to reexamine planned foreign direct investments, foreign MNEs found the U.S. environment more attractive and announced plans to open manufacturing facilities here. Cries of an impending capital shortage (or "capital crunch") in the United States caused a further looking inward: was it in the best interests of the United States for U.S. multinationals to export capital that was sorely needed at home? Hindsight indicates that the alleged capital crunch was dissipated by worldwide inflation, recession, and excess capacity. It can also reasonably be conjectured that the capital shortage forebodings were simply "cry wolf" tactics of businessmen: outcries against 10 percent capital when 3 percent money was desired; attempts to "politic" for additional tax concessions, and so forth.

Within the United States, attention was also focused upon the *tax loopholes* enjoyed by U.S. multinationals. The existing tax advantages increasingly were being equated with subsidization of foreign investment and further encouraging the export of capital. Foreign tax credits, tax deferrals, and other tax preferences afforded MNEs based in the United States were estimated to have cost the United States over $1.2 billion in tax revenues for 1974; lost tax revenues related to benefits accruing to individuals employed overseas by MNEs (and the U.S. government) were estimated at an additional $300 million for 1974.[11] While the average American is no tax expert, he has learned that, given an insatiable need for tax revenues by his government, if some $1.5 billion of potential tax revenues are waived from one source, so to speak, they must be collected elsewhere—and that elsewhere has historically been the individual taxpayer.

Groups of individuals, particularly labor unions and academicians, expressed their concern over the impact of foreign direct investment by multinationals upon *employment* in the United States. Were we in effect becoming exporters of technology and capital but importers of labor via goods produced overseas by cheaper labor? While little work was done in the area of cost-benefit analysis of exports versus sales by foreign subsidiaries, the comparative effects on the *international balance of payments* (IBOP) should have been readily apparent. Very simply, one dollar of IBOP credit was earned for every dollar of foreign trade (and we are totally ignoring the income benefits that would accrue to U.S. labor in manufacture of the item sold). A similar one-dollar-equivalent sale made to a third country by a wholly owned foreign subsidiary of an American MNC would probably generate less than ten cents in IBOP credit for the United States, and this would accrue only when and if the earnings were repatriated:

Sale of manufactured product	$ 1.00
Less: Cost of item sold and related expenses, say 60 percent	.60
Net income before foreign income tax	.40
Deduct: Foreign income tax at 48 percent	.19
Net income available for repatriation	$ .21
Assume a generous 50 percent dividend	$ .105
Deduct: Average foreign withholding tax at 15 percent	.016
Net remittance and IBOP credit	$ .089

Naturally, this example is constructed upon many conjectures; nonetheless, it should serve to illustrate the differential effects upon the IBOP of foreign trade and sales by foreign subsidiaries of MNEs.

Multinational corporations were placed on the defensive more and more as some writers equated the growth of the MNCs with a form of economic "colonization."[12] Others questioned whether concentration upon foreign direct investment rather than export trade continued to be in the best long-term interests of the United States.[13]

In addition to the foregoing causes for reexamination of the multinational corporation, groups collectively termed *environmentalists* joined the ranks of MNC adversaries, particularly in the United States. To be sure, the environmentalists had no specific reason to challenge the MNC per se. It just so happened that "big business" was considered to be scourging the environment in pursuit of profits—or at least the perpetrators seemed indifferent to the environmental impacts of their operations—and most of the perpetrators were MNCs. Examples abound. Ocean-marine pollution was dramatically highlighted by massive oil spills and the removal from consumption of certain fish due to dangerous levels of mercury content. The damage by industrial wastes was publicized by exposures in the media that made the chemicals Kepone and PCBs familiar household words. The Alaskan Pipe Line, commercial cutting of national forests, strip mining, and the oil-shale controversy are examples of problem areas in land use. Undoubtedly the most controversial and ongoing environmental concerns involve the air pollutants in coal conversion and the disposal of nuclear wastes in the search for alternatives to oil as an energy source.

Perhaps the final stroke of disrepute for the multinational fell with the *disclosures and admissions of bribes*, overt and covert political payoffs, "slush fund" operations, and other assorted activities considered to be illegal, questionable, or unethical business practices.

Ironically, some of the concerns expressed in the United States over multinationals finally adopted a different orientation—that of a host country fearing a *takeover* of some key industries and financial sectors by foreigners. First, the Japanese multinationals were cited as certain to take advantage of the dollar devaluations in 1971 and 1973 and acquire a good portion of American industry. Next, it appeared even a "greater certainty" that the Arab nations would virtually "buy us up" with their windfall gains. Neither event came about, but foreign investments in the United States did increase significantly in the 1970s, as compared with the 1960s, according to the Commerce Department. Also, the traditional foreign investment pattern changed somewhat: manufacturing overshadowed the usual interests in retailing, foodstuffs, and petroleum; existing firms were increasingly being acquired rather than constructing new plants. Dollar devaluations made U.S. production, or at least assembly, of many hitherto imported products a necessity if the items were to be competitive in U.S. markets. It was also alleged that depressions in the U.S. stock markets tended to make acquisitions more attractive than forging new enterprises and constructing new facilities. The influx of OPEC dollars did not occur and the investments that were made were in portfolio and not in direct control of manufacturing. Several reasons can be conjectured: many OPEC members chose to invest their windfalls in armaments, others concentrated upon long-over-looked internal needs, still others were governed by their legacy of conservatism and, not given to risk-taking, elected portfolio rather than direct involvement in business.

More than 75 percent of direct foreign investments in the United States continue to flow from six countries—Japan, Canada, United Kingdom, Switzerland, Germany, and the Netherlands. Political stability, relative economic freedom, dollar devaluations, favorable unit-labor-costs, and lower inflation rates have regularly been cited as the major U.S. attractions. Keeping up with the competition is also an ever-present yet seldom-admitted motivation. For example, Sweden's Volvo opened a U.S. assembly plant; Volkswagen of Germany announced similar plans shortly thereafter; and Japan's Toyota and Nissan companies are thinking of following suit.

There is little doubt that studies of the effects of multinational corporations, initiated by the developing countries in defense of criticism by the Third World and other developing nations, were transformed by a chain of events into critical reexaminations, if not direct challenges.

In the European Economic Community, new antitrust measures were introduced, and Articles 85 and 86 of the Treaty of Rome (the EEC counterpart of the U.S. Sherman Act) tended to be interpreted much more strictly. These actions represented a tougher attitude toward MNCs, although the EEC laws still retained their several loopholes.[14]

In the United States, the suggestions made by some segments of the populace reflected a changed role: from a home-country to a host-country attitude; from demands for more freedom in international business to proposals for new, but selective, barriers. Other studies confirmed (or at least supported) the contention that the increased presence of multinationals in industrialized countries—and that includes foreign MNEs in the United States—effectively enhanced competition, reduced oligopoly control, increased consumer choice, and supplied capital needs.[15]

To date, the questions raised still exceed the solutions obtained. The number of possible trade-offs and accommodations have been identified, examined, and clarified; therein lies the real accomplishment.

Notes

1. For an excellent exposition, see David G. Bradley, "Managing Against Expropriation," *Harvard Business Review*, July-August 1977, pp. 75-83.
2. The term *Third World* is actually a politicoeconomic concept used today to describe those emerging nations which are not parts of the Western

World (the U.S. hegemony) or of the Eastern World (the Russian hegemony). The socioeconomic concept of a *Fourth World* has also been suggested by writers such as Irving S. Friedman, "The New World of the Rich-Poor and the Poor-Rich," *Fortune*, May 1975, pp. 244-248, 250, 252. This world encompasses the poorest of the poor nations; those which not only are poor economically and socially today but for whom the future holds no visible promises for improvement in their fortunes.

3. Thomas P. McCann, *An American Company: The Tragedy of United Fruit*, edited by Henry Scammell (New York: Crown Publishers, 1976).

4. An interesting example surrounds the creation of a profitable shrimp industry in India, as an ancillary activity of the Union Carbide Corporation; described by F. Perry Wilson, Union Carbide's Chairman of the Board, in his article, "The Highest Self-Interest," *Newsweek*, November 24, 1975, p. 23.

5. Hans B. Thorelli, "Management Audit and Social Indicators: The MNC Through the Glasses of the LDC," in *The Multinational Corporation: Accounting and Social Implications*, edited by V.K. Zimmerman (Urbana, Ill.: Center for International Education and Research in Accounting, Department of Accountancy, University of Illinois, 1977), p. 3.

6. *Restrictive Business Practices* (United Nations Document TD/B/399), p. 26, cited in *A Discussion of Provision of Data on MNC Operations* (New York: USA-BIAC Committee on International Investment and Multinational Enterprise, November 1974), p. 11.

7. For a look at the intricacies of both sides, see Louis T. Wells, Jr., "Negotiating With Third World Governments," *Harvard Business Review*, January-February 1977, pp. 72-80.

8. For an interesting analysis, see Carl T. Rowan, "The War that OPEC Started," *The Reader's Digest*, September 1976, pp. 152-156.

9. It seems that the accounting and reporting requirements of the newly established Energy Department will accomplish what a recalcitrant Congress has not been able to do—provide adequate data to support both vertical and horizontal divestiture. See "Help for the Divestiture Drive," *Business Week*, August 15, 1977, p. 141.

10. *Witnesses for Oil: The Case Against Dismemberment* (Washington, D.C.: American Petroleum Institute, 1976).

11. G.C. Hofbauer and J.R. Nunns, "Tax Payments and Tax Expenditures on International Investment and Employment," *The Columbia Journal of World Business*, Summer 1975, pp. 12-20.

12. R.J. Barnett and R.E. Muller, *Global Reach: The Power of the Multinational Corporations* (New York: Simon and Schuster, 1974).

13. Robert Gilpin, *U.S. Power and the Multinational Corporation* (New York: Basic Books, Inc., 1975).

14. For an extensive review, see Robert T. Jones, "Executive's Guide to Antitrust in Europe," *Harvard Business Review*, May-June 1976, pp. 106-118.

15. Summary description of the results of the Multinational Enterprise Project (a large-scale, ongoing study begun by Harvard University in 1965) is given in an address by Frederick T. Knickerbocker in "Proceedings: First Annual International Business Conference," Saint Louis University, December 1, 1975. Unpublished, © Saint Louis University School of Business and Administration.

3 Socioeconomic Development

Socioeconomic development is both fascinating and frustrating. It is a process involving economic growth, income, and people; the last ingredient provides the fascination as well as most of the frustration. It is a process requiring change; and change is often uncomfortable, at best, since familiar habits and ways of thinking become altered and interlaced with uncertainties. It is a process not universally accepted as desirable, per se, since there usually are cost trade-offs which must be weighed: industrialization begets cities and their usual problems in the form of slums, pollution, dehumanization, and so on; cottage industries, family farms, corner stores, and the like, often must yield to the wake of progress; simple ways become structured and mechanized.

All too often, socioeconomic development is couched in economic or quantitative terms alone, and this is unfortunate. One example is the per-capita income statistic, long-used since it is relatively simple to calculate. The primary fallacy, of course, is the assumption of an even income distribution. The extraordinary distortions in this statistic produced in the countries of our OPEC friends may finally have deemphasized this measure. Even in so-called normal times, per-capita income data were blunt measuring devices, at best, since they were seldomly related with the costs of living in the respective countries or, for that matter, within sectors of a given country, such as the United States.

Concentration upon economic development alone has also caused too much emphasis to be placed upon external factors, whereas, in the author's opinion, such externalities are much less influential than the internal factors and their interrelationships. Assistance from outsiders—whether the one-shot, discontinuous forms of aid from other countries, or the more ongoing benefits of foreign direct investments by MNCs—can go only so far in helping the development of a nation. The primary impetus for bettering the lot of the average citizen must come from within the nation itself.

The premise of this chapter is the assumption that the primary goal of every country is ongoing socioeconomic development, defined as a continuous improvement in the average standard of living for the people as a whole.

Constraints

In the main, social scientists have emphasized the following constraints facing underdeveloped countries:

41

Low productivity rates

Excessive population growths

Capital scarcities

Unfavorable trade positions

Poor social structures

Archaic social institutions

Inadequate education systems.

This listing is a presumptuous oversimplification, to be sure. It is neither an ordering by degree of importance nor a sequence of hurdles to be overcome. It is simply a listing of factors having many interrelationships. Not all need be present in every instance and those that are will tend to vary in importance.

Low Productivity Rates

People in the United States and other industrialized countries enjoy higher standards of living because they produce more. But productivity in contemporary societies is dependent upon several other prerequisites as indicated by the following diagram:

Standard
of   ← Productivity ← Technology ← Innovation ← Education
Living

The proximity of the relationship depicted between technology and productivity explains the emphasis placed upon technology by many host nations. Some nations, however, are contemporary only in the sense that they exist in the present time frame; their methods and ways are virtually the same today as they were in the fifteenth century and, in some countries, time has virtually stood still. For many of these nations, the most immediate challenge remains feeding the populace.

Economists classify nations as underdeveloped if more than 50 percent of the people are engaged in primary activities, such as agriculture and the extractive industries (in some countries this percentage ranges between 80 and 90 percent today), and if less than 33 percent of the people are employed in secondary activities, such as manufacturing, processing, and construction. In addition to being tied to the land, the people in many struggling nations cultivate the same small parcels passed down through the generations, using the same antiquated methods as their forefathers. Yields are low and, in some areas, continue to decrease due to the lack of fertilizer for the tired soil and/or no machinery to clear additional arable land. There tends to be little, if any, impetus for change from within: the world-space for the majority is composed of their own and contiguous villages; things are as they always have been; the good life is a closely knit family circle with enough to eat. Productivity for many poorer countries is a static concept. For some of the poorest, it is a process of regression.

Excessive Population Growths

In recent years the name of Thomas R. Malthus has appeared with increasing frequency in the media. References to the Malthusian theory have caused more than a few copies of long-neglected introductory economics texts to be revisited. In his *Essay on the Principle of Population*, published in 1798, Malthus theorized that populations tended to increase geometrically if left unchecked. He cited famine as one of the natural restraints since, due to the law of diminishing returns, he could not envision food production keeping pace. Other natural checks on population he mentioned were war and pestilence. According to Malthus, societies could best help themselves by encouraging marriage in later years and exercising "moral restraint."

Many social factors ran counter to Malthus's advice. In the poor, rural areas, the family unit that was tied to the land associated many benefits with a large family size: a source of help or labor; a sense (and possibly the only one) of accomplishment; and, in many societies, a virtual necessity for security in later years. Religious teachings also tended to keep births constant in many societies. In India, many factions venerated life in all forms, and unnatural restrictions or barriers were seen as breaches in the chain of rebirth. To the Moslem, the preferred number of children was considered to be as many as Allah would send—on the average, seven. The frequency of local wars also decreased, thereby diminishing the effects of one of the so-called natural constraints.

Technology has played a dual role with conflicting results. On the one hand, medical science has significantly reduced the number of epidemics, increased life expectancies, and, in general, increased the number of mouths to be fed. Agricultural technology, on the other hand, has enabled fewer people to feed increasing numbers on a given quantity of land. For the majority of the poor nations the problem has been, or still is, that technology has not kept pace with increasing populations. (For example, the life expectancy at birth is less than 40 years for the populace in the majority of the poor African nations.) In short, it has been said that the challenge today is to bring production up to the level of reproduction—Malthus revisited!

Most writers and sources argue that, in the short run, the world's foodstocks are adequate and that we have "hunger amidst plenty" solely because of distribution problems. There is also a consensus that growing conditions improved throughout most of the "hunger belt" in 1975 and 1976, but no source would confirm a definite long-term trend toward self-sufficiency.

There also does not seem to be any real consensus on the projected scope of the population problem or the appropriate solutions.[1] Should the world food supply become overshadowed by world population, famine and/or triage (feeding only those who have a likely chance to survive) have been forecast. Barring a world food shortage, some groups in the developed nations are beginning to question the continuance of aid in the form of massive food shipments to those countries which have not helped themselves.

Most agree that, in the short run, populations will tend to increase. However, it is argued that, over time, population stability will result from improved standards of living. The best evidence may be drawn from population trends in developed countries today; the maze of interrelated social causes, however, remains moot.

Capital Scarcities

Capital is said to result from postponed consumption. For the underdeveloped world it is hardly possible to save or put off consumption of resources that are at the outset below the level of subsistence. Also, once the subsistence level has been achieved, capital formation tends to be an agonizingly slow process in most developing countries for a multitude of reasons. The usual process calls for initial investments to improve agricultural efficiency, and manufactures must wait. When an agricultural surplus does enable the beginnings of industrialization, the traditional emphasis tends to be toward consumer goods first at the expense of capital goods.

The foregoing treats capital as a *stock concept* and the deficiencies as quantitative factors. But capital also has a dynamic side, which should be viewed as a *flow concept*, which requires examination in qualitative terms. Not everyone in the poorer nations is destitute; the rich and their capital wealth exist in all countries. However, more often than not, those in the rich strata in the underdeveloped nations are not prone to be risk-takers. Tradition, habit, and many other sociocultural factors have led the affluent to invest in land and gold, or other forms of money, which are safer stores of wealth but not economically productive. Thus the dynamic cycle of capital (which Samuelson considers an output as well as an input of an economy[2]) is effectively retarded; the economic surplus accrues to the landed elite and virtually stops there.

Unfavorable Trade Positions

Many underdeveloped countries did not or could not follow Adam Smith's "natural order of things"[3] and engaged in international trade before turning to manufacturing. Consequently, many countries today are faced with the serious disadvantages of exporting relatively low-value basic resources and importing the more expensive manufactured products needed. Some countries voluntarily adopted this practice. Other countries were induced to follow this course of action by outsiders, such as their colonizers or the multinationals, and now consider themselves as having been exploited. The effect remains regardless of cause.

Cartels formed by some nations either were short-lived or, if successful, encouraged their own technological obsolescence. Petroleum, likewise, seems determined to create its own replacements. Coal appears destined to regain its earlier supremacy over oil and gas, particularly in the United States. The atom and the sun are being examined as energy sources. Also, witness the new synthetic oil recently marketed by one of the large U.S. oil companies.

Petroleum has not as yet been dethroned for three probable reasons, all of which are conjecture: (1) American industry has not yet been adversely affected to the extent required to spur massive research and development; (2) the international community has weathered the wave of oil-induced inflation and has, thus far at least, considered it to be nonrecurring; and (3) due to the effects of interrelated corporate ownerships, much of the research devoted to new energy sources has been performed by the oil industry or those industries in which it has some interest or relationship—motivation can only be suspect.

Poor Social Structures

A characteristic stigma of underdeveloped countries is a social structure consisting of a rich stratum and a poor stratum with a wide gulf in between. Wealth is generally represented by large land holdings, and the income produced by the land accrues to and perpetuates the landed elite. Internally, a state of social inertia exists. Large-scale land reforms rarely occur without some form of revolution. External aid becomes dissipated and almost always undergoes a process of filtration with relatively little benefit accruing to the poor majority. Foreign trade, while also a "trickle down" approach, usually benefits the poor more than aid, since the workers at least receive some compensation for whatever is produced.

In other developing countries, the social strata may include a relatively small middle-class segment. In some cases, this stratum was created in one or more coastal towns during a period of colonization. In other cases, the small middle class was painstakingly created over time and is composed of small shopkeepers, cottage industries, and the like. In all cases, social mobility is severely restricted if it exists at all.

In such societies, if nationalistic barriers to foreign capital are erected, for whatever reasons, the countries must look to the capital and initiative of the wealthy class for economic growth. All too often the businesses operated by family dynasties develop little economy of scale since the introduction of labor-saving technology in a labor-intensive society can cause havoc. Consequently, the productivity of labor and its income remains relatively constant—and so does the standard of living of the worker.

Archaic Social Institutions

Social institutions can be defined as ways of thinking. These ways of thinking tend to change slowly yet constantly. They function as guides for the interactions of people within a given society, and in this respect, relative stability is a necessary virtue. On the other hand, that very stability makes it virtually impossible to superimpose the successful methods of one culture upon another that is totally different.

The institution of religion has functioned as an effective means of social control in India and the poor Latin American countries. Hinduism helped millions to tolerate a miserable existence, confident that, if they obeyed the rules of their respective castes, they would be reborn within a higher step in the Brahmanic hierarchy. (It is interesting to note that the Hindu concept of heaven, called *nirvana*, could only be entered by those who achieved the highest caste, that of the Brahmin or priest, and consisted of a state of nothingness—nothing good but, more important, nothing of the misery of everyday life either.) However, the caste system was composed only of archaic functionaries (such as warriors), made no provisions for contemporary social roles (such as managers), and preempted the possibility of social mobility or advancement in one's lifetime. Catholicism also receives "bad marks" for its role in Latin America. While it stressed humility and deemphasized insurrection, Catholicism also encouraged larger populations, to which God would attend, and discouraged materialism, seen by many as an important stimulus for improvement in living standards. Thus, religion helped make life more tolerable for the individual but did not motivate him to seek any short-run improvement.

Governments are social institutions also, and the underdeveloped countries often have the added disadvantage of ineffective governments. Some have not changed since the days of colonization; independence simply changed the faces but not the methods. Many poor nations, the old as well as the new, are still searching for governments with stability and vision.

Socioeconomic growth and ideology have had recurring conflicts in some nations, large and small. Various forms of economic incentives have been used over time by the Russians, admittedly or not, in order to spur the productivity of managers of selected activities. These incentive methods and Russian technology were also credited for the substantial development of the Chinese economy during its first five-year plan (1952-1957). The managerial and technical middle class created in the process, however, ran counter to the Chinese goal of a classless society. The Russians and their material incentives were cast out as China ushered in its "Great Leap Forward" (1958-1961). By 1962, it became apparent that each forward leap of the economy was followed by two backward. Material incentives were reintroduced, and economic growth was reacquired and sustained. But the class distinctions that resurfaced were, on balance, less palatable to the Maoists. Consequently, most individual incentive systems were phased out, beginning in 1966, in favor of socioeconomic growth, albeit somewhat slower, with the requisite of a classless society.[4]

There is ample evidence that closed societies and economies inhibit socioeconomic development. Some of these societies are faced with deficiencies in the internal stimuli and reagents necessary for change, both in number and quality. In others the factors persist in their roles as adversaries.

Inadequate Education Systems

It has been argued that education is the root cause of the problems confronting the poor nations; if they knew more they would do more. Of course, that is truly an oversimplification; while education is an important foundation, many of the previously surveyed constraints interact to retard development.

Lacking instincts, humans reflect behaviors and practices that have been learned. Development of the written word and the printed page not only enhanced the transmission and diffusion of knowledge but concurrently created the need for literacy. In some of the poorer nations, the major obstacle is the existence of many languages or dialects. In others, the people are widely distributed over the land to which they are tied; their world-space and learning environment is limited to their respective hamlets or tribes ; governments simply cannot provide schools where the needs exist. In still other countries, the equivalent of a fourth- or fifth-grade education is provided at no cost and is often required in order for the individual to obtain a work permit. Education beyond that level, although inexpensive according to American standards, is often beyond the reach of any except the upper-middle or wealthy classes.

Many nations are confronted by migrations from the countryside to the cities—either as the result of technological displacement or in the quest for a better life. All too often the migrants do not have salable skills and, lacking land from which to extract a subsistence, they become dependent upon government institutions for support, impose impossible burdens upon the services (including education) provided by the cities, and create urban slums as well as "circles of poverty" from which there is little hope of emerging.

While reasonable access to education is the major hurdle in some areas, in others the curricula remain rooted in the nineteenth century. Secondary schools and universities continue to prepare young people from the wealthier families for their traditional roles in law and the arts. At the university level, such practices have deprived developing countries of a crucial asset—a supply of managers capable of taking over after the colonial interests or the development-assistance teams leave. The literature over the last decade has been replete with references to the lack of managerial resources within developing nations and criticisms of higher-education systems that are more interested in the social niceties than in socioeconomic development. Little attention has been directed toward a rethinking of secondary-education practices toward the practical rather than the intellectual.

Necessary Internal Changes

The major constraints of the socioeconomic development of the poor nations of the world were necessarily presented in an oversimplified format, which examined them as separates rather than as a set of interrelated variables.

In some nations, one or two basic constraints are of such critical importance that the others seem inconsequential; feeding the populace is one example.

In this scenario, it appears that OPEC has turned the hourglass and has assumed the major role, whether intentionally or not. Thus far, at least, 90 percent of OPEC aid has been directed to Arab and Moslem countries in the Middle East; only marginal assistance has been furnished to other developing nations—certainly not enough to offset the exchange costs of oil increases.[5] Further imposed increases in oil prices will surely direct the attention of the industrial world internally rather than upon the problems of others. Unless the appetites of the OPEC nations become satiated with armaments and crash development projects, and they adopt the roles of benevolent *patrones*, the sands in the hourglass will run out for many peoples.

Assuming that a sane course of action is followed and that widespread famine is averted, then the underdeveloped countries will be faced with the real challenges—the *internal* changes that must come about. In these areas of social metamorphosis, external assistance is not very effective, and the will necessary for socioeconomic advancement must be generated from within. People must be willing to change many of their old familiar ways for new, untried, alien ones. Customs, traditions, religious doctrines—the very roots of societies—must be pruned and transplanted in new soils, enriched by progressive systems of education and equity that reemphasize the importance of the individual. Consequently, external help may be necessary and effective in the early stages of socioeconomic advancement, but the stimuli and the will for social change must come from within.

Role of the United Nations

The charter of the United Nations was ratified more than 30 years ago (in October 1945). Its primary purpose was the maintenance of peace and security throughout the world by encouraging nations to settle their disputes by negotiation rather than by force. Ancillary motives called for the promotion of international cooperation in matters of economic, social, cultural, and educational development, as well as the construction of international law. Over the years, countless agencies and committees of the United Nations have sponsored a seemingly endless number of studies, and the great majority have made recommendations concerning socioeconomic development.

United Nations Economic and Social Council (ECOSOC)

In July 1972, a "group of eminent persons" was appointed by ECOSOC to study the effects of multinational corporations on development and international relations. The report was completed in June 1974 and was generally critical of the effects of the MNCs upon developing countries.[6] General recommendations called for such actions as increased aid to the lesser developed countries; use by host countries of central negotiating groups; renegotiation and phase-out clauses in entry agreements; more regional cooperation; and increased assistance from the United Nations to improve the negotiating skills of developing countries. Other areas of the report dealt with political issues, control and ownership, labor usage, technology, transfer pricing, competition, and information disclosure. This last section specifically called for the formation of an "experts group" to develop international accounting standards.

Probably the most valuable contributions of the Report were (1) the airing of the salient issues and (2) the recommendation, adopted by ECOSOC, for the creation of a commission on MNCs.

United Nations Conference on Trade and Development (UNCTAD)

In 1964, when developed countries represented the majority of the U.N. members, UNCTAD was created to serve as a vehicle for making heard the problems of the poorer nations. As aid lost in favor of trade in the 1960s, UNCTAD succeeded in obtaining more favorable access to Western markets for the manufactures and semimanufactures of developing countries; this did not help the poorer nations that exported only raw materials, however. UNCTAD also succeeded in having its proposal calling for the creation of a "new international economic order" accepted in 1975 as an official goal of the United Nations. A commitment of seven-tenths of one percent (0.7 %) of the gross national product of the rich countries to "official development assistance" was extracted by UNCTAD in 1970 but has not as yet been met by any of the developed countries other than the Netherlands and Sweden.[7] In the case of the

United States, substantial contributions to other organizations, such as one-fourth of the capital of the World Bank, should be considered. However, if the 0.7 percent commitment is considered alone, U.S. participation has been at less than one-half the rate specified and is declining.

The Third World nations of UNCTAD resorted to a series of demands made during a conference held in May 1976 in Nairobi: a common fund to support prices of 18 basic commodities; a general system of rescheduling the debts of poor nations; and free use of patents and other technologies, which, in the main, were privately owned by firms in the industrial world. Agreement was reached to begin negotiations in March 1977 on a fund to support some ten raw materials;[8] to develop criteria for a case-by-case approach to debt rescheduling; and to hold further discussions on technological assistance, since privately owned patents and the like do not legally represent a free good.

On balance, UNCTAD has progressed slowly, and this is understandable. United Nations endorsement of a new international economic order does not automatically make it so for the more than 100 Third World nations whose people represent 2 billion of the 3.5 billion global population. During UNCTAD conferences, unanimity is easy for the poorer nations when the issues concern the rich versus the poor; however, special interests lead to divergent opinions where such specific issues as trade concessions or prices for particular commodities are being negotiated.

There is a general agreement that UNCTAD has performed three services: (1) it has emphasized the crises facing the poorest nations; (2) it has improved the economic positions of those developing nations which have begun to export manufactures; and (3) it has tempered the extremism advocated by the more radical countries.

United Nations Financial Institutions

Two specialized agencies were approved by the United Nations in 1947 to assist international economic development: the International Monetary Fund (IMF) and the International Bank for Reconstruction and Development (now commonly referred to as the World Bank).

The primary functions of the IMF were to promote reasonable stability in exchange rates of all currencies and to discourage competitive manipulations of exchange rates by governments. Naturally, stability in the exchange rates of the currencies of underdeveloped countries would generate investor confidence, both internal and external. The workings of the IMF will be examined in a subsequent chapter dealing with exchange rates. However, suffice it to say here that, on balance, the IMF was generally successful, particularly over its first 20 years.

The World Bank was established as the major international lending agency with objectives to assist the flow of investment capital needed to rebuild and/or develop national economies, to encourage international investment by the private sector, and to help promote an international trade balance. The World Bank accepts only the *best risks*—governments and those firms which can obtain repayment guarantees by their respective governments. Loans traditionally have been restricted to sound, productive projects that can repay themselves in from 10 to 30 years.

A World Bank affiliate, the International Finance Corporation (IFC), services the *higher risks* represented by nonguaranteed loans to private business enterprises in developing countries. The IFC has played a versatile role. It has participated in and arranged for the composite financing of multi-million-dollar industrial complexes. Typically, the IFC furnished about one-fourth of both share and loan capital and persuaded private firms and banks, in both host and foreign countries such as the United States, to finance the major portion.

The *poorest risks* have been assumed by a second subunit of the IMF, the International Development Association (IDA). The bulk of IDA loans flow to the world's poorest nations for improvements in infrastructures, housing, and similar projects in the social interest. Since such ventures require a long lead time before producing returns large enough to enable repayment, loans are typically for a 50-year period, with no repayments scheduled within the first 10 years or so, and, instead of interest, they usually bear a nominal (less than one percent) annual service charge. As can be imagined, the more conservative World Bank and IFC are healthy international financial institutions, whereas the IDA must continuously plead for additional funds from the richer countries.

In addition to these international lending agencies, a half-dozen or so regional development banks, together with national development banks (such as the U.S. Export-Import Bank), serve as sources of financing for developing nations.

Paradoxically, as the availability of financing effectively widened during the 1970s, more and more of the non-oil-producing underdeveloped countries found themselves at or near the limits of their borrowing power. The common problem was a mounting balance-of-payments deficit, which, for most developing nations, was significantly worsened by OPEC's 1973 price hike. External debts of the less-developed countries (LDCs) are estimated in excess of $200 billion, with private banks holding slightly more than one-fourth of the total. As interest payments become more difficult to meet, the private sector will become less receptive to additional requests, and governments will have to fill the voids if stability is to be retained. OPEC might even be persuaded (or shamed) into repairing some of the economic damage it has caused.

While recent statements emanating from the less-developed plurality of the United Nations have seemed more like demands, the responses made by some officials of the United Nations and the developed countries have generally been more critical of the LDCs' efforts to help themselves. Speaking before the

Habitat Conference held in Vancouver in June 1976, U.N. Secretary-General Kurt Waldheim charged the leaders of the less-developed countries with the responsibility to do whatever was necessary to provide minimum housing standards for their people. U.S. Treasury Secretary William E. Simon, in an address to the annual gathering of the IMF World Bank and the private banking community held in Manila in October 1976, criticized the LDCs for erecting barriers to the inflow of private foreign capital and for the lack of self-help efforts.[9]

Internal belt-tightening, sacrifice, and determination on the part of the poor nations were among the remedies for socioeconomic development prescribed in a recent study for the United Nations by a team of economists headed by Nobel-laureate Wassily Leonteif.[10] Probably the most significant finding of the study was the identification of the major growth constraints—social, political, and institutional defects—rather than the physical limitations so often touted. Recommendations called for the use of drastic measures by LDC governments to at least double food production.

Role of Private Foreign Enterprise

There is little doubt that foreign direct investment and other forms of assistance are necessary to generate socioeconomic development of the poorest nations at a pace rapid enough to enable them to overcome unemployment, hunger, poverty, and squalor. The larger multinational enterprises have the scope, the resources, the opportunity, and the talent to perform an active role. Their contributions to economic and social progress may have been overshadowed in recent years, but they have been substantial.

Not all writers give the MNE a good report card in the socioeconomic development process. Some stipulate that the differential contribution of a multinational corporation depends upon the development phase of the host country, the bundle of benefits offered by the MNE, and the price of the elements in that bundle.[11]

Others argue that the multinational is ill-suited for assisting in the development process and has no role to play. The profit motive of the MNE is considered the primary obstacle, since profitable activities seldom, if ever, address the two basic needs of the poor masses—full and efficient employment as well as increased productivity. This criticism is valid if and only if other private addressors of these basic needs are available to perform the services without profit or, if supplied by the government, at a lesser total cost.

The first basic need usually encompasses infrastructures, electrification, and health-care resources that are normally the obligations of government; MNEs can and will help, but not gratis. Concerning the second need for greater productivity in the normal, daily affairs of the masses, MNEs can certainly produce all the shovels, pushcarts, bikes, and wagons[1 2] needed, but, again, these articles will be produced for sale, at a profit, and not gratis.

Both of these needs depend upon one common denominator—money. If the developing country has the funds, it can be self-reliant; that is, it can purchase what it cannot provide internally.

In his statement before the United Nations Group of Eminent Persons on September 11, 1973, Emilio G. Collado, Executive Vice President of Exxon, explained that his corporation conducted international operations for 85 years and, as of September 1973, operated facilities in more than 100 countries. He cited the achievements of the ADELA investment company, a cooperative effort by MNCs and banks in the United States, Canada, Europe, and Japan. ADELA was designed to assist small business firms in Latin America by means of loans and/or minority investments. Over eight and one-half years, ADELA provided more than $1 billion in loans and investments. As of September 1973, Collado stated that current ADELA participation consisted of (1) loans to and investments in some 400 small businesses in Latin America, totaling about $350 million; and (2) support by more than 235 multinational firms and banks. He also announced that, in view of ADELA's success, similar cooperatives were being organized by MNCs to serve the African and Far Eastern regions.[1 3] Such assistance, while emanating from the MNEs, is not usually accompanied by concerns of exploitation or dependence.

Along similar veins, direct investments by smaller foreign firms tend to be welcomed by many developing nations, since these ventures do not carry the stigma of those proposed by the multinationals.

Participation in such ventures is becoming more practicable for smaller firms based in many industrial countries. In the United States, feasibility studies, long-term development loans and grants, and credit and investment insurance programs by agencies such as the Eximbank, the Foreign Credit Insurance Association, the Inter-American Development Bank, and the Overseas Private Investment Corporation are available, among others. Eurocurrencies provide similar opportunities for firms in Europe.

The Decades of Decision

It is certain that most of the developing countries will be faced with extremely difficult choices in action in the next 20 years. It is also probable that some of the poor nations will not survive.

Each nation must, in effect, assess where it stands today and where it wants to go. Given reasonable and attainable aspirations, each must choose the route it considers best. Existing models will be examined—capitalism, communism, and socialism. More often than not, each of the models will be found either wanting in certain respects or simply not workable without modifications. Many less-developed countries will resort to state control of the economy, or at least its vital sectors, in the initial stages of growth and dependence upon the multinational will diminish.

Nationalism will tend to spur growth only so far, and this realization, together with the degree of self-confidence that will have been acquired, should lead toward regional cooperation among countries with similar attitudes and aspirations. The sharings of ideas, the economies of scale, and the benefits of acculturation thus acquired can only further the realization that interdependent cooperation enhances the socioeconomic status of all peoples.

Role of Accounting

Since accounting is considered to be the language of business, its international role is that of communicating information, primarily financial, concerning the operations and fiscal positions of enterprises. In this context, governments are among the largest of enterprises. It appears that Communist China is learning this lesson belatedly. Recurring phases in China's history reflect unsuccessful attempts to attain economic growth while retaining ideological purity, or a classless society. A recent editorial in the *People's Daily Newspaper* of Peking reportedly urged the populace to generate the wherewithal for economic growth and blamed the current economic difficulties upon the fact that the necessary tools of accounting had lost their credibility. A policy of greater accountability within the public sector was stressed in the editorial as essential to growth within the socialistic economy today and not as a token of surrender to capitalism.[14]

In its travels around the globe, accounting evolved in response to the needs of the communities it served. In most instances the development and vitality of the accounting framework paralleled the growth and prestige of business within the national environs. Consequently, with the exception of India, accountancy today is rudimentary, at best, in the lesser-developed countries, whereas the needs for reliable and responsive financial reporting are becoming increasingly important.

Committees of the American Accounting Association have examined accounting practices and educational programs of lesser-developed countries and have concluded:

1. The problems require infusions of significant resources and interest.[15]
2. Accounting education cannot be considered or developed outside the general educational system in a given nation; therefore:
    a. Governmental accounting should be emphasized to assist in the efficient use of resources.
    b. Accounting and taxation should be improved by the establishment of legal requirements.

    c.   Selected forms of assistance should be pursued, such as textbooks, curricula development, and instructor-exchange programs.[16]

Without a single solution or an organization, either philanthropic or for-profit, that is capable and willing to provide it, the sources of help for accounting education within developing countries are open to conjecture. Some reasonable assumptions can be made, however.

Some developing nations will adopt communism, or one of its variant forms, as the preferable solution to socioeconomic growth. State ownership of *all* resources in closed economies will also close the door on help from free-enterprise sources. Accounting and reporting systems will be those imposed by the government to support its centralized, national planning. Nations choosing this course of action will have to depend upon internal resources augmented by assistance from countries with similar ideologies.

It is more likely that the majority of the developing countries will espouse national planning but with something less than total state ownership.

Nations that select state ownership of the *majority* of the economy, with little emphasis upon the private sector, will tend to adopt centralized planning from the top down, with much imposed uniformity. Here again, such countries will be forced to look to themselves for accounting expertise. However, accounting methodologies will tend to follow the imposed uniformity in the central planning, and this, as Mueller[17] has suggested, should assist in the construction of accounting systems, the preparation of accountants, and the transferability of accounting expertise.

Other developing nations will choose state ownership and/or control of *selected* areas of the economy, such as those concerning natural resources, agriculture, and basic industries. Central planning will also tend to be adopted as a necessary tool, but in cooperation with private enterprise, both domestic and foreign. Where finances are not immediate constraints, such as in OPEC, outside assistance in the improvement of accounting education can be afforded and imported. The less-fortunate nations may look to the larger foreign firms within the private sector as training grounds and resource centers for accounting expertise. The state, of course, will have to support the upgrading of accounting education with resources commensurate with its perceived importance.

Still other developing nations will depend upon private enterprise for economic growth, with the state attempting to recognize and fill the voids. These nations will usually approach national planning from the bottom up, depending more upon coordination than upon compulsion. The development of accounting education should benefit from a broader base and interest. In addition to the state itself, help could emanate from multinational enterprises, interested international organizations, and the multinational networks of professional accounting firms.

Regardless of the approach to socioeconomic development selected by the lesser-developed countries, accounting and accounting education will most likely be forced to play the game of "catch up." Economists, such as Goldsmith, Kuznets, and McKinnon, have established the relationships between economic growth and capital markets. Few will demand proof that viable capital markets, in turn, require dependable financial reporting—the contribution of accountancy. Thus the following linking relationship is developed:

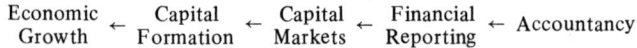

$$\text{Economic Growth} \leftarrow \text{Capital Formation} \leftarrow \text{Capital Markets} \leftarrow \text{Financial Reporting} \leftarrow \text{Accountancy}$$

Each arrow should be read as "is dependent upon." In this relationship, accountancy is on the "tail end" and will tend to develop only as a result of the preconditions and demands of the other stimuli.

Notes

1. Joseph Winski, "By 2000, Prevention of Starvation May Be a Chief Global Concern," *The Wall Street Journal*, March 25, 1976.

2. Paul A. Samuelson, *Economics*, 10th ed. (New York: McGraw Hill Book Company, 1976), p. 50.

3. In his *Wealth of Nations*, Adam Smith advised nations to follow the "natural order of things": first, feed the populace; next, produce manufactured needs; finally, seek out foreign trade. Smith regarded deviations from this pattern as "unnatural and retrograde."

4. Barry M. Richman, "A Firsthand Study of Industrial Management in Communist China," in Stanley M. Davis, *Comparative Management* (Englewood Cliffs, N.J.: Prentice-Hall, Inc., 1971), pp. 280-293.

5. See Roger D. Hanson et al., *The U.S. and World Development: Agenda for Action* (New York: Praeger Publishers for the Overseas Development Council, 1976).

6. *A Review of the Report: The Role of Multinational Corporations on Development and on International Relations* (New York: USA-Business and Advisory Committee, November 1974), 46 pp.

7. Hansen et al., *The U.S. and World Development*, Table E-7, p. 203.

8. Robert Prinsky, "Pacts to Stabilize Prices of Raw Materials Are Expected Eventually on Some Items," *The Wall Street Journal*, July 19, 1976, p. 14.

9. Editorial, "The One Billion Poor," *St. Louis Post-Dispatch*, October 16, 1976, p. 4A.

10. Comments of Wassily Leontief reported in "Poor Nations Must Sacrifice to Close Gap, UN Study Says," *St. Louis Post-Dispatch*, October 14, 1976.

11. Gustav Ranis, "The Multinational Corporation as an Instrument of

Development," in *The Multinational Corporation and Social Change*, edited by David E. Apter and Louis Wolf Goodman (New York: Praeger Publishers, 1976), pp. 96-117.

12. Harry Magdoff, "The Multinational Corporation and Development—A Contradiction?", in *The Multinational Corporation and Social Change*, edited by Apter and Goodman, pp. 200-222.

13. Emilio G. Collado, "The Multinational Corporation," in *Multinational Enterprise* (New York: The Exxon Corporation, 1974), p. 5.

14. "Chinese Are Asked to Raise 'Enormous Funds' for Growth," *The St. Louis Post-Dispatch*, August 28, 1977, p. 11A.

15. "Report of the Committee on Accounting in Developing Countries," *The Accounting Review: Supplement to Volume 51*, 1976, p. 211.

16. "Report of the American Accounting Association Committee on International Accounting Operations and Education, 1975-1976," *The Accounting Review: Supplement to Volume 52*, 1977, pp. 70-75.

17. Gerhard G. Mueller, *International Accounting* (New York: The Macmillan Company, 1967), p. 110.

4 Business Ethics

Business has earned little esteem in some societies, is held highly suspect in others, and is viewed with contempt in still others. Antiquity looked upon commerce—the simple interchange of goods for profit—as being base by definition. The values added in the form of time and place utilities were not considered. The esteem of business was assisted by the advent of manufacturing, since the conversion of a basic material into a more useful form or product lent a measure of credibility to the profit sought. In some areas the work ethic (or Protestant ethic, as it has sometimes been called) became socially acceptable, as well as the profit, in whatever form, that accrued from one's labor.

Today, few question the contributions of the profit incentive to the standards of living of the people in those societies which have subscribed to it in various forms. However, there is also abundant evidence that the profit motive has played the role of corruptor. Some thinkers, such as Adam Smith, looked upon outside intervention as harmful and unnecessary since the "invisible hand" of the marketplace in an environment of perfect competition would result in the greatest benefit for all. Unfortunately, the very quest for competitive advantage destroyed, or at least ameliorated, the checks and balances ascribed to perfect competition, and, consequently, most societies imposed some form of external sanction upon the marketplace. As a result, the basest form of corruption in these societies involved bribes—payments generating improper actions by those responsible for administering the sanctions designed to protect the public.

Ethics

The study of the right and wrong in human conduct is known as ethics. The term is derived from the Greek *ethos*, denoting character. Ethics is a normative study in that the judgment of an action as being right or wrong requires a standard or norm on which to base the judgment. Since these standards vary between and among societies, a given form of behavior may be frowned upon in one social environment yet be entirely acceptable in another.

Sociologists have devised a hierarchical pattern of rules or norms governing social conduct: folkways, mores, and laws. *Folkways* are simply customs or traditional ways of doing things, such as wearing shoes or sleeping in a bed. *Mores* are also customs, but more important ones in that they are considered to be basic to societal welfare; for example, the keeping of a mistress in addition to a wife and family in our society is considered immoral, since it poses a threat to the family institution and to society as a whole. *Laws* represent those norms which a given society considers important and vital enough to merit formal recording and enactment by legislative bodies.

Sanctions represent the means, in the form of rewards and punishments, that societies use to support or enforce the rules of behavior. Rewards may vary from a smile to the Nobel Prize. Punishments also vary. Deviation from a folkway may result in sanctions ranging from a frown to labeling as queer. Violation of mores brands the offender as immoral, with penalties ranging from ridicule to social ostracism. Violation of the law brings sanctions ranging from fine and/or imprisonment to death.

The preceding framework of social sanctions, though oversimplified, can be used as a basis for understanding the popular approaches for coping with unethical behavior within our society in general and business in particular.

One school of thought, which, for want of any other label, can be termed *legalistic*, favors a general strengthening of the laws: make the punishment sufficient and it will deter infractions. The use of negative motivators by the legalists faces several challenges. Within a given society, such as ours, there are those who regularly request proof that a particular punishment actually deters a specific illegal act. Naturally, given the multitude of possible social variables that exist as well as interact, it is no more possible to prove that a law is a deterrent than to prove that it is not. The point is moot. Also, laws tend to be interpreted strictly, and, divested from the reasonings underlying their original enactment, many laws become ineffective over time as the social or business environment changes. The usual response tends to be additional layers of regulations to cover the exceptions. In a society that takes pride in its foundation of personal freedom, each new law or regulation is at once at odds with the concepts of personal and enterprise freedom. Finally, what can be done about those individuals and organizations which, because of position or purse, are effectively "beyond the law" in that the prescribed sanctions can be ameliorated if not avoided altogether? Interactions between individuals and firms in different countries further multiply the problems confronting legalistic approaches to regulating behavior. In some nations, guilt is presumed upon accusation and justice is quickly done; in others, the accused is considered innocent until proved guilty, and proceedings can consume several years.

At the other end of the spectrum is a group, call them the "moralists," that points out that laws cannot be imposed upon a society. Instead, laws must be accepted if they are to be effective. In other words, the moralists argue that, without the existence of an adequate foundation of mores or morals in a given society, the enactment of additional laws tends to be rather useless. Their recommendation, then, is that the specific sectors of society—businesses, governments, professions, and so forth—should be tasked with putting their own houses in order. Accepting this advice for the sake of argument, what does it mean? The negative motivator of law—punishment—is rather evident and often measurable. The positive motivator of the moralists—reward—is subtle and usually unrecognized. Few ordinary folk and businessmen receive rewards for conforming to the mores of good citizens.

International business multiplies the problems in the moral milieu the same as in the legal environment. Since morals differ between and among societies, is it permissible to do as the Romans do when in Rome? Or should American morals be applied in business relationships transacted in other countries? Are business relationships subject to a moral code different from that governing individual relationships? These are only examples of the gamut of moral issues that have been brought to the fore in recent months.

For a variety of reasons, actions by individuals or firms may be accepted as commonplace in one country, disliked but condoned in another, branded as illegal in another, and condemned by dishonor in yet another. (The moralist would be quick to interject that dishonor was ranked above legal sanction in that ordering. Unfortunately, this tends to hold true primarily in those older societies in which the coming-of-age brought about a reconciliation between personal and general welfare. In this regard, America is still an adolescent.)

There is little doubt that if everyone followed the mores adopted by society there would be little need to formalize the rules in the form of written laws. At least for the present, that notion can be put aside. All that is necessary is a scanning of today's newspaper. Granted that the media accentuate the negative aspects of society under the guise that they are the most newsworthy, yet it requires a healthy constitution to review topics such as Watergate and the questionable payments made by business, which are continuously unfolding, and not become ill in the process.

Questionable Payments

Were the events not crucial to the very foundation of the free market system, the nuances applied to the corruptive practices of businessmen would be simply humorous. Payments uncovered and/or admitted by businessmen were not labeled right or wrong, legal or illegal, but rather, questionable. The only questionable factors regarding the payments were related to the passing of time and exposure. In short, the payments were considered to be questionable only after the fact, when they were publicized; at the time they were made, they apparently weren't considered to be questionable at all. Or, if they were, the participants relied upon not being caught.

The whole sordid mess of corruption within government and business gradually unfolded after two events: the Watergate fiasco, which began on June 17, 1972, and the suicide leap of Eli Black, Chairman of United Brands, on February 3, 1975. The first event brought to light corruptive domestic practices of government and business, primarily with political overtones, that culminated in the crushing disgrace and fall of the president of the United States. In the second event, Eli Black, described as a "quiet rabbi,"[1] chose death over disgrace and focused attention on overseas corruption of business and government.

The ensuing investigations directed by the U.S. Special Prosecutor, the SEC, and foreign governments have implicated hundreds of the largest U.S. corporations—the number seems to increase almost weekly—as well as some highly respected personages in the United States and abroad. The amounts involved certainly can't be considered petty cash either, since millions of dollars of these so-called questionable payments have been traced to dozens of the largest U.S. corporations. Lockheed Aircraft Corporation has thus far earned the dubious distinction of "biggest spender," having been charged with more than $250 million of such payments.

The numbers of these covert payments and the magnitude of the amounts have sunk business to the lowest level of credibility since the stock exchange scandals of the 1930s. Yet, in reading the accounts brought to light thus far, the ultimate disgrace for the corporate community comes not from the wrongs perpetrated on this and other societies, but rather from the audacity of those corporate officers (and government personages) who attempt to defend their actions on ethical or ideological grounds.

Some distinguished experts, such as Peter Drucker,[2] believe that the recent clamor over corporate behavior has confused ethics with aesthetics. In short, business was given, or assumed by default, a leadership role. It chose not to employ the prudence expected of leaders in our culture. Consequently, business has forfeited its leadership in an era literally clamoring for the socioeconomic improvements only industrialization can provide, at least in the near future. This is the grievous crime.

Political Contributions

In the United States, it is illegal for corporations to make political contributions in federal elections from company funds (U.S. Criminal Code, section 610).[3] The second member of the business-labor-political triumvirate was likewise enjoined by the Labor-Management Relations Act of 1947 (section 304). Both acts prescribe criminal penalties upon the contributor and the recipient. Few articles indicate that these contributions are criminal, not merely questionable, in the United States.

There are legal avenues for business and labor contributions to political campaigns in the United States. These usually take the form of political action committees to which voluntary contributions can be made by individuals. (Given the pressures that can be exerted upon individuals within business and labor organizations, the voluntary nature of these contributions requires application of a great deal of confidence or, alternatively, a vivid imagination.) Donations are subsequently made to the campaigns of those candidates whose positions are considered to be friendly in the opinion of the administrators of the committee. The candidate, or his campaign committee, must disclose the sources of contributions in excess of $100, in accordance with the Election Campaign Practices Act of 1972.

In other countries, such as Canada and Italy, political contributions are not illegal. However, they are not deductible business expenses for tax purposes, either.

Legal and other constraints aside, disclosures over the past several years clearly indicate that a myriad of the largest U.S. corporations, as well as many of the most prominent U.S. political personages, either believed they would not be caught or that they were effectively beyond the law.

Accounts of slush-fund operations seem much like James Bond scenarios. One of the largest tire manufacturers falsified accounting records and consented to an SEC charge of maintaining a political slush fund in excess of $300,000, which was reportedly under the personal control of the company's chief executive officer.

A multinational oil company similarly consented to the operation of a clandestine subsidiary in the Bahamas used for the "laundering" of capital contributions from the U.S. parent. Illegal political contributions were made in the United States, as well as unknown payments to foreign recipients. In this case, knowledge was traced to the top executives, including one board member.

Another giant U.S. oil company admitted making some $27 million of political contributions in the United States and several other countries; that amount was more than doubled upon subsequent audits. More than 40 secret bank accounts were maintained, none of which appeared on the company's records, and the funds were reported to have been accumulated by illicit rebates, overdrafts, and the like. A panel of directors subsequently recommended that the stockholders should not sue the company's officers (who had resigned) for their errors of business judgment.

Thorny issues can arise even in those nations where political contributions are legal. For example, consider the case in which British Petroleum (which was 69 percent government-owned) contributed $1.5 million to political parties in Italy.

Bribes and Extortions

In law, a bribe is the offering of something of value to a government official in order to improperly influence his action. Extortion is similar, except that the demand for payment originates from the official. In actual instances, it is often difficult to distinguish one from the other over time.[4] In any case, both practices are crimes under the laws of all countries.

Disclosures of bribes and/or extortions paid by large American firms, particularly the multi-million-dollar payments admitted by aerospace and munitions companies, have enraged the public and disgraced American industry.

The Lockheed Aircraft case appears destined for notorious citation in textbooks for decades to come. Not only were hundreds of millions of dollars involved, but the cesspool of infamy uncovered thus far has tainted national governments, including our own, as well as royal families and prestigious personages.

Lockheed Aircraft, the largest defense contractor in the United States, also consented to SEC charges of falsifying accounting records, using its subsidiaries to launder funds, and making bribes and other clandestine payments from secret funds and Swiss bank accounts. Payments made by Lockheed to Japanese government officials have been denounced as bribes and have resulted in the loss of face as well as influence of the Japanese political structure that has, historically at least, been most favorable to the United States. Planned acquisitions of military hardware from the United States have been canceled or postponed indefinitely by Japan. According to the Japanese view, if Lockheed stooped to these immoral practices, so did their competitors, and all U.S. military suppliers were held suspect. Italy, which is traditionally slow to react and often ready to lend a deaf ear to internal scandal, indicted several government officials for reportedly accepting bribes from Lockheed. Prince Bernhard of the Netherlands was forced to resign in order to preclude his prosecution and the abdication of the Queen. Bernhard's disgrace was not the result of accepting bribes from Lockheed—that would have required admission or proof by additional investigation—but rather stemmed from written evidence that he directly solicited favors in writing. Undisclosed Saudi Arabian officials have reportedly led the field in amounts received from Lockheed—more than $160 million in a five-year period. Other governments are also looking into transactions with Lockheed; West Germany, South Africa, Nigeria, Spain, and Greece are examples.

American interests in the Lockheed affair have gradually, and painfully, turned inward. There is a valid concern that, given the actions that have been disclosed abroad, similar crimes may have been perpetrated in the United States.

On the one hand, it is reasonable to assume that, given the authorizations required to conduct arms sales to foreign governments, certain U.S. agencies and officials would have been privy to the transactions and, if so, would have indirectly, if not directly, condoned them.

On the other hand, Lockheed was the first large American firm to be bailed out of its financial difficulties by means of a $250 million federally guaranteed loan approved in 1971. (The potential impact of political contributions by big business firms may be assessed when one considers that the Lockheed loan proposal passed the Senate by three votes and the House by only one.) In many ways Lockheed acquired not only the endorsement necessary for its loan but the government as a bedfellow as well; during investigation of the Lockheed payments made abroad, several government sources recommended that amounts and locations of payments not be disclosed, since such exposure might cause the firm to default on its loan. Other government representatives, recognizing that the firm apparently paid virtually as much in bribes and similar payments as the amount of the loan, have demanded that a monthly pay-as-you-go schedule be used in lieu of the existing balloon-type loan repayment.

One lesson should be evident. Those who might argue that bribes and similar illegal payments are necessary for the economic survival of a major firm in the international realm would be well advised to consider the Lockheed example first—virtual bankruptcy is not the reflection of a winner.

Agent Commissions

The third prominent category of questionable payments refers to fees paid to sales agents in foreign countries as commissions. A payment made as compensation for the selling of a product or service has long been considered a legitimate business expense, subject only to the criteria of all business expenses—that they be reasonable, customary, and necessary. Defenses presented in recent months have ranged from the ridiculous to the sublime. *Reasonable* has been defined as "the least that we could get by with." *Customary* meant that "everybody does it." *Necessary* was simply, "if we didn't pay, we couldn't survive."

Here, again, some of the alleged perpetrators obtained the U.S. government as a bedfellow. At the request of the SEC, the U.S. District Court directed the Boeing Company to disclose the names of 18 foreign sales agents (reportedly government officials—including a prince—and close associates) to which Boeing allegedly paid $77 million in fees over a five-year period. The Department of State joined the Boeing Company in an appeal to reverse the order. The State Department feared the disclosures might be damaging to international relations; Boeing contended that the persons in question were men of prominence in their countries.[5] In cases such as this, in which firms or individuals appear to be above the law, disclosure seems to be a penance that is more effective—or at least more feared—than legal penalties.

In some payoff cases, it was found that commissions were added to the customer's billings in a variety of ways. Upon collection by the selling corporation, the agents' commissions were often directed, at the agents' requests, to third-country bank accounts, presumably to avoid publicity and/or taxes. Accounting entries engineered to conceal these payments were more common than not.

The use of an agent as middleman was also broached as a defense in some cases involving bribes paid to foreign officials. Some corporations argued that it was difficult, if not impossible, to control the actions of agents in such matters.

The defense is good only because the offense is moot. In the law of agency, application of the general rule imputes knowledge of the agent to the principal, except in those cases involving crimes; criminal law requires actual knowledge, rather than merely constructive knowledge, of the principal.

The issues surrounding agent commissions are not nearly as clear-cut as those concerning political contributions and bribes. Cases involving commissions and similar fees will have to be judged by the circumstances and the actions of the participants concerned. One point that is clear, at least to this author, is that any transaction that cannot stand the light of disclosure but must be concealed by falsification of records or other devious means is judged as illicit by those most qualified to make that assessment—the participants.

What Can Be Done?

Since, in the course of a lifetime, few individuals have not done something of which they are not proud, should society collectively refrain from casting the first stone? Are the norms and mores governing individual conduct, and hence the determinants of social values, different from those applying to the conduct of institutions? Is there a separate and distinct "organizational imperative," as suggested by Chamberlain,[6] that sometimes prevails over individual morals?

In short, is there a business ethic separate, distinct, and different from an individual ethic? If not, then society can evaluate recent events using standards for behavior that are as old as time itself. If there is a separate business ethic, then the task becomes one of definition and redefinition, since the world of business is much broader in scope and more volatile than the world-space of most individuals.

Whether or not a separate business ethic exists in fact is not altogether that important, since it appears that many businessmen believe it to be so and act accordingly. Based upon this premise, our society and others cannot sit back and expect individual values to trickle down and regulate the organizational imperatives. The international society cannot be dissuaded in its initial prescription of the business ethic, nor can it acquiesce to those business executives who are quick to caution that we cannot expect to improve upon the Bible yet are just as eager to remind that business is too pervasive to be circumscribed by rules of individual conduct.

International business has come of age sufficiently within the industrialized world to permit those nations to collectively prescribe the perimeters of acceptable business conduct and national relationships. A thus-far-and-no-further delineation of international business practices would place the burden of proof upon those multinationals and nation-states which constantly elect to tread the perimeters. Those which operate extraterritorially, so to speak, would clearly become earmarked as undesirable world partners. Developing nations would also have guidelines to follow in negotiation and in action.

The United States has earned the respect and envy of the world for at least three major achievements: a relatively high average standard of living for its people; a reasonable accommodation between industrialization and the individual; and the maintenance of a delicate, though undulating, balance between private enterprise and the public interest. The image of the United States has fallen to its lowest levels in both the private and public arenas. Before the United States can reattach its former weight of credibility to international issues, it faces the chore of first looking inward and setting its own house in order. Decisiveness will aid its cause.

Internal Issues

Watergate, political slush funds, and the South Korean influence-peddling scandal have defamed important public figures as well as the legal and accounting professions. Little action has been taken thus far by the Justice Department in response to information furnished by the Special Prosecutor. One reason could well be the ambiguities within existing laws. These ambiguities need to be removed.

With the exception of two or three individuals, the Watergate and CREEP (Committee to Re-elect the President) figures were professional men of some stature. The various bar associations and the AICPA gained little public favor through their efforts, which seemed more intent on saving face than on admonishing offenders of codes of professional conduct.

Also, something is inherently wrong with a system in which American senators and congressmen (and those individuals seeking election to public office) can accept money and other gifts, from U.S. or foreign sources, or can place themselves in positions of apparent compromise and walk away with their skins intact. John McCloy, for one, considers reactions to the disclosures of political contributions to be primarily one-sided. A political contribution is a two-party act and, consequently, McCloy cautions that it is not reasonable to condemn one party (the contributor) and hold the receiver guiltless, either legally or morally.[7] In the wake of the Watergate debacle, politicians have fallen to such low esteem that public opinion has ceased to represent an effective deterrent now or for the immediate future. Ethics committees of the Senate and the House have also proved to be ineffectual, to say the least.

It is apparent that business is no more likely to clean up its own house than are our elected officials. It is also apparent that something more effective than the current round of slaps on the wrist will be necessary. According to Nader and Green: antitrust fines have been trivial; fines imposed upon Watergate offenders averaged only a mere $7,000; SEC consent decrees do not require the admission of past wrongs, but merely promises to obey existing regulations in the future; and most executives cited by the SEC and the Special Prosecutor still retain their prestigious positions.[8] For the myopic executive who didn't realize that he authorized or acceded to a wrong, wrong will have to be described. For those firms (and accountants) that ducked behind the shield of materiality, materiality—at least in this context—must be defined.

Traditionally, moral and legal codes affecting business have functioned in much of a seesaw fashion: each time society has perceived a general lessening in the importance of ethical conduct by businessmen, laws have been enacted to fill the voids considered to exist. This is the situation that presently exists.

National remedies that have been recommended and seem appropriate, in order to be most effective, must begin with efforts to clean up the remaining sectors of the political process. Sufficient funds now exist to bring senatorial and congressional campaigns under the same fund restrictions that govern presidential campaigns. Contributions from political action committees of both business and labor should be prohibited. Firms and labor unions should have the same privilege as individuals—to earmark one dollar of tax liability to the national election fund. Congress has not expressed any immediate concern to restrict its own sources of campaign funds; some arm-twisting and effort by the newly elected junior members and the general public will be necessary. Illegal activities, disclosures, and penalties will require more precise definition. Although, as artificial persons, corporations have not enjoyed the right to vote, many have apparently bought the benefit. The changes suggested would at least make political corruption more difficult and, by use of adequate penalties, much more costly.

Corporate crimes, unlike those of desperation or passion, have been described as "sophisticated and deliberative."[9] Furthermore, the executive perpetrators have been able to hide behind the corporate curtain. It seems logical that some lifting of this curtain is required, much like the corporate veil of the past.

Although multinational firms are effectively beyond the control of any single government, Nader and others have recommended that (1) all giant firms in the United States at least be brought under federal chartering; and (2) a Division on Corporate Crime be established in the Justice Department.[10]

In the area of national legislation, it would also seem appropriate to prohibit the employment of former commissioned military officers and former federal civilian personnel (above the grade of GS-9) by firms that they acted to regulate or control while in government service.

There is certainly no unanimity for legislation of business morality. The chairman of an MNE with operations in more than 30 countries has termed current actions to stem corporate corruption as "commendable" but has urged that efforts center upon the guilty individuals, particularly top executives, rather than blunting our international competitive position by imprudent legislation.[11] Unfortunately, no suggestions were made for lifting the corporate curtain in order to reach the presidents and other top executives.

Following the initial settlement between the SEC and Lockheed, the chairman of the SEC, Roderick M. Hills, stipulated that he was not in favor of pervasive new laws, such as requirements for outsider boards, federal charters, or special rules for MNCs. Hills did favor the adoption of tougher and more expeditious penalties for officers of those firms maintaining false records.[12]

It is rather evident that all too many executives and politicians have embraced a double standard as necessary and inevitable: they can be moralists in their private lives but pragmatists in business and government affairs. Based upon disclosures in recent months, new federal legislation could do much to bring the two standards closer together.

International Issues

For a multitude of obvious reasons, ethical business conduct on an international scale has been difficult to delineate, much less to administer. The veritable collage of customs, value systems, religions, and trade practices represent an uncertain environment to some businessmen and a convenient shield to others.

International business decisions are not basically different from those of domestic enterprise; both involve selection of courses of action from competing and often conflicting alternatives. Differences are primarily those of degree, in such areas as risk, uncertainty, and illegality.

Executives of some multinationals, confronted with uncertainties on the one hand and potentially profitable opportunities of some magnitude on the other, elected to make moral compromises in foreign environments that they probably would not have made in domestic affairs. Yet these were considered actions; few executives were duped or unaware.

International payments collectively described in the literature as questionable include "grease money" to expedite foreign transactions, bribes, political contributions, and outsize commissions. SEC regulations do not prohibit grease-money payments so long as the transactions are accurately recorded and described in the accounts, and if top managements and boards of directors are not deceived. In many countries, gratuity payments within reason and for services rendered have been customary business practices, even where minor government officials, such as port authorities or customs agents, were involved. So long as such payments are not meant to induce improper behavior, they are every bit as acceptable as the costs associated with entertaining customers in the United States.

Foreign bribes, as noted previously, are considered to be illegal everywhere. They clearly are also acts of unfair competition. On these grounds, there does not appear to be any valid reason why U.S. law cannot or should not clearly stipulate that bribes in excess of a specified amount, say $1,000, paid by American firms anywhere will be punishable as crimes. Prosecution of offenses might be vested in the Corporate Crime Division of the Justice Department (as Nader and others have suggested) or jointly with the SEC.

Given the pathetic results of Watergate, the author has no qualms whatsoever about recommending legislation that would declare political contributions illegal when made by U.S. firms and their controlled subsidiaries anywhere in the world.

Fees and commissions paid to foreign agents should not be branded as *malum per se* any more than are similar payments made domestically. However, when such payments are made to officials of foreign governments, they should be considered as bribes, prima facie. Otherwise, foreign payments should be subjected to the same tests applied to domestic fees and commissions: customary, necessary, and reasonable for the level of services performed. Enforcement of such regulations would require disclosure to some agency, such as the SEC, of the details of all such payments in excess of a specified amount, say $1,000 with the burden of proof of legitimacy placed upon the firm making the payment. Naturally, to be effective, the SEC should also be required to report the details of the payments (payer, payee, date, amount, and so forth) to the government of the nation of which the recipient is a legal resident.

Some nations today have retained archaic laws requiring local agent representation in all foreign transactions; Iceland and some of the Middle Eastern countries are examples. In these environments, U.S. firms would be well advised to disclose the agent and his proposed fee to the governments of the country making the purchase and to the United States before the agreement is consummated.

A final refinement and clear indication that the United States supports the return of integrity in international business could encompass such actions as: (1) banning corporate violators, U.S. and foreign, from eligibility for U.S. government contracts; (2) denying U.S. support of those U.S. firms that commit transgressions abroad; and (3) prohibiting foreign transgressors, including those firms guilty of bribing foreign business away from American firms, from conducting operations in the United States. These refinements would also make it easier for those American firms that are "fence-sitters" to say no to unethical propositions made here and abroad.

Is this legalistic? Possibly so. However, approaches similar to those mentioned would be evidence that the United States applies more than lip service in efforts to clean up its own house and to regain its former position of credibility in the international realm. It would not be surprising if the majority of the industrial countries that really matter—the OECD—would concurrently adopt the same approaches if requested to do so. Other countries would soon recognize the economic sense of joining the club as well.

International Code of Conduct

On June 21, 1976, after more than a year of active negotiations, the OECD adopted a Declaration on International Investment and Multinational Enterprises. The declaration is a package of documents that, taken together, represent a code of conduct for multinational firms and host governments. Guidelines applicable to MNEs cover business conduct, disclosure of information, competitive practices, taxation, and industrial relations. Among activities designated as illicit are bribes (payment, solicitation, and expectation—both direct and indirect) and political contributions (except where permitted by law). Government responsibilities relate to fair treatment of MNEs (the same treatment afforded national companies), cooperation with respect to incentives and disincentives for investment, and member consultations.

Codes of ethics have traditionally been ridiculed as unnecessary, useless unless enforced, window dressing, and shams to reduce pressures for new legislation. Whether or not the OECD declaration earns a similar description remains to be seen. However, the OECD effort has some interesting aspects. It represents the first concerted and collective attempt by the industrial countries to affect the operations of MNEs. The guidelines, though voluntary, are expected to bear considerable weight, both moral and political, in view of the widespread impacts of corporate and government corruption. Success in this initial collective effort might well lead to the creation of an international regulatory body having and operating from a meaningful basis of international business law. Another important first surrounds the delineation of responsibilities of host governments, and, presumably, these guidelines will also favorably affect the behavior and investment climates of the developing nations that are not OECD members. Also significant is the applicability of the code to government-owned as well as private companies.[13]

For some observers, the OECD declaration indicates the willingness of the industrial countries to surrender voluntarily some of their options as nation-states. Clearly the next move rests with the developing nations. When taken together with agreements in process by other powerful international organizations—such as the World Bank's Convention on the Settlement of Investment Disputes—there is much to support the premise that an effective system of international business law and conduct can become a reality within the next decade.

Accounting Implications

Illegal payments and related issues have permeated and challenged the very foundation of accountancy. This is not a new experience. Accountancy rose in professional stature in the United Kingdom as an aftermath of the "bubble period" and in the United States in response to the stock-exchange scandals of the 1930s. In each instance, the accounting profession championed the protection of the investing public. The independent accountant assumed, whether desired or not, something of an adversary position in relation to client managements. Some proponents as well as critics of the profession have expressed concern that, in the United States at least, this role has softened over time in that the emphasis of the profession, and consequently its interest, has shifted from investors to managements. Causative factors cited were the income tax, systems, management advisory, and similar services furnished to client managements. Fees for these services collectively have for some time now far outweighed the billings for primary auditing engagements of most large public accounting firms. Discourses over the past decade in professional journals have questioned the impact of such services upon the independence of public accountants but have, in the main, advocated approval of their retention.

It is not surprising, therefore, that disclosures of corruptive business practices have prompted the question, "Where were the auditors?" and have generated two suggested courses of action affecting auditors: (1) hold them coliable with management in criminal or civil actions, and (2) reinforce their roles as adversaries of corporate managements.

Emphasis upon assertion of an adversary role for independent auditors has been generated primarily by the SEC. The commission concluded that, in the recent past, the auditors, attorneys, and outside directors within the private sector have been unable to supply the level of self-protection upon which the SEC relies. Consequently, much of the commission's emphasis has been directed toward improving corporate accountability via assurances that all corporate transactions are properly reflected in the accounts and that none are concealed from auditors or directors.

A seemingly unrelated event, the Moss Report, was scathing in its references to public accountants. The report, named after Representative John E. Moss, who chaired the House Subcommittee on Oversight and Investigations, covered a review of nine government agencies and commissions, one of which was the SEC. The report recommended that the SEC should prescribe and enforce accounting principles, auditing standards, and ethical codes for independent auditors. The report also considered the fairness standard to be deficient and suggested that auditors attest to the quality and enforcement of internal controls. Related recommendations called for outsider majorities on corporate boards and making negligence of auditors a criminal act where audits covered by the Securities Act were concerned.[14]

The effectiveness of the Moss Report was diminished because the subcommittee did not solicit the opinions of concerned organizations, particularly the AICPA and the Financial Accounting Standards Board. Nonetheless, the report bore the weight of a subcommittee of the House and could not help but aggravate the ongoing discourse between the SEC and the accounting profession.

Representative Moss moderated the tone of his report somewhat in his address before the AICPA's Fourth National Conference on Current SEC Developments held in Washington, D.C., in January 1977.[15] He stated that his committee was particularly concerned over the lack of credibility in corporate reports; monotonous reiterations that financial reports are those of managements; and the lack of any assurance for shareholders, who are risking their capital, that the selected accounting standards result in fair reports. Moss assured the conference that he did not favor, or recommend, vesting sole authority for accounting and reporting practices in the SEC, although the SEC presently had the authority to implement his recommendations. Instead, he said he envisioned the SEC and the FASB cooperating as partners rather than adversaries.[16]

In 1975, the Senate also examined accounting practices through its Subcommittee on Reports, Accounting and Management of the Committee on Government Operations. The report of the study, entitled "The Accounting Establishment" (also known as the Metcalf Report after the chairman, the late Lee Metcalf) was submitted to the Senate Operations Committee, on December 7, 1976. Hearings were scheduled, beginning in 1977, and reverberations will continue for some time.[17]

The Metcalf Report criticized the federal government for not monitoring the accountability of public corporations and recommended that Congress or the appropriate Federal agency should:

1. . . . exercise stronger oversight of accounting practices. . . . [The SEC was chastised for delegating its authority to others.]

2. . . . establish comprehensive accounting objectives for the Federal government. . . . [As an example to abet the reduction of alternative accounting standards for the private sector.]

3. . . . amend the Federal securities laws to restore the right of damaged individuals to sue independent auditors. . . . [To reverse the effects of the Hochfelder case in 1976.]

4. . . . consider methods of increasing competition among accounting firms for selection as independent auditors for major corporations. . . .

5. . . . directly establish financial accounting standards for publicly-owned corporations. . . .

6. . . . establish auditing standards used by independent auditors. . . .

7. . . . itself periodically inspect the work of independent auditors. . . .

8. . . . restore public confidence in the actual independence of auditors . . . by promulgating and enforcing strict standards of conduct. . . . [Client representations and management advisory services should be prohibited.]

9. . . . require the Nation's 15 largest accounting firms to report basic operational and financial data annually. . . .

10. . . . define the responsibilities of independent auditors so that they clearly meet the expectations of Congress, the public, and courts of law. . . .

11. . . . establish financial accounting standards, . . . auditing standards and other accounting practices in meetings open to the public. . . .

12. ... act to relieve excessive concentration in the supply of auditing and accounting services to major publicly-owned corporations. ...

13. ... retain accounting firms ... only to perform auditing and accounting services. ... [Not for consulting, management services, etc.]

14. ... treat all independent auditors equally in disciplinary and enforcement proceedings under the Federal securities laws. ...

15. ... [prevent domination of the Cost Accounting Standards Board] by representatives of industry and accounting firms which may have vested interests. ...

16. ... [prohibit] Federal employees [from serving] on committees of the American Institute of Certified Public Accountants or similar organizations. ...[18]

During hearings in April 1977, the Financial Accounting Foundation and the Financial Accounting Standards Board presented their joint *Statement of Position*[19] to the Metcalf subcommittee. Briefly, the *Statement* defended the existing structures for establishing and maintaining standards within the private sector with "review and participation of the SEC." With reference to "questionable" payments, the *Statement* argued that most instances concerned fraudulent, dishonest, and ill-advised management actions that were concealed from auditors—not inadequate accounting or auditing standards.[20]

Members of the financial community and the accounting profession also testified before the Metcalf committee. Proposals emanating from the profession were, primarily, those that were anticipated: support voluntary peer review as it existed or by means of a private-sector board; retain the standard setting in the FASB but with provisos for greater public participation and responsive action; upgrade the responsibilities of audit committees. Suggestions by various sectors of the financial community were not surprising either: some called for a new private-sector body other than the FASB; others asked that the ban on advertising be loosened to increase competition; still others advocated the prohibition of management and executive recruiting services.[21]

Two proposals were unexpected. First, the recommendations by John C. Biegler, senior partner of Price Waterhouse and Company, that the control of the SEC be increased by requiring:

1. Registration with the SEC by CPA firms that audit registered companies;
2. "Peer reviews" of registered CPA firms to be established and supervised by the SEC;
3. Guidance (including any limitations) to be developed by the SEC for management advisory and consulting services performed for clients by registered CPA firms; and
4. Accounting firms registered with the SEC to publish financial statements annually.[22]

Second, the recommendation by the late Manuel F. Cohen, then chairman of the AICPA Commission on Auditors' Responsibilities, calling for a "continuous audit," instead of the present practice involving brief annual visitations by independent auditors. The intended purpose, of course, was to provide auditors the time necessary for them to develop a greater familiarity with and assurance of the fairness of reporting systems in use.[23]

Prior to the closing of the Metcalf hearings, the SEC commissioner, Harold M. Williams, expressed support for the retention of standard-setting in the private sector. However, he also advised that the SEC would probe certain issues (for example, the extent of CPA services to clients, various methods of peer review, and possible registration of auditors). The SEC report, together with any recommended legislation, was planned for completion by July 1978. At such time the Metcalf subcommittee would also be reconvened.[24] In effect, the accounting profession was given one year to put its house in order.

The article in the *Journal of Accountancy* that reported the closing of the Metcalf hearings was entitled "Metcalf Finale."[25] To the contrary, the issues raised by the report and hearings will be reverberating through the halls of accountancy for some time to come.

One example, pertinent to the issue of illegal payments, is apparent in the personal views expressed by Dr. Carmichael, the research director of the Commission on Auditor's Responsibilities (the Cohen commission). Carmichael considers the auditor to be an intermediary serving both users and issuers of financial statements. Consequently, in Carmichael's opinion, independent auditors *do* have responsibilities for seeking out management acts that might be fraudulent, illicit, or questionable. Users have come to rely upon auditors for such examinations. Furthermore, if questionable acts are discovered, they cannot be set aside as trivial, since there are no degrees of abrogation where management's accountability is concerned.[26]

The AICPA chairman, Michael Chetkovich, also acknowledged the pressures mounting from many directions for changes in the auditing function in an effort to reduce corporate corruption. In an address on accounting for multinationals given at California State University in Northridge, Chetkovich stressed that CPAs cannot be expected to play multiple roles. He emphasized that the profession must determine its role exactly as well as delineate who it serves—issuers or users.[27]

Since accountancy is a profession, it would be appropriate for the individual investor and the public interest to regain ascendancy—by the voluntary action of the profession rather than by imposition from without. But this is not likely to happen. The individual investor has become a faceless person. The advent of the large corporation changed the role of the individual from that of an investor with a personal interest in and relationship with a firm to that of a remote speculator. Dependence upon a return in the form of dividends has largely been supplanted by an expectation of gain by appreciation within a market system often described as fickle. Corporate management has largely become a process of self-perpetuation only infrequently challenged by proxy skirmishes. The accountability of management as well as its indiscretions have become indeterminates. Business interrelationships and combinations have permitted instant earnings, improved earnings-per-share ratios, and increased volumes simply by acquisitions. Colossal size has rendered inept decisions harmless, ineffective systems operable, unfair competition practicable, and outright bribery defensible as not material. Small wonder, then, that the large firms of attorneys and accountants, who collectively should function as the conscience of big business, have found it much more practical to support the interests of the clients who pay their fees and with whom a direct contact and relationship is maintained.

The SEC, primarily, and the IRS, secondarily, have stepped in over time to fill the void. To date, the SEC has employed disclosure and publicity as means of safeguarding stockholder interests. Also, requirements for soft data are being emphasized by the SEC. Unfortunately, given the options in accounting principles used by reporting firms and the multitudes of footnote materials now necessary to comply with ever-increasing disclosure requirements, accounting reports have become virtually incomprehensible by all but the most sophisticated individuals, analysts, and institutional investors.

There appears to be a consensus that the SEC has been awakened since the Watergate affair and has begun to flex its muscles. Little stretching of the imagination is needed to envision the SEC's assuming the role of interpreter for the investor in the near future. If the average investor has grown disinterested or disillusioned by annual reports, the SEC has the professional and legal capabilities needed to protect the public interest.

It is not at all difficult to cast the SEC in the dual role of sounding board and interpreter. The first function would involve limiting the number of alternative accounting procedures that now exist as well as blessing future proposals submitted by the FASB (if it survives) or by the AICPA, CASB, and the like. As interpreter, the SEC could and would replace the accounting profession as attestor of fairness and conformity. Since the SEC could sanction offenders or nonconformers itself or in concert with the Justice Department, there would be little reason to doubt its power or its independence.

In the international realm, the SEC could also be the obvious repository and disseminator of the information necessary to comply with the disclosure requirements of the OECD "Guidelines for Multinational Enterprises" (see appendix 4A). The attestation of the SEC to OECD disclosures presumably would bear more weight with foreign governments than that of the various CPA firms. The SEC also presumably could assist the multinationals and their CPAs in definition of geographical areas and could devise standardized formats for reports in order to minimize cost and duplication while improving public understanding. Most of the data specified in the OECD disclosure-of-information guidelines are and have been routinely provided by U.S. firms, either to the SEC (in Form 10-K and other reports) or to the public in the annual reports and financial statements. Since the United States has traditionally excelled in financial disclosures, the major impact of the OECD guidelines will fall upon those multinationals based in other countries. There will be, of course, some minor complaint and resistance from the business community,[28] and it will be most interesting to see what evolves regarding the required disclosure of transfer-pricing policies.

Summary

Ethical conduct, whether on an individual or a business plane, is a bother. Without resorting to religious tenets—and these seem to be of lessening import, if not interest—there is no real framework for reference.

Most of the benefits accruing to American society have been the results of individuals and businesses pursuing their own best interests with relative freedom of action. Consequently, the freedoms that exist are highly valued and have only been constrained when they negated the concurrent responsibilities of individuals and firms to the extent that the public interest was impacted. The 1970s represent such a time.

Perhaps the United States would benefit by looking back, as it begins its third century, to the ideals expressed by some of its original commonwealths. Those ideals attributed to Massachusetts, for instance, permitted freedom of individual economic actions so long as they also benefitted the larger society. In short, business was to be a positive-sum game—similar to the suggestions made by Adam Smith. A simple ethic such as this would go far in clarifying, if not reconciling, the interests of the individual, business, and public communities.[29]

There is little doubt that new laws will be devised to dissuade future transgressors. However, there is also little likelihood that sanctions for recent offenses by a relatively small but prestigious group of persons and firms will be adequate deterrents. Since many other countries have acted directly and forcefully toward their citizens who were participants in international scandals, the United States will be conspicuous by its absence.

Multinationals based in the United States will be well advised to recognize that ethical business conduct does not really vary materially between and among environments, even though the international community is just beginning to reduce that fact to writing. A good corporation is a good citizen in any community; those few that are too lazy to compete, that make a mockery of free markets, and that must resort to bribes will soon find themselves not welcome anywhere.

Disclosure requirements will be added to the existing paperwork and reporting burdens of all firms—not just the 350 or more that have admitted questionable payments to date. Reporting practices in some countries will be upgraded significantly and in one giant step. American multinationals and the influential CPA firms should examine the forthcoming disclosure requirements with recent circumstances in mind. Instead of expressing self-serving objections, members of industry and the profession should seek out methods of reducing multiplications of efforts. Recommending consolidation of government reports to a single agency such as the SEC would be one step in that direction. Approval would not be an easy task, but few worthwhile things ever are.

The accounting profession should be well aware that, if it does not act to reduce the numbers of methods by which the same economic event may be recorded, and does not aggressively support fairer financial reporting, the SEC will be forced to do so. And, though social accounting is a relatively new area of interest, accountants might serve themselves well by recognizing that their collective efforts to upgrade the social responsibility of business may represent the best form of social accounting today.

Businessmen may profit from the advice of A.W. Clausen, president of the Bank of America, who observed:

> Integrity is not some impractical notion dreamed up by naive do-gooders. Our integrity is the foundation for, the very basis of, our ability to do business.
>
> If the market economy ever goes under, our favorite villains—Socialist economies and government regulators—won't be to blame. We will.[30]

Notes

1. Gordon McKibben, "A Story of Human and Corporate Tragedy," *Business Week*, November 22, 1976, p. 8.

2. Peter F. Drucker, "New Demands on Top Management," *The Third Annual Distinguished Guest Lecture Program*, Saint Louis University School of Business and Administration, May 17, 1977, p. 31.

3. Section 610 is basically a codification of the Federal Corrupt Practices Act (1925), which, in turn, represented an expansion of the Tillman Act (1907). Many progressive states have enacted similar prohibitions.

4. Yerachmiel Kugel and Gladys W. Gruenberg, *International Payoffs* (Lexington, Mass.: Lexington Books, D.C. Heath and Company, 1977), pp. 11-15.

5. "State Department Seeks Secrecy for Boeing Co.," *St. Louis Post-Dispatch*, January 9, 1977, p. 2E.

6. Neil W. Chamberlain, *The Limits of Corporate Responsibility* (New York: Basic Books, Inc., 1973), p. 205.

7. John J. McCloy, "On Corporate Payoffs," *Harvard Business Review*, July-August 1976, p. 16.

8. Ralph Nader and Mark Green, "What to Do About Corporate Corruption," *The Wall Street Journal*, March 12, 1976.

9. Ibid.

10. Ralph Nader, Mark Green, and Joel Seligman, *Taming the Giant Corporation* (New York: W.W. Norton and Company, Inc., 1976), 312 pp.

11. F. Perry Wilson, "The Highest Self-Interest," *Newsweek*, November 24, 1975, p. 23.

12. Stephen J. Sansweet, "Lockheed Settles Foreign-Payoffs Case with SEC, but U.S. Payments Are Hinted," *The Wall Street Journal*, April 14, 1976, p. 3.

13. The United Nations is also preparing a code of conduct to govern multinationals and, reportedly, is under pressure from some socialist and Third World nations to exempt state-owned enterprises. "World Roundup," *Business Week*, February 7, 1977, p. 50.

14. "News Report—Government," *The Journal of Accountancy*, December 1976, p. 26.

15. "News Feature: Current and Future SEC Actions Outlined at AICPA Conference," *The Journal of Accountancy*, February 1977, pp. 34-37.

16. Ibid., pp. 35, 36.

17. The letter of transmittal, a glossary, and the summary of the Metcalf report, including recommendations, were reproduced in "The Accounting Establishment: A Staff Study," *The Journal of Accountancy*, March 1977, pp. 104-120.

18. Ibid., pp. 118-120.

19. A copy of the *Financial Accounting Foundation's and the Financial Accounting Standards Board's Statement of Position on the Study Entitled "The Accounting Establishment,"* April 14, 1977, without the supporting exhibits, was distributed to AICPA members. A complete copy is available from the FASB, file number SOP 477.

20. Ibid., p. 4.

21. "News Report: Metcalf Update—Accountants Discount Plan for Greater Control by SEC," *The Journal of Accountancy*, July 1977, pp. 4, 8, 12, 14.

22. Ibid., p. 4.

23. "Late Developments: Metcalf Finale," *The Journal of Accountancy*, July 1977, p. 3.

24. Ibid.

25. Ibid.

26. D.R. Carmichael, "The Report of Tentative Conclusions of the Commission on Auditors' Responsibilities: What Does It Say?", *The Journal of Accountancy*, August 1977, p. 56.

27. "Chetkovich Discusses New Illegal Payments Guide," *The Journal of Accountancy*, November 1976, p. 22.

28. See, *A Review of the OECD Guidelines for Multinational Enterprises:*

Disclosure of Information (New York: USA-BIAC Committee on International Investment and Multinational Enterprises, November 1976), 24 pp.

29. Gordon C. Bjork, *Private Enterprise and Public Interest* (Englewood Cliffs, N.J.: Prentice-Hall, Inc., 1969), p. 236.

30. Bill Kester, economic comment, "Corporate Bribery," *St. Louis Post-Dispatch*, May 14, 1976. Reprinted with permission.

Appendix 4A:
OECD Guidelines for
Disclosure of
Information

Annex to the Declaration of 21st June 1976 by Governments of OECD Member Countries on International Investment and Multinational Enterprises

GUIDELINES FOR MULTINATIONAL ENTERPRISES

Disclosure of Information

Enterprises should, having due regard to their nature and relative size in the economic context of their operations and to requirements of business confidentiality and to cost, publish in a form suited to improve public understanding a sufficient body of factual information on the structure, activities and policies of the enterprise as a whole, as a supplement, insofar as necessary for this purpose, to information to be disclosed under the national law of the individual countries in which they operate. To this end, they should publish within reasonable time limits, on a regular basis, but at least annually, financial statements, and other pertinent information relating to the enterprise as a whole, comprising in particular:

i) the structure of the enterprise, showing the name and location of the parent company, its main affiliates, its percentage ownership, direct and indirect, in these affiliates, including shareholdings between them;

ii) the geographical areas* where operations are carried out and the principal activities carried on therein by the parent company and the main affiliates;

iii) the operating results and sales by geographical area and the sales in the major lines of business for the enterprise as a whole;

iv) significant new capital investment by geographical area and, as far as practicable, by major lines of business for the enterprise as a whole;

v) a statement of the sources and uses of funds by the enterprise as a whole;

vi) the average number of employees in each geographical area;

vii) research and development expenditure for the enterprise as a whole;

viii) the policies followed in respect of intra-group pricing;

ix) the accounting policies, including those on consolidation, observed in compiling the published information.

---

*For the purposes of the guideline on disclosure of information the term "geographical area" means groups of countries or individual countries as each enterprise determines is appropriate in its particular circumstances.

Part II
Accounting Problems
of Multinationals

5 Inflation

Inflation is most often defined as a persistent, upward trend in the general level of prices. It is also considered to represent an insidious tax, particularly upon those with little or no means of defending themselves—the poor (both individuals and nations) and persons who must exist on fixed incomes. The causes and consequences of inflation, as well as the remedies suggested, have provided room for controversy. For accountants, both managerial and financial, the challenges involve how to report, or account for, and cope with inflation. This chapter will examine, albeit in summary form, the general theories of inflation, some of the major causes of inflation in the United States, the effects of inflation, and remedies suggested by noted economists.

Theories of Inflation

The complexity of an issue such as inflation can be appreciated from a review of some of the numerous theories of inflation that have been advanced, not to mention their myriad hybrid forms. The ideas remain theories since, while they are conceptually sound and supporting evidence can be gathered, the economic and social milieu are such that the theories can be neither proved nor disproved. One reason, of course, relates to the nature of the environment itself. In addition to the economic variables, the behavior of individuals and firms is affected by psychological, social, political, and legal factors—both real and perceived. It simply is not possible to hold all other things equal, as is done in the classroom, in order to isolate cause-and-effect relationships.

Some of the more familiar theories of inflation will be presented here in simplified form. An understanding of such basic concepts, as well as an appreciation of the overall complexities that exist, is necessary if accountants are to assess the merits of the many proposals advanced for price-level accounting and reporting.

Demand-pull theorists agree that inflation is caused by excess demand. The general price level rises because the demand for goods and services exceeds the supply when the economy is at or near the full employment of men and capital. These theorists also contend that inflation could not progress very far without an increase in the supply of money with which to bid up prices. But at this juncture agreement ends.

The *monetarists*, such as Milton Friedman and others argue that inflation tends to accompany increases in the money supply without corresponding increases in goods and services. Usually the increase in money supply is cast in the form of banks increasing loans to business, and, without an increase in the supply of goods and services, the excess demand bids up prices. Money is treated as a *stock concept*. Proposed solutions stress control of the supply of money. In symbol form, $MV = PQ$, where M = quantity of money, V = velocity of money, P = price level, and Q = quantity of output traded. If V is considered fixed or given, then the money supply (M) determines PQ.

On the other hand, the *Keynesians* consider demand-pull inflation to be more closely related to changes in the velocity of money and liquidity preferences. Money is treated as a *flow concept*. A typical example would involve the government issuing bonds for cash, resulting in no change in the money supply. However, when the government spends the cash (deficit spending), prices are bid up without corresponding increases in output. In this model of $MV = PQ$, the price level is considered to be a *political phenomenon*; thus, PQ is exogenously determined and MV must adjust itself to PQ.

Cost-push theorists argue that inflation results from higher costs as factors of production try to increase their shares of total product by raising their respective prices. These stipulations assume that monopoly and/or oligopoly elements exist in the product market (if a profit push) or in the labor market (if a wage push). Cost-push inflation discussions have become synonymous with wage push, and wage push has been equated with union push. The effects upon the economy tend to be dependent upon the sector in which wages increase. Normally, wage hikes given to production workers usually are accompanied by, or result in, some increase in productivity. Conversely, wage increases for service workers tend to produce little, if any, additional output. This latter point is important for certain economies, such as that of the United States, where more than one-half of the labor force is employed in services, and that sector is increasing steadily. Another often-cited cause of cost-push inflation occurs when, during periods of rapid economic growth, bottlenecks develop in certain material or labor stocks and result in specific price increases.

Structural or *sectoral* inflation is said to occur when, although total demand is unchanged, there is a strong increase in demand for one particular good or class of goods within a given industry. Prices, profits, and wages increase within the industry affected. Other sectors, while not directly affected, press for increases as well in order to keep up. Such movements are assisted by the fact that, in most industrial economies, prices tend to reflect upward flexibility and downward rigidity. This seems to be particularly true of processed materials and services; many raw materials tend to have some downward price flexibility because of their greater susceptibility to the effects of substitution.

Bail-out inflation is said to result from the government's sensitivity to unemployment. As supply increases in response to monopoly or union pressures, the government acts to increase demand in order to prevent unemployment. The net result is higher prices and wages but no change in real income.

Markup inflation, as the name implies, results from management's practice of applying a constant rate of markup on the costs of goods and services produced or acquired for sale. As material, labor, and overhead inputs increase in cost, application of a stable markup percentage produces absolute price increases larger than the cost increments—and larger profits. Prime recent examples are gasoline and other petroleum products.

Stagflation is a relatively new economic sobriquet, characterized by rising prices and growing unemployment occurring simultaneously. Stagflation can occur only when market mechanisms become violated by oligopoly or monopoly forces.

Expectations have been cited as (1) causative factors and (2) means whereby the public renders systematic economic policies impotent. As inflation continues, people begin not only to expect it, but to anticipate certain government actions.[1] Sellers develop the habit of charging normal prices plus an increment to cover expected future inflation; in this scenario, inflation breeds inflation.

Greed as an incubator for inflation is seldom mentioned but is ever present. Vertically integrated industries, cartels, cooperative oligopolies, regulated monopolies, and national labor unions serve as typical spawning grounds. Each of these actors in the economic arena continuously—if not methodically—escalates prices beyond what the traffic will bear but seemingly just short of widespread consumer revolt and consequent government intervention. In the author's opinion, the obvious reluctance of the government to exert pressures on upward price movements from 1973 to early 1977 served as the green light for all those wishing to get as much as they could as quickly as they could; that is, before the lid would eventually fall in the form of price controls. The fear within industry was evident. In the area of big-ticket items, a prime example was the auto industry. Manufacturers offered discounts from inflated list prices since they did not want to be caught short when and if price controls were established. Producers of small consumer goods increased the use of cents-off-coupons to obtain the benefits of lower prices without formally reducing them.

It is a fallacy to believe that cartel actions can escalate prices only so far and that market forces will serve as effective constraints. Those days are long gone, if they ever really existed after the industrial revolution.

Causes of Inflation

Inflation can rarely be attributed to any single cause. Given the benefit of hindsight, however, certain factors can be logically considered as having played the major roles.

In the EEC, overemployment and labor shortages have received the most recent blame. Burdensome social costs together with excessive labor demands have been cited as the malefactors in Britain. On the global scene, OPEC has been charged with creating or adding to inflation within all nations using imported oil to any extent. Finally, within the international realm, few (if any) economies are truly isolated, even controlled economies such as that of the USSR.

Inflation that occurs in one country, particularly within the major industrial and trading nations, tends to spill over and impact the economies of others. In effect, it could be said that countries export and import inflation as well as goods and services.

Historically, in the United States and elsewhere, inflations and depressions were most often associated with wars and their aftermaths. The pattern normally followed was one in which price levels would be driven upward by wartime pressures and then would recede in peacetime, if not to their previous levels, at least substantially. This pattern changed after World War II insofar as the United States was concerned. The following is a simplified scenario:

1948-1950: Prices lost their downward flexibility as consumers acted to fill needs that were postponed during the World War II years.

1950-1952: Korean conflict produced sharp increases in price levels.

1953-1955: Relative price stability; moderate increases.

1956-1958: An unusual period: significant inflation (two and a half to three times that of the prior three years) during a business recession. Coining of the term *stagflation.* Emergence of the military-industrial complex.

1959-1965: A period of reasonable stability; the GNP deflator reflected increases ranging from 1.2 percent (1962) to 2.1 percent (1965).

1966-1969: Sharp escalations in prices, fueled by the Vietnam conflict.

1969-1972: The beginning of the nightmare of inflation for Americans. Price increases greater than during the Vietnam period. Runaway inflation led to price controls (Phase I: temporary freeze on wages, prices, and rents; Phase II: mandatory controls, dividends included).

1973: A burst of price increases following the relaxation of price controls under the Phase III program of voluntary compliance. Devaluation of the dollar caused a surge in world demand as U.S. prices decreased in world markets. Food prices soared. Prices frozen a second time (Phase III and a half). OPEC raised oil prices from about $2.50 to more than $11 a barrel. Mandatory controls on prices, wages, and profits reimposed (Phase IV).

1974-1975: Double-digit inflation—a first in the memory of living Americans. Escalating oil prices literally wrecked many economies and currencies. Strong labor unions pushed to increase their relative positions. Increasing price and production collusion by large firms: prices were raised in the face of declining demands (steel, for example). Inflation became *the* topic for the first time in the United States.

1976 to date: Record business profits maintained; prices continued to be determined by what the traffic would bear. The effects of bigness of industry— national and multinational—began to be seriously examined outside the govern- ment sector, and belatedly by the governments of the United States and other nations.

In sum, until the late 1960s, Americans were not overly concerned about inflation, which had averaged slightly less than 2 percent per year. Since 1970, however, consumer prices have more than doubled, and Americans are con- cerned. They have begun collectively to pressure the government toward responsive action. Their efforts have met with little success for several reasons, which merit examination.

Both government action and inaction can act to fuel the fires of inflation. Inaction in the form of refusal to control and regulate problem sectors of the economy was mentioned previously. Government actions have also served to engender inflation. By intervention, such as the Employment Act of 1946, the government accepted the responsibility for directing the economy in order to avoid major depressions, as well as inflations, and to promote full employment of resources. One result has been the amelioration of the so-called business cycle—fewer and shallower bottomings of the economy occur to reduce price levels. This is analogous to banking the fires of inflation.

Government spending actions, in both quantity and quality, often kindle the fires. Deficit spending is the most familiar quantitative aspect about which much has been said, but little has been done. The qualitative content of government expenditures—what the government spends our monies on—is not as widely discussed, yet it seems to be much more relevant.

Military spending is the most pernicious of all government expenditures, and it is a difficult dragon to slay. College freshmen learn that the government is primarily a consumer; it produces very little for the marketplace. Defense spending is an excellent example, since it competes for and siphons off material and other resources, adds significant dollars of purchasing power, yet fails to produce goods for purchase in the market. This would induce inflation with no other causative factors present. The industrialists that produce the military hardware operate from an entrenched position. Arms races, once begun, can be halted only by intelligent and determined efforts. The real opponent is the public fear of two mythical losses—security and jobs.

Although the attitude of the Russian populace is not known, many Americans seem unconvinced that, in the present stages of overkill, additions to arms stockpiles are not only stupid but self-defeating. The situation is analogous to that of a homeowner who wishes to keep others from trespassing or crossing his property. He hires a guard, then another, and another until he completely encircles his domain. He eliminates trespassers, but, in the process, he expends his resources on security to the extent that he can no longer maintain his house, and it crumbles—not from onslaught, but from decay within.

Many Americans also equate defense cutbacks with the loss of jobs and resulting recessions. Such fears are fostered by the assumption that such reductions would not be preceded by planning in the form of alternative government expenditures. The government's contribution to the economy is that of a consumer; the net effect would be a change from one form of consumption (highly inflationary, at that) to other forms, with economic benefits. For example, there is no logical reason why the technology commanded by our military hardware and aerospace giants (now one-fourth of U.S. technological resources) could not be diverted to solving the problems of mass transit, energy, pollution abatement, and housing, to name but a few. Military bases and installations, which blanket the map of the United States like a pox on a pox, could be objectively examined insofar as essentiality is concerned. Those serving no real military purpose could be converted readily to fill social needs: training facilities for the trades and crafts; auxiliary correction institutions, commercial airfields, and civilian hospitals are cases in point. These represent nothing new. They are simply examples of the restructuring of priorities that is often mentioned.

Such restructuring is a political phenomenon, however. And most politicians, either openly or secretly, will agree that military expenditures are inflationary cankers and should be reduced—but in somebody else's district.

The total magnitude of military expenditures is difficult, if not impossible, to aggregate and analyze, since many related costs are hidden in other portions of the government budget and/or include significant future costs. Approvals of hardware-development programs made today carry with them, as history will vouch, implicit commitments of future resources, most of which are open-ended and subject to cost escalations and overruns.

There also are multitudes of attendant costs in the form of fringe benefits—present and future—particularly for military personnel. Subsidized department stores (base/post exchanges), commissaries, housing complexes, hospitals, and the like, are provided wherever troops are stationed throughout the globe. Significant future costs are represented by the retirement benefits afforded the military (at least one-half the pay of the rank earned at retirement with twenty years' service). Such retirement pay begins at retirement, not at age 60 or 65, and is not reduced or affected by subsequent earned income; and a portion or all of the retirement pay received, more often than not, is free of taxes.

Some congressmen have had the fortitude to call for reassessment of the hidden burden of the costs of military pension programs as well as the practices now employed. In 1965, military pension costs were $1.2 billion, or 2.5 percent of the military budget. Following the military pay escalations in the late 1960s, these pensions swelled to $8.4 billion, or 8.5 percent of the defense budget, by 1975. Annual costs projected for the year 2000 were $34 billion. One reason for the dramatic increase is the fact that percentage retirement formulas were left unchanged when military pay rates were hiked to achieve comparability with those of their alleged civilian counterparts. In reality, there are few comparable functions indeed and, more important, no allowances were made to offset the security inherent within the military tenure system.

There are two key issues surrounding growing military pension costs: (1) the absence of current funding, and (2) the early retirement age. The lack of current funding makes military pensions a favorite promise-now-pay-later scheme of politicians that passes the costs to future generations. The absurd retirement ages—41 for the average enlisted person and 46 for the average officer—enable military personnel to collect more in retirement than while in uniform: 132 percent for enlisted personnel, 146 percent for officers. Although the retirement age is ridiculous, it becomes more flagrant when one recognizes the growing practice of *pseudoretirement*—retiring military personnel simply changing from the uniform to civilian clothes and accepting employment (often with 100 percent disability retirement from the service) within the civil service or in agencies using nonappropriated funds. This practice is known as double-dipping. Clearly, issues of funding, contributory requirements, retirement ages, and reemployment practices require examination and change.[2]

Given the pigeonholing of many current defense costs, and the failure to consider future costs, the total magnitude of defense spending and its inflationary impact upon the economy is almost impossible for the average citizen to assess. It would not be impossible, however, to demonstrate that total defense-related expenditures, including military retirement benefits and fringes (as past-service costs), and the related interest costs, for each and every budget year following the Vietnam conflict equaled or exceeded the total dollars collected in federal income taxes from *every individual taxpayer in the United States.*

Some wise man is credited with the observation that the problem with managing an economy the size of ours is the enormity of the amounts involved. A billion or even a million dollars is beyond the comprehension of most legislators and ordinary citizens. Revelations such as those that follow, however, clearly demonstrate some of the economic and social costs of the military-industrial complex:

> Every gun that is made, every warship launched, every rocket fired signifies, in the final sense, a theft from those who hunger and are not fed, those who are cold and are not clothed.
>
> This world in arms is not spending money alone.
>
> It is spending the sweat of its laborers, the genius of its scientists, the hopes of its children.
>
> The cost of one modern heavy bomber is this: a modern brick school in more than 30 cities.
>
> It is two electric power plants, each serving a town of 60,000 population.

It is two fine, fully equipped hospitals.

It is some 50 miles of concrete highway.

We pay for a single fighter plane with a half million bushels of wheat.

We pay for a single destroyer with new homes that could have housed more than 8000 people. . . .

This is not a way of life at all, in any true sense. Under the cloud of threatening war, it is humanity hanging from a cross of iron.[3]

These are not the outpourings of some naive pacifist but rather the warnings of the most respected of experts—a five-star General of the Army and the 34th President of the United States, Dwight D. Eisenhower. The military burdens that concerned President Eisenhower in 1953 are minor when compared to current levels of expenditures. Not only do they aggravate present inflation, but they prevent the allocation of resources to productive, necessary sectors of the economy.

The interest costs of the military-industrial complex are also of increasing concern. To the extent that defense costs are financed by deficit spending, the interest costs are placed upon future generations. After deduction of "phantom dollars" (those interest costs which the federal government pays to other federal agencies holding government securities), the $44.6 billion interest cost of the national debt reflected in the 1977-1978 budget still comes to about $30 billion, or roughly 8 percent of the total proposed budget. This amount is reportedly larger than General Motors' annual sales, the total Swedish budget, or the GNP of New Zealand or Greece.[4] Aside from its magnitude, the interest cost never comes to a vote, since it is considered an automatic necessity, as if it were covered by some sort of "permanent indefinite appropriation."[5]

There appears to be a growing awareness today that inflation is, for the most part, a political phenomenon. From the viewpoint of an accountant, Paul Grady is convinced that the general public "confuses cause and effect" where the disease of inflation is concerned. Emphasis is placed upon symptoms—rising prices—rather than on the disease itself—the erosion of the purchasing power of the dollar, which in Grady's opinion is essentially a de facto program of the federal government.[6]

If, in fact, inflation is largely a political phenomenon, the prospects for a short-run cure do not seem bright. External pressures upon the government from the military-industrial complex and the effective cartels in the oil, steel, energy, and other giant industries point toward continued inflation. Internally, government coffers would also be diminished if inflation subsided. According to Milton Friedman, government revenues benefited by some $25 billion in 1973 due to inflation.[7] These additional revenues were generated "without legislation," Friedman points out, and, if inflation were ended, the government would be required to reduce its expenditures or, alternatively, replace these funds by increasing taxes or through borrowing, actions which Friedman terms "politically unattractive."[8]

Effects of Inflation

Although the impact of inflation is readily visible in the supermarket and elsewhere in the consumer sphere, other effects are often not as obvious.

In the *short run*, inflation is widely recognized as having an immediate and great impact upon those who have no defense. For persons with fixed incomes, inflation has often been called the cruelest tax. Worse yet, this segment of society can claim few effective champions for its plight. Economists, and others, hold that inflation tends to be less damaging than severe unemployment upon the populace as a whole.

From income producers, both individuals and firms, inflation extracts "confiscatory taxes,"[9] at least in countries such as the United States. While real incomes represented by purchasing power do not increase (and may in fact decline), inflated paper incomes thrust taxpayers into higher tax brackets. Some sources have stated that the total tax bite has reduced the real incomes of individuals as much or more than rising prices. Confiscatory taxes act to reduce (1) the purchasing power of the capital base of a firm and (2) the standard of living of an individual.

Within industry, investment is retarded (as risks increase with extended payoff periods for projects); allocated to inflation-inducing projects (those with lesser risks afforded by technological or oligopolistic positions); or allotted to equipment (fleets of cars, for example) that does not enhance industrial capacity or productivity.[10]

Medium-range effects are less obvious. Four examples serve as illustrations. First, a trend from savings to consumption occurs as consumers are forced to dip into savings and investments more frequently. Second, inflation tends to breed upon itself in that the rate existing today helps determine the rate of the succeeding period much like an upward spiral. Dusenberry has called this the "ratchet effect"; prices and consumption reach a certain level, then pause temporarily while the producers and wage earners with sufficient power regroup to devise ways to reestablish their relative positions, and then it's off and running again.[11] A third trend is evidenced by a movement of savings from soft currencies (those with declining purchasing power) to hard or stable currencies. Investment capital moves from those countries needing it most to those with near or existing surpluses. Finally, businesses are increasingly confronted with capital and liquidity crises.[12]

Because of favorable leverages and tax shields, debt becomes increasingly more attractive, and more readily accessible, than equity. Federal Reserve data indicate that debt financing grew from 38 percent of total capital in 1965 to 53 percent in 1974.[13] Policies of growth at any price lead to positions of overextension of debt, financing of long-term projects with short- or mid-term sources of funds, and similar forms of financial suicide. In the 1970s, debt service costs and similar pressures on liquidity led to the reorganization or demise of many established corporations.

The *longer-term effects* of inflation are more insidious since they tend to be even less noticed.

One change is the gradual but steady weakening of public confidence in money and money-forms. As the popular favor turns to more tangible assets, capital for investment needs becomes increasingly scarce and costly. The United States has not been confronted with this change of attitude to the extent existing in Europe and the lesser-developed countries. However, certain items, such as land, diamonds, gold bullion, and Kruggerands increasingly are being touted as inflation-proof investment forms. Also, the so-called small investor allegedly has divorced himself (or has been driven) from the stock market. The ridiculous costs of trading a small number of shares, and the minuscule returns in the form of dividends, place total emphasis upon market appreciation. For the small gambler, the odds are better at the racetrack.

A second dilemma surrounds the estimating and adequate funding of pension programs. In these cases, the cumulative effects of even moderate inflation extract a significant toll upon future buying power. An extended period of rampant inflation mandates stiff increases in contributions from employers and beneficiaries if the purchasing power of retirement dollars is to be protected.

A third far-reaching problem, one which accounting has been charged with perpetuating, concerns the distorted decisions made by governments, firms, unions, and the general public based upon the illusory profits shown in income statements. Governments, by taxing these illusory profits, extract a portion of the economic substance of the firm; in effect, it represents a tax on capital. Also, the probability of government intervention increases as reported profits escalate. Management decisions may be distorted as well. Lulled into a sense of growth and well being by reported profits, dividend declarations may unwittingly, in whole or in part, represent distributions of capital. Paper profits also readily serve as support for union demands for a larger share of the benefits, overshadowing considerations of productivity and fiscal integrity. Within the larger society, reports of inflated earnings of the business sector generally produce two results: (1) big business is charged with creating inflation and (2) a credibility gap develops as industries preach capital needs while enjoying an apparent earnings glut.

The most elusive enigma of inflation surrounds the redistribution of purchasing power that occurs—not every firm or individual is worse off. Two types of price movements are encountered during inflation. Changes in *specific (or relative) prices* may or may not be inflation-induced. Technology, for instance, may very well drive prices of certain items downward; electronic calculators and minicomputers are examples that come to mind. Changes in *general prices* are averages and, as such, are rather blunt measuring tools. The various indices that have been constructed represent attempts to measure price movements among broad spectra or market baskets of goods and services. As is peculiar to averages of data, some elements will be more or less volatile than others, and it is quite possible that no single element will reflect the specific value of the index in question.

Among the firms and individuals not isolated from inflation, some will be in position to boost their prices and money incomes at higher rates than rising costs and will realize net benefits in purchasing power. Although generalizations always run the risk of exceptions, as a rule, inflation redistributes purchasing power from net creditors (who lose) to net debtors (who gain). In our economy, the traditional net-creditor sectors are households and financial institutions.

With few ways to insulate themselves against inflation, the poor tend to congregate in cities and add to the financial burdens of municipalities already taxed by inflation themselves. Judicious planning and fiscal integrity (now largely dependent upon federal revenue sharing) will be mandatory if our larger cities are to continue to function and to minimize civil strife as they have, at least thus far.

Suggested Economic Remedies

Both economists and accountants are concerned about inflation. Economists have pursued the loftier motives, since they have sought and suggested remedies whereas accountants have been bickering over methods of accounting for the effects of inflation. Suffice it to say at this point that the efforts by economists to cure the patient have been more laudable than the accountants' attempts at maintaining the patient's chart. Space naturally restricts us to a few cursory overviews of proposals made by distinguished economists to ameliorate the effects of inflation.

Milton Friedman and others[14] of the monetarist and laissez-faire schools, argue that ending inflation is not a technical problem but rather a political one. They recommend indexation as a necessary first step. If all government transactions (taxes and borrowings as well) were indexed, then taxes would tend to be levied on real income only, at least to the extent that the real income of each taxable entity would be affected by movements of the index applied. For holders of government securities particularly, the purchasing power of both interest and principal payments would be maintained. Similarly, wage increases should be tied to specific increases in productivity. They point out that, while indexation would not eliminate inflation, of itself, the process would render inflation somewhat more tolerable, especially in the near term. Downstream, the reductions in government tax revenues from indexation, plus the increases in absolute dollars for debt servicing and/or reduction, would call for reductions in government spending or, alternatively, efforts to increase explicit tax rates. Assumptions are that increasing tax rates or debt levels would be difficult and expensive, respectively, and that reductions in government expenditures would fall within the more inflationary sectors.

Wassily Leontief has long been a staunch advocate of national economic planning supported by input-output analyses applied to economic models. Leontief defends the profit motive but wishes to civilize it, much the same as man has tamed rivers and streams by using the force of gravity rather than trying to do away with it. He cautions that macro approaches, such as those followed by the Council of Economic Advisers, are no longer practicable. Instead, microdata, much of which is not yet collected, must be harnessed by input-output techniques in order to foretell shortages and to guide the economy toward its social goals.[15]

In Leontief's view, an economic planning board, using facts and models, is a necessity for the United States. Professor Leontief has used the analogy of a sailing ship to illustrate his concept of national economic planning. The profit motive serves as the wind to propel it, while national economic planning serves as the rudder to steer the ship and keep it on course and off the rocks.[16]

Other noted economists have advocated forms of indicative planning as methods of improving the market system and for coping with shortages of exhaustible resources. Kenneth Arrow advocates planning as the means to minimize future uncertainty and market failures. In his view, since capitalism depends upon the market system, the performance of capitalism can be improved and economic throes can be reduced by the stability that indicative planning can provide.[17] Robert Solow suggests that such planning should be centered upon exhaustible resources, such as oil, in order to minimize the traumatic economic effects of shortages of critical resources. In this case, indicative planning would coordinate the exploitation and use of essential resources as well as encourage the development of alternate materials and the requisite technologies.[18]

Advocates of a return to laissez-faire have not been silenced by the economic planners. Events that have transpired in the recent decade or so have simply made a hands-off policy unrealistic. Only the most naive would continue to champion the invisible hand of the marketplace. Today's multinational corporations have rendered the concept of free, open competition useless, not only in the United States but in the world market as well. Oligopoly theories are the only relevant bases for economic models today.[19] The giant firms within the military-industrial complex have long since attracted the government as a partner, and to consider them as private enterprises requires a vivid imagination. And, last but not least, the multinationals themselves have come to recognize that economic planning tends to reduce the risks of uncertainty far more than it inhibits corporate operations by means of outside intervention.

Summary

Inflation is a complex phenomenon. Human elements include demands, expectations, uncertainty, and greed. Material and intangible elements encompass money-forms, goods, and services—present and future. Processes involved are political actions or inactions, as well as monopolistic and oligopolistic coercions. Decisions that become distorted pertain to policies of pricing, capital investment, and redistribution of income and wealth; the first two are discretionary, the last occurs without due consideration. The effects of inflation spill over to other nations and plague future generations.

Small wonder, then, that economists are unable to predict inflation accurately, even in the short run. There are too many variables to unravel, and, unfortunately, the all-important human element has proved to be the most elusive.

To the extent that inflation is a political phenomenon and related to the military-industrial complex, it can be eliminated by the stroke of a pen. But this calls for common sense, determination, and confidence—not often found in combination in the political arena. Consequently, the most that can be reasonably expected is an effort to ameliorate the effects of inflation.

If economic planning becomes the "rudder" selected to guide the economy and reduce the frequencies and effects of economic traumas, such as inflations and shortages of resources, then the "courses" selected, as well as the changes to be made en route, will depend upon data that are reliably, timely, and efficiently generated. That is the realm of the accountant.

Notes

1. See the synopsis of the theory of rational expectations developed by economists Lucas, Wallace, and Sargent and described in "How Expectations Defeat Economic Policy," *Business Week*, November 8, 1976, pp. 74, 75.

2. "The Secret Debt: Government's Pension Obligations Now Total 300 Billion Dollars," *St. Louis Post-Dispatch*, February 20, 1977, p. 2D.

3. *Public Papers of the Presidents of the United States* (Washington, D.C.: Office of the *Federal Register*, National Archives and Records Service, 1953-), Dwight D. Eisenhower, 1953, p. 182.

4. Arlen J. Large, "U.S. Debt Costs Now Bigger than GM's Sales," *The Wall Street Journal*, January 21, 1977, p. 8.

5. Helmut A. Merklein, "Can the U.S. Economy Collapse?" in *World Oil*, December 1975, pp. 76, 79-80, 82, 86, 88.

6. Paul Grady, "Purchasing Power Accounting," Price Waterhouse & Co. *Review*, 1975, No. 3, pp. 2, 3. Mr. Grady is a retired partner in the Price Waterhouse firm.

7. Milton Friedman, "Monetary Correction," in *Essays on Inflation and Indexation* (Washington, D.C.: American Enterprise Institute for Public Policy Research, 1974), p. 30.

8. Ibid., p. 25.

9. *Client Inflation Clinic* (Chicago: Arthur Andersen & Co., September 1975), p. 2. It is interesting to note that, among all the literature examined from the AICPA and the large public accounting firms, Arthur Andersen is the only source in which the plight of the individual is considered (or even mentioned) to any extent.

10. Alan J. Mayer and Pamela Lynn Abraham, "A Ticking Time Bomb," *Newsweek*, August 29, 1977, pp. 57-58.

11. See James Dusenberry, *Income, Saving, and the Theory of Consumer Behavior* (Boston, Mass.: Harvard University Press, 1949) and "The Mechanics of Inflation," *Review of Economics and Statistics* 32, May 1950, pp. 144-149.

12. "The Capital Crisis: The $4.5 Trillion America Needs to Grow," *Business Week*, September 22, 1975, pp. 42-48.

13. Reginald H. Jones, "Why Business Must Seek Tax Reform," *Harvard Business Review*, September-October 1975, p. 51.

14. Milton Friedman, "Monetary Correction," in *Essays on Inflation,* pp. 25-61. In this same source, Herbert Giersch discusses uses of indexation by other countries in "Index Clauses and the Fight Against Inflation," pp. 1-24. Also, see G.E. Lent, "Adjustment of Taxable Profits for Inflation," in *IMF Staff Papers* 22, No. 3, November 1975, pp. 641-679, for a summary of indexation measures applied in selected countries from 1946 to 1975.

15. Interview with Wassily W. Leontief, "What an Economic Planning Board Should Do," *Challenge*, July-August 1974, pp. 35-40.

16. Wassily Leontief, "National Economic Planning," *The Second Annual Distinguished Guest Lecture Program*, Saint Louis University School of Business and Administration, April 23, 1976, 40 pp.

17. Kenneth J. Arrow's presidential remarks to the American Economic Association, in the *American Economic Review*, March 1974, pp. 1-10.

18. Robert M. Solow, "The Economics of Resources or the Resources of Economics," *American Economic Review*, May 1974, pp. 1-14.

19. Adolf A. Berle and Gardiner C. Means, *The Modern Corporation and Private Property*, rev. ed. (New York: Harcourt, Brace & World, 1968).

6 Price-Level Accounting

Inflation and price-level accounting attempt to do the impossible with bad theory ill-applied. Small wonder, then, that neither approach has been (or will be) adopted in the United States.

Accounting for changing price levels has been the most discussed, least understood, and most abused topic in the literature over the past decade. Paradoxically, the disease in question—inflation—remains virtually untreated, although inflation represents the only real threat to capitalism and free enterprise.

The Setting

It is vital to emphasize that *accountants can record, report, and interpret economic events in any way, so long as someone is willing to pay the attendant costs.* Accounting for inflation is no exception. Problems result when constraints are added:

1. Methods should be applied uniformly.
2. Procedures should be objective and verifiable.
3. Presentations should be fair and not misleading.
4. Reports should make economic sense.
5. Reports should be useful and worth their costs.

The constraints upon the accounting model could be relaxed or ignored in order to simplify the issue. If so, the results would tend to be no more realistic nor useful than the products of most other model-builders, and generally not worth the costs and efforts invested.

The language of business, as accounting is often called, is fast becoming one of many dialects. In less complex times, *normative* methods of accounting served the needs of business and other users reasonably well. The growth of the giant conglomerate and the multinational enterprise have forced accounting to become more *situational* in nature. Accountants, particularly those in the United States, have resorted to supplementary schedules and footnotes to prevent normative reports from being misleading.

An article on this subject, entitled "What's Wrong with Price-Level Accounting," appeared in *Harvard Business Review*, November-December 1978, pp. 111-118.

Over time, accountants (who normally are cautious people) have also bent their normative methods under the pressures of business or Congress (or both). Accelerated methods of depreciation, investment tax credits, last-in-first-out (LIFO) inventories, and the deferred income tax myths that result represent the effects of changing from rational accounting to "practical politics and tax relief."[1] In the process, the common sense and usefulness of financial statements have been prostituted. The long-legged accountant's stool has become rickety.

While trying to maintain at least a semblance of reason within financial reports (and his posture on his stool), the accountant has seen inflation rear its ugly head and challenge the validity of the basic tenets of accounting.

The accountant has been forced to leave his stool and return to his workbench to examine his conceptual framework[2]—and how to mend his stool before it collapses.

Challenged Assumptions

The invention of money as a medium of exchange facilitated the conduct of business. It became a convenient store of wealth and value—not for its intrinsic value, but rather for the representative value of the goods and services for which it could be exchanged, its purchasing power. The use of money as a common denominator was also a prerequisite for the developing of bookkeeping.

The practice of accountancy in the United States has also been predicated upon the assumption that the dollar is a stable measuring unit. Assets are to be recorded at their historical or acquisition costs. As these assets are used or expire, their related costs are matched with the revenues earned or received in the same time period. During periods of significant inflation or deflation, the stable-dollar assumption becomes suspect.

Since historical cost is founded upon the stability of the dollar as a unit of measure, the use of historical cost also becomes questionable. Financial statements reflecting changes in numbers of dollars are not incorrect, however. They simply are less useful since they commingle dollars of various purchasing power.

From the 1930s to the present in the United States, historical cost has always emerged as the victor in cost-versus-value encounters. Cost has been considered the only practicable method *to account for* the activities of large, complex, capital-intensive firms. Cost and value are synonymous only at the time a transaction occurs. Thereafter, their equality is happenstance, since the worth of a thing is what it will bring. The value of a firm as an entity and the values of specific assets (with minor exceptions) are not customary concerns of accounting for ongoing enterprises. Values are determined by future events (expectations of or changes in markets, competitive conditions, demands, tastes, technologies, and so forth) and not by accounting reports of past events.

To the extent that management uses data in external financial reports as the basis for making future decisions, are they being misled by historical cost information? Similarly, to the extent that third parties evaluate management's stewardship and the entity's performance based upon these financial reports, are the depicted results fair, useful, and relevant?

If traditional financial statements and reports are rendered defective by inflation, should the underlying accounting methods be revised? Should uniform (normative) methods be considered, or are entities affected differently? Should only the financial reports themselves be adjusted to reflect the impacts of changing price levels? Should the primary statements be revised, or should supplemental statements be prepared? Should the effects of changes in both general and specific price levels be disclosed? Are the remedies worth the costs?

Such questions challenge the basic foundations upon which the profession of accountancy has been developed in the United States. The combination of these issues served as the major, but not sole, motivation for the FASB to engage in efforts to reexamine the whole of accounting, as evidenced by its discussion memorandum on the *Conceptual Framework*.[3]

Professional Perspectives: U.S.A.

Probably no other single issue in accounting has generated as much written comment as price-level accounting. And yet, serious interest in the matter, at least in the United States, did not occur until the era of chronic inflation began in the early 1970s. This section will touch upon chronological events, focusing upon major studies and recommendations, in order to place the present controversy in proper perspective.

The father of price-level accounting in the United States is Henry W. Sweeney. He was concerned over the use of what he termed "rubber units of measurement"[4] in accounting reports around 1936. Sweeney's concern was accentuated by his studies of accounting in the more volatile German economy during the previous decade and by the influence of German professors Schmalenbach and Schmidt. Professor Sweeney's proposal, in capsule form, called for the following steps:

1. Apply the cost-of-living index at year-end to the historical cost amounts in opening and closing balance sheets, using surplus (retained earnings) as the balancing amount. This restatement in homogenous units of purchasing power was the basis of Sweeney's term *stabilized accounting.*
2. Separate the gains and losses resulting from Step 1 into realized and unrealized categories. Realized amounts (those actually represented by cash receipts and disbursements) were to be reflected in income of the period. Unrealized gains and losses were to be presented in a separate portion of the income statement after realized net income.

3. Obtain replacement costs for real-value assets (inventories, plant, equipment) by appraisals or other means. Superimpose these replacement costs on the stabilized amounts obtained in Step 1 for balance-sheet purposes only. Differences were to be shown in the unrealized section of the income statement.

The latter two provisos were designed to reflect real values of plant and inventory assets on the balance sheet, to prevent changes in the specific price levels of such assets from affecting realized net income, and to use the unrealized gain or loss increment as a connecting link between the adjusted balance sheet and the price-level-adjusted statement of realized income.

Sweeney's proposal is of particular interest since it effectively combined the purchasing-power concepts advocated by Schmalenbach with the current-cost approaches of Schmidt. Thus, the controversies surrounding price-level accounting today are rooted in suggestions made more than a half-century ago.

Professor Sweeney's ideas were ahead of their time in the United States. Asset appraisals were still contaminated by memories of the abuses of the 1920s and early 1930s. The computations required were laborious. And, most likely, inflation at that time was not really a very great concern.

Interest in the rising costs of replacing plant and equipment after World War II reawakened some interest in price-level accounting in the United States. This interest has continued, though intermittently, as reflected by the following scenario.

In 1947, the Study Group on Business Income was organized by collaboration between the Rockefeller Foundation and the American Institute of Accountants (the forerunner of the AICPA).

Also in 1947, the Committee on Accounting Procedure (predecessor of the APB) issued *Accounting Research Bulletin No. 33*, which examined but disapproved the use of increased depreciation charges (based on current values) as impracticable and undesirable.[5]

On October 14, 1948, the Committee reaffirmed its position in *ARB No. 33* by letter to members of the AIA; deferred consideration of changes in depreciation pending the report of the Study Group; and placed responsibility for coping with, interpreting, and disclosing the effects of inflation squarely upon management.[6]

In 1949, George O. May (a member of the Study Group) issued his separate monograph aimed at correcting the approximate effects of inflation. May suggested LIFO costing to offset inventory profits plus depreciation charges in two increments: (1) based on historical costs (and credited to the normal accumulation accounts), and (2) based on the increment obtained by adjusting historical acquisition costs by the consumer prices index (this amount to be credited to a special reserve for replacement).[7]

In 1951, a committee of the American Accounting Association recommended that financial statements continue to be based upon historical costs and that information on the effects of changes in price levels be presented in supplementary statements. The committee encouraged further study and favored methodology that would consistently apply a general price index to all items on both the balance sheet and income statement.[8]

In 1952, the Study Group on Business Income issued its summary report, which stated that inflation was causing reporting problems and that something should be done, but it supplied no consensus on approach.[9]

When *ARB No. 33* and the reaffirming letter were restated in 1953 as part of *ARB No. 43*, there were dissenting opinions that supported the recommendations made earlier by George May.[10]

Following a ten-year lull in pronouncements, in October 1963 the AICPA published its prodigious *Accounting Research Study No. 6: Reporting the Financial Effects of Price-Level Changes.*[11] The study did not examine the soundness of various possible systems of reporting the effects of changing price levels. It did assemble a uniform approach to the application of a general price index to financial statements. *ARS No. 6* recommended that:

1. The primary financial statements should continue to be based upon historical cost.
2. The effects of changes in general price levels should be disclosed in supplementary statements, restated in terms of the purchasing power of common (not constant) dollars as of the latest balance-sheet date. (In comparative statements, prior years would have to be rolled forward; that is, the numerator in the multiplier shown below changes—no constant base is used.)
3. The Gross National Product Implicit Price Deflator index should be used to restate historical costs, using the following multiplier:

$$\frac{\text{numerator}}{\text{denominator}} = \frac{\text{index at latest balance sheet date}}{\begin{array}{l}\text{index at time of transaction, but}\\ \text{not earlier than 1945.}\end{array}}$$

(The research group considered the market baskets of goods and services existing prior to 1945 not comparable to those in 1963.)
4. Only gains and losses on net monetary items (amounts fixed by contract or statute) were relevant and should be reflected in the income statement for the period. Nonmonetary items (all others) were not affected by changing price levels, and no gains or losses should be recognized.

Few firms voluntarily furnished the supplementary statements recommended by *ARS No. 6*.

Since accounting research studies are meant to encourage discussion and carry no weight of authority, the Accounting Principles Board decided to sanction the recommendations in *ARS No. 6* under the Board's *Statement No. 3* (so-called *APBS No. 3*), issued in 1969.[12] No new concepts or procedures were introduced. On balance, *APBS No. 3* may best be described by what it did not do. It did not really encourage the reporting of price-level-adjusted information. The *Statement* did refer to the cumulative nature of inflation over time, and it alluded to the importance of its impact upon financial reports. However, the recommendations depicted a lukewarm interest at best: the supplemental information could be disclosed but was not required at that time. The business community mirrored the lukewarm interest, since inflation had not yet come to centerstage.

By 1973, inflation had become a real concern in the United States. Accounting professions and governments in other countries were recommending specific actions. Motivated by these and other factors, the Financial Accounting Standards Board (successor to the APB) issued a discussion memorandum in February 1974. After public hearings and more than 130 written comments, the FASB published an exposure draft on December 31, 1974, entitled *Financial Reporting in Units of General Purchasing Power.*[13] Comments received during the nine-month exposure period indicated division among the large accounting firms as well as within the business community. Further action was tabled by the FASB in June 1976 pending completion of its conceptual framework project.

In retrospect, the FASB exposure draft had little chance at the outset. Despite the information gathered during the discussion period (February to December 1974), and the mountains of literature accumulated on the subject matter in this and other countries, nothing new was contained in the exposure draft. The FASB virtually dusted off the five-year-old *APBS No. 3*, changed its title, and reissued it. For all intents and purposes, the exposure draft merely echoed the recommendations of *ARS No. 6*, circa 1963. If little support for an idea could be garnered after eleven years of discussion, little hope existed for its reissue under a new cover.

Actions in Other Countries

Inflation has been described as not only an international disease but a pervasive one as well, since it spills over national boundaries. International trade is the carrier agent, and few economies can (or will) effectively isolate themselves from contamination. In general, the more dependent an economy is upon imports, the more susceptible it is to imported inflation; or, stated another way, the less effective internal measures will be to cope with inflation.

Recent comparative inflation rates (as measured by increases in general price levels) for selected countries are shown in table 6-1. Many of the countries listed

Table 6-1
Inflation Rates, Selected Countries, 1975-1977
(percent)

Country	Increase in General Price Levels		
	1975	*Est. 1976*	*Proj. 1977*
Argentina	335.0	400.0	150.0
Australia	17.0	15.0	11.0
Brazil	30.0	40.0	25.0
Canada	9.7	9.1	6.8
West Germany	7.9	4.1	4.0
Italy	19.4	17.2	9.3
Netherlands	11.0	9.0	7.0
Sweden	13.3	10.0	6.5
United Kingdom	22.1	16.5	9.3

in table 6-1 have revised accounting and reporting systems, are considering revisions, or have adopted alternative means of reporting the effects of inflation.

In *Argentina*, runaway inflation rendered the monetary unit useless as a measuring device. General-price-level financial statements, based upon the purchasing power of the peso, have been required as the primary statements since 1975.

The accounting profession in *Australia* touched most of the possible bases. In December 1974, general purchasing power was recommended; in June 1975, current-replacement-value accounting was proposed; in December 1976, current-cost accounting was required to be used after July 1, 1977. (This last requirement was provisional in that the information could be presented in the form of supplemental statements until July 1, 1978. Thereafter, statements based on current-cost accounting methods would become the basic reports.)

Brazil has been plagued by inflation to a greater extent and over a longer time span than most other nations. Consequently, the Brazilian government has concentrated upon reducing the effects of inflation rather than merely accounting for them. Indexation methods, mentioned in chapter 5, have been used as a basis for most of the Brazilian economy for more than a decade.[14]

Canada's Institute of Chartered Accountants considered the adoption of a combination approach, which differs from the methods proposed by her British, Australian, and American cousins. The CICA discussion memorandum requested comments by June 30, 1977, on a proposal that combines both current-value and general-purchasing-power accounting.[15] Previous considerations in July 1975 focused only upon general-purchasing-power accounting.

In *West Germany*, the Company Acts mandate the use of historical costs in official statements. Whether for that reason or, more likely, because of the German penchant for placing responsibility where it is due, the German Institute has not seriously considered revising the primary reporting practices. Instead, the responsibility for disclosing and explaining the effects of inflation in annual reports was placed squarely upon the shoulders of management in February 1975. In addition, management was charged with stating what was being done to minimize the effects of inflation upon the firm. The suggested disclosure is a simple, supplementary schedule of inflationary profit, consisting of three figures: additional amounts to reflect current costs of depreciation and inventory maintenance, less gearing (an adjustment for that portion of fixed assets and inventories which is financed by external debt).

The Netherlands has become synonymous over the past 50 years with current-replacement-value accounting (CRVA). The theory of replacement value was developed and advocated by Theodore Limperg, Jr., professor at the University of Amsterdam from 1927 to 1949. Also, as a relatively small country at the hub of international maritime commerce, the Netherlands has long been forced to deal with fluctuating prices, both internally and in foreign exchange. Replacement-value accounting is permitted in the Netherlands, but it is not as widely used as is often believed; it is used by only 39 of some 200 Dutch firms quoted by the Amsterdam Stock Exchange.[16]

Undoubtedly, the use of replacement-value theory in the Netherlands has been publicized as a result of the widespread exposure given the modified version in use by the N.V. Philips Company, the sixteenth largest industrial firm in the world (1976). Headquartered in Eindhoven, Netherlands, Philips has maintained manufacturing or marketing functions in almost all countries of the free world since 1960.

To control its maze of operations, Philips has employed an elaborate system, which combines a modified version of CRVA, indexation, standard costs, budgeting, and responsibility accounting for both cost and profit centers.[17] Although space prohibits a more detailed review, Philips and its subsidiaries use CRVA to maintain owner's equity in the form of productive capacity. Both specific and general price indexes are used, depending on the item to be costed. Although changes in the purchasing power of monetary items are calculated, they are never recorded in times of inflation because of the firm's financial structure and accounting policy. Philips traditionally employs heavy debt-financing (from 50 percent to 60 percent of total assets), and purchasing-power gains normally result from its excess of net monetary liabilities. However, company policy recognizes monetary gains only to the extent of monetary losses recorded previously, and since, in times of rising prices, no monetary losses are sustained, gains are never recorded.

It must be emphasized that Philips' methods collectively represent a very costly, sophisticated management accounting system that uses whatever devices, including CRVA, that are best suited for internal evaluation and decision making. External reporting is considered of secondary importance, although statements contain excellent supplementary information, enabling users to restructure data to historical cost and other bases.

Two other points should be noted: CRVA methods are not acceptable for tax purposes in the Netherlands; and replacement-value accounting systems, even those less ambitious than Philips', are considered to be beyond the expertise and means of all but the larger firms. Those factors could account for the limited application of CRVA in the Netherlands.

Events in the *United Kingdom* generated the third popular method of accounting for inflation—current-cost accounting (CCA). Actually, CCA is a derivation of replacement-value theory in that it attempts to maintain owners' equity in terms of money or general purchasing power rather than in the nature of productive capacity, the goal of CRVA. The following sequence of events summarizes the recent history of inflation accounting in the United Kingdom:

January 1973: The Accounting Standards Steering Committee (ASSC), composed of the five major accounting groups in the United Kingdom, issued *Exposure Draft No. 8, Accounting for Changes in the Purchasing Power of Money (ED-8).* ED-8 was patterned after *APB No. 3* (AICPA) and the FASB exposure draft that followed it, except that the United Kingdom favored use of the Consumer Price Index. Resistance developed within business and government.

January 1974: A Committee of Enquiry, headed by Sir Francis E.P. Sandilands, was appointed by the government to consider the matter—reportedly an example of a "common delaying tactic."[18]

May 1974: The ASSC issued its provisional *Statement of Standard Accounting Practice No. 7 (SSAP-7)* bearing the title and recommendations of *ED-8.* The provisional feature made adoption voluntary. Few firms adopted.

September 1975: The Sandilands report[19] was issued and recommended:

1. Current-cost accounting should be used as the basis of primary financial statements effective December 23, 1978.
2. General purchasing power adjustments were not necessary or appropriate.
3. A steering committee of the ASSC should be appointed to develop the SSAP necessary for implementation.

November 1976: Following more than eight revisions to satisfy concessions demanded by many sectors, the ASSC released *Exposure Draft 18*, which proposed a combination of current-cost and general-purchasing-power accounting.[20]

November 1977: The Accounting Standards Committee (successor to the ASSC) issued "Inflation Accounting: An Interim Recommendation." Patterned after the German guidelines, only minor supplementary amounts are required: the impacts upon cost of sales and depreciation, less gearing.

Before leaving this tour in the United Kingdom, it is appropriate to point out that the Sandilands report was unique in several respects:

1. It represented the first attempt by the U.K. government in modern times to determine accounting and reporting practices.
2. It was recognized as a salutary contribution by a group, primarily non-accountants, in a very short period of time.
3. Psychologically, it came during a time of indecision in the United States.

This abbreviated visit to other environments indicates that two primary methods of accounting for changes in price levels were advocated. Each deserves closer scrutiny.

Purchasing-Power or Value Accounting?

In many respects the structure of the problem, as depicted in table 6-2, is similar to that of a menu in a Chinese restaurant. Once the FASB made a selection from Column A (purchasing power as a measuring unit), its choices in Columns B and C were limited if a logically valid structure were to be developed. Similarly, the Sandilands committee recognized that the selection of money as the yardstick also limited its choices in the other columns—even though the number of options was greater. The courses selected were parallel, with no possibility of converging in the future. One focused upon changes in general prices, the other upon changes in specific prices. To the extent that inflation consists of both elements, each of the approaches selected must be considered deficient.

Characteristics of General-Purchasing-Power
(GPP) Accounting

Since inflation was defined as a persistent, upward trend in the level of general prices, advocates of GPP accounting argued that inflation accounting should account for general price-level changes. Other forms of proposals should not be considered as accounting for inflation.

Advocates further argued that GPP methods were objective, verifiable, and represented the least departure from historical-cost accounting (table 6-3).

Dissidents, on the other hand, cited their concerns that, among other complications, changes in general price levels were macro phenomena that could affect micro units (individual firms) in different ways. Accounting was concerned with micro units. Therefore, accounting for the effects of general price-level changes upon the individual firm using any normative method would make economic sense only by accident. In fact, some firms suffering from

**Table 6-2
Price-Level-Accounting Alternatives and Combinations Proposed
in Selected Countries**

Price-Level-Accounting Alternatives		
Column A: *Unit of* *Measurement*	*Column B:* *Basis for* *Measuring Assets*	*Column C:* *Definition of Profit*

1. Money
2. General pur-
   chasing power
   of money
	1. Historical cost
	2. Replacement cost at
	   current purchasing
	   prices
	3. Net realizable value
	4. Economic value
	   (the discounted
	   present value of
	   future cash flows)
		1. Amount which may be
		   distributed while main-
		   taining:
		a. Monetary amount of
		   shareholders' interest
		   at beginning of year
		b. Purchasing power of
		   shareholders' interest
		   at beginning of year
		c. Productive capacity
		   of assets
		d. Purchasing power of
		   assets at beginning
		   of year
		e. Value of assets less
		   value of assets
		   consumed

Combinations Proposed in Selected Countries				
		Alternatives Selected		
Country	*Method*	*A*	*B*	*C*
Netherlands	CRVA (modified)	1	2,3,4	1c
United Kingdom	Historical-cost	1	1	1a
	SSAP #7 (CPP)	2	1	1b
	Sandilands (CCA)	1	2,3,4	1e
United States	Historical-cost	1	1	1a
	Exposure draft (GPP)	2	1	1b

specific critical ailments (high leverage or cash and capital deficiencies) would be diagnosed not only as healthy but as steadily improving. Financial reports could be confusing, if not misleading, and simply not worth their costs (table 6-4).

Characteristics of Replacement-Value Accounting

As table 6-2 indicates, replacement value theory has several variant forms dependent upon the concept of profit employed.

Two general concepts have been developed, based upon the following asset measurements:

Table 6-3
Advantages of General-Purchasing-Power (GPP) Accounting and General-Price-Level Financial Statements (GPLFS)

1. Measures changes in general price levels now ignored. Discloses impact of inflation on the general purchasing power of the dollar.
2. Reliable enough for reporting purposes. GPLFS are primarily oriented toward third parties.
3. Sufficiently objective and verifiable.
    a. All firms will use same index.
    b. Results are auditable.
4. Relatively easy to apply.
    a. Accounting standards not changed, only the unit of measure.
    b. Restatement of prior years is simpler than with CRVA.
    c. Practices have been field-tested.
5. Common unit of measure facilitates comparability.
    a. Revenues/expenses are matched using common or constant dollars.
    b. Interperiod comparisons are more meaningful.
6. GPP unit (a "dated dollar") replaces the "rubber" dollar. GNP Implicit Price Deflator is the best comprehensive index.
7. Discloses effective or "real" tax rates. Enhances progress toward favorable changes in tax laws.
8. Less drastic departure from historical cost.
    a. Historical costs must be retained in accounts for tax, legal, and other purposes.
    b. Few ongoing changes in accounting necessary; adjustments arise mainly in preparation of reports.
    c. Reports are basically historical costs adjusted or restated in common (or constant) dollars.
9. More realistic income relationships are possible.
    a. Relates dividends paid to "real" income.
    b. Helps develop logical dividend policies.
    c. Helps prevent accidental distribution of capital.
10. Aids management evaluation and use.
    a. Provides more realistic return-on-investment rates.
    b. GPP gains/losses reflect management's response to inflation.
    c. Supplies better idea of purchasing power needed to replace assets consumed.
    d. Helps internal management of cash.
    e. Aids in union negotiations by separating inflation and productivity gains.
    f. Can serve as public relations tool for certain industries.

1. *Input* costs or *entry* prices—current costs
2. *Output* values or *exit* prices
    a. net realizable values
    b. present values of future cash flows

Theorists tend to agree that the discounted present value of future cash flows is technically the most appropriate basis for measuring assets, since the accounting income that is produced is closest to economic income. That aspect also makes it the least practicable as a total approach. If net income is determined by the expiration of the current values of assets, and if these current values are determined by discounting future net income streams, the model is

Table 6-4
Disadvantages of General-Purchasing-Power (GPP) Accounting and General-Price-Level Financial Statements (GPLFS)

1. GPP does not account for changes in specific prices.
   a. Should account for changes in general and specific prices.
   b. GPP indices applied to assets do not reflect the specific prices of those assets.
   c. Gains/losses on nonmonetary assets are ignored.

2. GPP is not logically consistent. While specific price changes are said to be ignored, price-level-adjusted amounts reported for assets cannot be greater than their net realizable values.

3. General indices are not always appropriate.
   a. Not all goods and firms are affected in the same way.
   b. Specific indices are more appropriate in some cases.
   c. Relevance of index depends upon user. For management, wholesale or industrial indices seem to be preferred. For stockholders, consumer price levels should be more meaningful.
   d. Indices are not exacting measures.

4. Results could be misleading.
   a. While replacement costs of assets are not depicted, users will tend to make those assumptions.
   b. GPLFS are not directly comparable with historical-cost statements.
   c. Presented with multiple statements, users may wonder which set is "real."
   d. Single net income figure includes paper gains/losses on monetary items as well as holding gains, which will be difficult for the layman to understand.

5. Distorts "normal" income.
   a. Highly leveraged, debt-laden firms will look good.
   b. Paper gains on long-term debt are not necessarily equivalent to good management; funds are not provided for anything.
   c. Forecasting is hindered, since focus is on past events.
   d. Gains/losses on monetary items should be separated into realized/unrealized segments, the latter deferred until they can be matched with expirations of costs of related assets.

6. Confuses profitability and liquidity.
   a. Firms willing or able to risk higher levels of borrowed working capital will be able to hedge.
   b. Firms with few nonmonetary assets are, by nature, automatically in a hedged position.
   c. Ability to hedge, either natural or created, will be combined with measurements of profitability.

7. Ignores other effects on prices, such as technology, competition, economic environment of some firms, and the like.

8. Use of GPP of the dollar as the measuring unit mandates the use of unsound procedures for the translation of foreign operations.
   a. Prohibits the use of restate/translate/restate procedures.
   b. Assumes that all effects of inflation upon foreign currencies are recognized by exchange rates.

9. Costs are not worth alleged benefits.
   a. May lose the ability to use LIFO for tax purposes.
   b. May result in higher property-tax assessments.
   c. Must roll forward (restate) prior years each time comparative statements are prepared if common dollars are used.
   d. Must also provide replacement-cost information to the SEC.
   e. Investors may not attempt to understand the GPLFS.
   f. There are better ways to disclose the effects of inflation upon a specific firm, its assets, its operations, and its future.

insoluble. Present values are useful as partial approaches, however, especially in the measurement of selected monetary items.

Variations in replacement-value accounting also result from motives to protect either the productive capacity (the Dutch aim) or the current cost or value of the entity's assets (the British goal). Differences in approaches aside, the methods are similar enough that they can be collectively termed *replacement value.*

Supporters were convinced that replacement-value accounting reflected general and specific changes in the condition or worth of the important, productive parts of an entity (these are the only concerns of consequence) while retaining the familiar unit of measure (money). Theoretically, accounting for changes in specific price levels applied micro concepts to micro units and thus related concepts with entities (table 6-5).

Critics (table 6-6) were quick to challenge the subjectivity necessarily related to assessments of condition (value or current cost) to be reported. Second, the focus was upon current replacement costs or values. Such an

Table 6-5
Advantages of Replacement-Value or Current-Cost Accounting

1. Statements are interpretable.
   a. Familiar monetary unit is retained as the unit of measurement.
   b. Assets will approximate the values often assumed by users of historical-cost statements.

2. Provides closer approximation of real income.
   a. Revenues are related to costs in common dollars.
   b. Income is not contaminated by changes in price levels, since these are excluded and set up in capital-maintenance accounts.

3. The capital of the enterprise, however defined, is protected from involuntary diminution by management.

4. Measures real effects of inflation.
   a. Balance-sheet items reflected at current values take into account changes in both general and specific prices on these items; no additional price changes are relevant to the firm.
   b. Will correct prostitution of balance sheets by LIFO inventories while retaining current matching benefits on income statements as well as protecting continued use of LIFO for tax purposes.
   c. Current values can also recognize the effects of technology, competition, industry peculiarities, and the like.

5. Effective or real tax rates are disclosed.

6. Value accounting is a better management tool. Concepts are future-oriented, which is the realm of managers, analysts, and other informed users of financial statements.

7. Value accounting is gaining support.
   a. The SEC requires certain replacement-cost information now, may require supplemental statements later.
   b. Professional groups in other countries and regions (such as the EEC) are considering adoption/trial in various forms.

Table 6-6
Disadvantages of Replacement-Value or Current-Cost Accounting

1. Defective income statements.
   a. Changes in the purchasing power of money are not reflected in the period in which they occur.
   b. Comparability is impaired.
2. Defective balance sheets.
   a. Subjective evaluations and asset appraisals may signal a return to the abuses of the 1920s.
   b. No uniformity; combinations of current cost and current value will be used.
3. Problems and costs of implementation and administration.
   a. Nonavailability of necessary specific indices.
   b. Complete departure from historical costs; two sets of records will be required.
   c. Costs and problems of implementation will seriously impact small firms; no practicable way to implement in large firms.
   d. Replacement values may result in increased property-tax assessments.
   e. Audit costs will increase.
4. May initiate price increases to further aggravate inflationary conditions.
5. Systems are not logically sound.
   a. In a competitive environment, company survival cannot be taken as a "given."
   b. Maintenance of productive capacity is neither a necessary nor a sufficient condition for survival and growth of an enterprise.
   c. Increases in assets on balance sheets are not reflected in income statements.
   d. Recovery of historical costs plus costs of capital will produce a "steady-state" firm so long as selling prices are based upon historical costs.

approach was considered to be appropriate for items with rapid turnovers (such as inventories) but illogical for items that would be replaced far into the future (such as plant), possibly in different economic circumstances (such as in another country), and maybe in different form altogether (due to changes in technology or need). Third, changes in the vigor or purchasing power of the unit of measure (money) were ignored. Finally, in market-based economic systems, the survival of an economic entity could not be taken as a given. (The narrow agreement was also presented that, given the definition of inflation mentioned earlier, accounting for changes in specific price levels—which can occur for all sorts of reasons other than inflation—is technically not accounting for inflation.)

The heading of this section posed the question, "Purchasing-power or value accounting?" The disadvantages attributed to both proposed methods indicate that each has significant deficiencies, both theoretical and practical. Reason dictates a search for a better way.

Hybrid Proposals

The literature of price-level accounting is replete with suggestions of that better way. Space does not permit references to the efforts and contributions of countless individuals, and fairness precludes the mention of some to the exclusion of others. Virtually all the peers of the accounting profession examined the basic methods and found each of them wanting in certain respects. Many recommended hybrid proposals, which combined the desirable aspects of GPP and the current-value or current-cost methods.

Many organizations were particularly concerned, since they were practitioners. Not only did they have to practice what was to be adopted, but, given their personal contact with clients, they were concerned about the usefulness and the attendant costs of the remedies to be administered. Two examples, one at each end of the spectrum, are worthy of mention.

One organization[21] sought economic reality by combining the best features of both major proposals into a hybrid form of accounting system. The method proposed was eclectic, situational (it related measurement techniques with the nature of items), and experimental. Unfortunately, combining two methods, each having serious practical deficiencies, could hardly be expected to produce a single practical method.

Another practitioner[22] made an interesting and very practical proposal. The disease of inflation was said to infect primarily two physical parts of the economic organism—inventories and fixed assets. The medication of LIFO arrested (or had reportedly reduced the tax pains of) the first affliction. Why not simply administer a similar balm to the fixed assets? A medication akin to one proposed by George O. May thirty years ago[23] was suggested—depreciation based upon current costs (historical costs adjusted by official indices) for reporting and for tax purposes. No, neither medication would cure the disease, nor would one of the patient's charts (the balance sheet) fairly reflect his economic position. But with more money in his pockets, the patient would at least feel more comfortable.

No reproach is intended nor should it be inferred from the two examples mentioned. The point to be made is that accounting for inflation or changing price levels is intractable by any reasonable means. Those means which are logically consistent are not worth their costs. Those which are practical are primarily pain relievers, not accounting methods.

Consequently, the agency charged with overseeing the general health and welfare of all public entities was forced to require that something be done, even if it was not the most desirable something, while the discourse continued. The Securities and Exchange Commission required in its Accounting Series Release No. 190 (ASR-190)[24] that certain large public entities disclose selected replacement-cost information in their 1977 reports as an interim experiment. Other effects of inflation were also encouraged to be included in the disclosures.

The ASR-190 disclosures could appear in footnotes or in separate sections of the financial statements. The information could properly be labeled as "unaudited"; however, it was considered a part of the financial statements, and the independent auditor was "associated" with the information regardless of label, form, or location.

The selection of replacement-cost information as a frame of reference is interesting but not really important, since the many variables affecting asset replacements, particularly for multinational enterprises, rendered the information virtually useless. The real significance of the requirement lies in the fact that the SEC chose not to revise the accounting process. Instead, emphasis was placed upon disclosure of the effects of inflation by those in the best positions to do so—management, primarily, and the independent auditor, secondarily. It forced managements and accountants to start thinking about the effects of inflation upon specific entities.

The mechanisms, as well as the necessary motivators, have been put in place to encourage rational internal examination and diagnosis upon which to base external disclosure.

Toward a Cure

If physicians concentrated on maintaining charts rather than curing illnesses, their patients would either die or heal themselves by natural means. In either case, there would be little need for physicians. Accountants and economists are now facing a similar dilemma. They should concentrate their immediate efforts upon curing inflation in the United States. Naturally, charts must be maintained to assess the patient's progress, but the charting process must be recognized as only one of several means rather than as the end in itself.

Inflation was laboriously examined to illustrate that, as a disease, it is pervasive and pernicious. It not only afflicts the living but is transmitted to generations yet unborn. It is an extremely complex malady, affecting some but not all, and in various ways and degrees. It respects no national boundaries or economic systems. It is known to afflict the poor and the weak more readily and to a greater extent than the rich and powerful, be they individuals or nations. While it is known to affect artificial persons as well as real persons, the corporate forms of artificial persons are furnished certain medications called investment tax credits, accelerated methods of depreciation, LIFO systems of inventory costing, and related deferrals of income taxes. Some of these artificial persons serve as carriers of the disease and, having acquired a degree of relative immunity by various means, are suspected of forming groups that serve to spread and intensify the disease, whether intentionally or not. Some of these artificial persons have become closely associated with the government—a sort of supra-artificial person. It has also been reported that the government uses the disease as a "political and social force"[25] to accomplish several ends, some of which are suspect.

The disease known as inflation can be perceived by accountants and economists as a threat to their existence—and it may well be if they continue to be ineffectual. Or they can consider the challenge of inflation itself (and its many ramifications upon economic entities) as an opportunity to render genuine public service, not only to their clients and national governments, but to the international community as well.

Inflation spills over into many aspects of business operations: exchange rates, currency translations, transfer prices, performance evaluations, consolidated and segmented reportings, and taxation practices. Inflation also impacts the larger business environments: the legal, political, and (by insidious redistributions of income and wealth) the sociocultural sector.

Prevention and cure for the disease of inflation would be efforts worthy of the profession, as Wilcox advocated more than twenty years ago:

> . . . when the problem [fluctuating price levels] is placed in appropriate perspective, it will not be forgotten that a solution of its effects on accounts is in the nature of a drug to lessen pain, rather than a cure for the disease. The disease is inflation, itself, and its prevention would not only eliminate the accounting problems which result from it, but would also be of greater social usefulness than any conceivable adjustment of accounts.[26]

The profession of accountancy and the discipline of economics, acting together, can exercise considerable influence. They must convince the business community that its best long-run interests will be served by joining their cause, since inflation represents the only real threat to capitalism and free enterprise. Collectively, political influence could be applied to cure and prevent the disease of inflation.

In view of the virulent nature of inflation, control must begin at the fount. The most desirable first step requires indexation of federal taxes and government obligations.[27] Although not a cure in itself, indexation is an essential starting point. First, the government would join the ranks of those who are adversely affected by inflation instead of standing off to one side and/or benefiting from the problems of others. Second, the government would be forced to consider seriously some trade-offs among planned expenditures as revenues shrink and borrowing costs increase. Third, indexation would effectively serve to prevent practical politics and tax considerations from determining accounting practices.

It is not logical to assume that the government would voluntarily adopt this abbreviated form of indexation. It will have to be convinced that such action is desirable. The job of convincing should be assumed by business and the accounting profession. No special-interest charges could be levied, since the pressures for change would benefit individuals and businesses alike—those present and yet to come.

While the medicine prescribed is effective, it would not result in an instant cure. Time would be required. During this interim (and thereafter, it is hoped), accountants could devote their full attention to chart-keeping.

The government would certainly require charts to measure its own health and the pulse of the economy. A significant initial step in this direction was represented by the second annual prototype report of the consolidated financial statements of the U.S. government for the fiscal year ending June 30, 1976. These statements were prepared, using accrual methods of accounting and historical costs, by the Treasury Department, assisted by an advisory committee of CPAs, businessmen, academicians, and government officials. For decades it has been generally considered ridiculous to expect to manage or report the financial affairs of the world's largest single business entity using cash-basis accounting methods not much more sophisticated than those used by individuals managing their checking accounts. Yet not much was done to change matters, since compliance reporting was considered to be of overriding importance, rather than a necessary but ancillary function of the government accounts. Accrual-basis reporting will highlight rather than conceal the present and future obligations of present and past political decisions.

A second essential chart that must be provided is in the form of a road map for the national economy. Call it national economic planning or indicative planning (or common sense), those who profess to steer the economy should know where it is, where it wants to go, the available routes, and the obstacles that exist or may appear. This chart need not necessarily be an integrated model, for such concoctions are often awe-inspiring but not very practical. However, the charting system at least must be able to recognize and anticipate significant roadblocks, be they shortages of critical materials, greedy businesses or unions, uncooperative trading partners or multinationals, or similar national concerns. So long as the traditional mechanisms of the free market system are not effective in certain sectors of our economy, the public interest mandates government intercession in wage and price decisions in the recalcitrant sectors.

Data for such ventures will necessarily be in physical as well as monetary units; perhaps the activity will also teach accountants and economists to pull in the same harness again. Regardless, these planning ventures will require data: some in different forms and in different time-frames than are now available; in other cases, new data needs will arise; in all cases, the accountant will have the opportunity to become associated with the information.[28]

A third chart needed to assist governmental operations is an effective program of zero-base budgeting.[29] As the name suggests, a zero-base budgeting system requires each government agency requesting appropriations of funds to start from scratch, that is, as if it did not previously exist. This tends to require each activity to justify its operation, and to deemphasize standard procedures of taking last-year's costs (and inefficiencies) and adding thereto. To be effective, a zero-base budgeting system must be designed to prevent a one-page request for funds from being accompanied by a ream of narrative justification. A two-page limit is a sound rule.

Contributions such as those mentioned would help government assess proposed expenditures, reduce waste and inefficiency, and thus stretch a stable or reducing stream of revenue dollars that would result from indexation.

Ultimately, difficult value judgments would be necessary if budgets were to be balanced. Although these represent political decisions, they can nonetheless be translated into dollars and financial impacts, before and after the decisions are made. Undisclosed debts and future costs would be illuminated for consideration and, later, for accountability by public reckoning. To consider certain decisions as political is one thing; to assert that they are political and therefore not accountable is quite another matter.

The foregoing steps toward a cure for inflation are the most difficult. Dealing with the reporting problems in the private sector is more or less child's play in comparison.

Interim Medication

Even if the requisite leadership and determination miraculously blossomed today, time would be required to affect a cure for inflation. In the interim, accountants, with the help of the economists, would still be faced with the tasks of chart-keeping and reporting the operations of economic entities. Neither group needs a new charting process or a new measuring unit. What is needed is a change in attitude.

1. No changes are necessary in the present financial reporting systems based upon historical cost and the dollar as the unit of measure. Historical costs have served us well, and there is no other practical way of reporting the account-ability of management. Legal and other regulatory processes are also dependent upon historical-cost relationships, which must be maintained in any case. (However, if indexations of federal taxes and obligations were adopted, then such artificialities as LIFO, accelerated depreciation, and similar tax concessions should be prohibited. They belong on tax returns and related schedules, not on financial statements.)

2. No changes in traditional accounting or reporting are necessary to prevent management from making irrational economic decisions. Management does not (or surely should not) use financial accounting reports as the primary basis for decision making. Managerial data should be future-oriented; financial reports are, by necessity, couched in historical terms. Managements are not constrained by the precepts of financial accounting and can design internal information systems to serve their particular needs, whatever they might be.

3. Capital maintenance is not a given. It is a function of management and the factors of the marketplace. No system of financial accounting can, or should, assure capital maintenance; that is management's responsibility. Furthermore, Anthony[30] has demonstrated that historical cost will maintain a "steady-state" company in times of inflation so long as selling prices are based upon historical costs.

Along a different vein, the alleged inadequacy of depreciation based upon historical costs (through 1974) is a myth that has finally been disposed of by Schiff.[31] However, since 1974, historical-cost depreciation (together with the sweetenings of accelerated methods for tax purposes plus investment tax credits) has become slightly less than straight-line depreciation on current costs, only because business reduced new capital investments, for whatever reasons. That is exactly the rationale underlying tax allowances to spur capital investment—they will benefit only in times of expansion. Business may well ask for but cannot expect to have its cake and eat it too.

4. Management must be charged with explaining the effects of inflation upon the enterprise in financial reports, together with what actions have been taken (or are planned) to cope with rising price levels.

SEC-imposed experiments will prove to be beneficial, since they will have initiated some internal thought and examination. Although ASR-190, as an experiment, has not produced meaningful information, it did encourage management to evaluate existing facilities. Inflation was only one of the factors examined, along with technological change and location, among others. Adequate explanations of inflation could make continued use of ASR-190 unnecessary. However, ASR-190 will have to be contended with until the SEC is satisfied that other equivalent (and more useful) disclosures have been implemented.

A second SEC experiment—segmented reporting—will not go away, since it was effectively adopted by *FASB Statement No, 14*, "Financial Reporting for Segments of a Business Enterprise" in December 1976. Although segmented reporting is addressed in chapter 13, it is relevant to mention here that it will prove to be helpful in inflation explanation as soon as managements and accountants stop complaining about lifting the corporate veil and start putting the new tools to use. Since all parts of enterprises are not affected by inflation in the same way, whether they be diversified domestic or multinational, looking at the several parts rather than at the whole should help put the impacts of inflation into more manageable contexts.

Not all firms are adversely affected by inflation; those that are can be affected in various ways and degrees. Managements, aided by their accountants and economists, are in the best positions to make the necessary assessments. Independent auditors are in position to evaluate the fairness of the assessments made. Such evaluations would certainly be in line with the recommendations of the recent Cohen commission on the responsibilities of independent auditors.

No particular factor or factors can be recommended above others, since each firm and segment occupies a unique niche in the economic realm. All relevant factors, domestic and foreign, having a material net effect should be considered: changes in the specific prices of goods and facilities; changes in the purchasing power of money; and leverage or gearing realized by external financing.

This recommendation would require some changes in attitude on the part of economists and accountants. Economists would be required to return to the realm of social relevance and to divorce themselves from habits of modeling the social environment mechanistically "as if it were a branch of physics."[32] Accountants, on the other hand, would have to shed their reluctance to interpret or explain events. Accountants have traditionally been content to furnish reports and to leave the interpretation and understanding to others. This characteristic represents a poor hallmark for a profession.

Users of financial statements would, at long last, be given reasoned explanations in addition to raw data and a maze of footnotes.

5. Some additional information should be supplied as well. Reconciliations of statutory and effective tax rates and amounts should be furnished. Additional disclosures considered to be necessary in the particular circumstances should be encouraged, to keep the information, taken as a whole, from being misleading.

Inflation Explanation

Analyses such as the foregoing would place the phenomenon of inflation into context. Many myths would be laid to rest, and new interrelationships would surely be discovered. Some firms would be identified as incubators or carriers of the disease of inflation, and some practices possibly would be changed.

In the process, accounting methods that have proved to be of value would be retained; others would be changed over time. Users of financial reports would be provided with reasoned explanations in addition to cold data interspersed with myths. (It will be a sad day when only accountants can understand financial reports—they will be communicating only with themselves.)

Accountants would free themselves from pressures to do the impossible—to account for something as nebulous as inflation. Accountants would not be placed in positions as adversaries of management, but rather would be professional associates attesting to the reasonableness of explanations of economic events. That is much more the role of a profession.

Two choices face accountants today. They can continue to play the game of practical politics and tax relief and wrestle with attempts to account for something that cannot be accounted for (or reported meaningfully) using any normative means. Or they can trade inflation accounting for inflation explanation—and reasoned explanation may represent just the glue needed to stabilize the accountant's rickety stool.

Notes

1. Leonard M. Savoie, "Price Level Accounting, Practical Politics, and Tax Relief," *Management Accounting*, January 1977, pp. 15-18.

2. Financial Accounting Standards Board, *FASB Discussion Memorandum*, an analysis of issues related to *Conceptual Framework for Financial Accounting and Reporting: Elements of Financial Statements and Their Measurement* (Stamford, Conn.: FASB, December 2, 1976), 360 pp.

3. Ibid.

4. Henry W. Sweeney, *Stabilized Accounting* (New York: Harper & Brothers, 1936), preface.

5. "Depreciation and High Costs," *Accounting Research Bulletin No. 33* (New York: American Institute of Accountants, 1947).

6. The Accounting Principles Board, *Accounting Research and Terminology Bulletins: Final Edition* (New York: American Institute of Certified Public Accountants, 1961), p. 69.

7. George O. May, *Business Income and Price Levels* (New York: American Institute of Accountants, 1949).

8. American Accounting Association Committee on Concepts and Standards, "Price Level Changes and Financial Statements," *The Accounting Review*, October 1951, pp. 468-474; also in *The Journal of Accountancy*, October 1951, pp. 461-465.

9. Study Group on Business Income, *Changing Concepts of Business Income* (New York: The Macmillan Company, 1952).

10. *Accounting Research and Terminology Bulletins: Final Edition* (New York: AICPA, 1961), pp. 70-71.

11. Staff of the Accounting Research Division, *Accounting Research Study No. 6: Reporting the Financial Effects of Price-Level Changes* (New York: American Institute of Certified Public Accountants, Inc., 1963).

12. Accounting Principles Board, *Statement No. 3: Financial Statements Restated for General Price-Level Changes* (New York: American Institute of Certified Public Accountants, Inc., June 1969).

13. Financial Accounting Standards Board, *Financial Reporting in Units of General Purchasing Power*, Exposure Draft of a Proposed Statement of Financial Accounting Standards (Stamford, Conn.: FASB, December 31, 1974).

14. See *The Brazilian Method of Indexing and Accounting for Inflation* (Chicago: Arthur Andersen & Co., May 1975).

15. "Canadian Institute Issues Current Value Accounting Memo," *The Journal of Accountancy*, November 1976, pp. 32, 34.

16. R. Burgert, "Reservations About 'Replacement Value' Accounting in the Netherlands," *Abacus*, December 1972, p. 125.

17. A. Goudeket, "How Inflation Is Being Recognized in Financial Statements in the Netherlands," *The Journal of Accountancy*, October 1952, pp. 448-452, and "An Application of Replacement Value Theory," *The Journal of Accountancy*, July 1960, pp. 37-47. A somewhat more detailed version was available as "Philips NV," 1968, Case No. 9108003, from the Intercollegiate Case Clearing House, Boston. Although the financial statements in the case are dated, the managerial philosophies and systems are timeless.

18. Brian D. Smith, "Sandilands Report," *The Arthur Andersen Chronicle*, April 1976, p. 26.

19. *Inflation Accounting: Report of the Inflation Accounting Committee*, F.E.P. Sandilands, chairman. (London: Her Majesty's Stationery Office, September 1975), 364 pp.

20. "U.K. Approves Current Cost Accounting Exposure Draft," *The Journal of Accountancy*, January 1977, pp. 24, 26.

21. *Economic Reality in Financial Reporting* (New York: Touche Ross & Co., 1976), 29 pp.

22. Ernst & Ernst, *Accounting Under Inflationary Conditions*, 1976, 28 pp. Retrieval No. 38474.

23. George O. May, *Business Income and Price Levels.*

24. Securities and Exchange Commission, "Notice of Adoption of Amendments to Regulation S-X Requiring Disclosure of Certain Replacement Cost Data," Accounting Series Release No. 190, March 23, 1976.

25. *Client Inflation Clinic* (Chicago: Arthur Andersen & Co., September 1975), p. 14.

26. Edward B. Wilcox, "Fluctuating Price Levels in Relation to Accounts," in Morton Backer (ed.), *Handbook of Modern Accounting Theory* (Englewood Cliffs, N.J.: Prentice-Hall, Inc., 1953), p. 271. © 1953, Prentice-Hall, Inc. Reprinted with permission.

27. Indexation is one concept reportedly under consideration as a result of the 1976 Tax Reform Act. See Joel M. Forster et al., "Tax Reform: The New Perspective," *The Journal of Accountancy*, April 1977, pp. 79-88. Also see Ernest J. Oppenheimer, *The Inflation Swindle* (Englewood Cliffs, N.J.: Prentice-Hall, Inc., 1977).

28. Wesley T. Andrews and Charles H. Smith, "A Role for Financial Accounting in National Economic Planning in the United States," *The International Journal of Accounting* 12, No. 1, Fall 1976, pp. 133-145.

29. Peter A. Pyhrr, "Zero-base Budgeting," *Harvard Business Review*, November-December 1970, pp. 111-121.

30. Robert N. Anthony, "A Case for Historical Costs," *Harvard Business Review*, November-December 1976, pp. 69-79.

31. Michael Schiff, "Depreciation Short Fall: Fact or Fiction?", *The Journal of Accountancy*, March 1977, pp. 40-42.

32. Robert L. Heilbroner, "Sterility of Modern Economics," in Gerhard G. Mueller and Charles H. Smith (eds.), *Accounting: A Book of Readings* (New York: Holt, Rinehart and Winston, Inc., 1970), p. 187.

7 Currency Exchange Rates

International operations are conducted in an environment in which there is no universal currency or common unit of account. Consequently, firms transacting business with companies in other countries are usually confronted with two problems:

1. Conversion—the actual exchange of one currency for another to settle business transactions.
2. Translation—the expression of financial transactions and reports recorded or denominated in one unit of account into another.

In a specific international business transaction, neither conversion nor translation will be a problem for one of the parties concerned. If the transaction is denominated (stated) in the local currency of the seller, he will receive, upon settlement, the stipulated amount in his domestic currency. He (the seller) has no problem of converting a foreign currency into his customary money of account. Also, the seller in this case is able to record the transaction in his domestic currency, much as if the sale was transacted with a local firm.

But what of the buyer in this situation? He has to contend with both problems. First, he must translate the amount of the transaction from that agreed upon in a foreign currency to its equivalent amount in his local currency in order to record the transaction in his accounts. Then, at the time of payment, he must convert a quantity of his local money to the amount in foreign currency needed to settle the account.

Both procedures—translation and conversion—are accomplished by means of exchange rates, ratios by which one currency is traded for others. Exchange rates, in turn, are determined by the foreign-exchange mechanisms of the international monetary system.

It follows logically that, if businessmen and accountants choose to operate in the international arena, they should have a general understanding of the characteristics of foreign exchange rates and the system within which they are determined.

Accountants, particularly, should understand the vagaries of exchange rates if they are to be used as yardsticks to measure and evaluate foreign economic activities.

Background

The problems of converting and translating foreign transactions have been managed routinely since the dawn of trade between nation-states.

Money-changers and their activities are recounted in the early histories of Babylon, Greece, and Rome, and of course they earned disrepute for their hagglings in the temples of the New Testament. Systems of money-changing (now called foreign exchange markets) were created in response to the needs of trade between nations and followed in the wake of that trade. Consequently, by accident of history and location, the complexities of foreign exchange are treated as commonplace by the peoples of some nations, while others are relative neophytes in foreign money markets. For example, Europeans, as a matter of course, have regularly crossed national boundaries and have used different currencies. Americans, on the other hand, although they live in a large country composed of many states, benefit from the use of a single national currency. As a result, the average American is not as familiar with foreign exchange as is the average European today.

Some countries, such as the Netherlands, were forced by location and resources to engage in international commerce. For them, operating within foreign-exchange markets became commonplace. Even relative newcomers to the international sphere, such as the United States, experienced little difficulty in learning the rudiments of converting and translating foreign transactions.

The advent and growth of the multinational corporation complicated matters. No longer were individual transactions the primary concern. Parent corporations found it necessary—internally as well as by external mandate—to translate the financial reports of affiliates domiciled throughout the free world. Not one or two but a host of foreign currencies (and their fluctuating prices) had to be dealt with.

The processes of adjusting, translating, and—particularly for U.S. firms—consolidating financial statements were time-consuming and troublesome but were not sources of real concern, for several reasons. Most companies developed standardized systems of translation and consolidation procedures. These systems were governed by people and by human judgment, with computers relegated to the supportive functions of detail storage and manipulation. Second, the exchange rates of most currencies were rather stable until 1973, at least insofar as short-term volatility was concerned. Finally, accounting and reporting conventions in most countries, the United States included, were flexible enough to permit the use of reserves to smooth out the effects of most large-scale fluctuations caused by translations—often called accounting, paper, or translation gains and losses, as opposed to real, economic (conversion) gains and losses.

In 1973, the managed or pegged system of exchange rates was discontinued, and currencies were permitted to float to levels determined by the financial marketplace. Unfortunately, 1973 also saw the OPEC price orgy wreak havoc in that marketplace. The subsequent period of inflation and fluctuating exchange rates caused doubt to be cast upon the usefulness of many accounting concepts.

This chapter will address the international monetary system in order to (1) examine some of the determinants of exchange rates and (2) determine what factors cause fluctuations in exchange rates in the short and the long term.

The International Monetary System

Monetary systems are those collections of procedures designed by societies to serve two functions: (1) to facilitate the exchange of goods and services and (2) to settle or discharge obligations or debts. Primitive societies had no need for monetary systems, because the limited trade that was necessary was conducted directly, by means of barter. As division of labor and specialization altered subsistence methods, a more convenient system became necessary, and man invented money.

Money is anything that is generally accepted in exchange (payment) for goods, services, and the settlement of debts. The acceptance of money as a medium of exchange is dependent upon two attributes. First, it must be capable of serving as a store of value, at least temporarily. That is, a farmer will accept money in exchange for his wheat so long as he is confident that the money can later be exchanged for other goods or services he might require. Second, money must also serve as a common denominator by which the relative prices of goods and services can be measured and expressed. The latter attribute is most important, since, if money cannot function as a common denominator, it cannot serve as a medium of exchange or as a store of value.

Money has taken many forms, from useful commodities, such as salt and spices, to precious metals, such as gold and silver. These commodity forms of money merely represented more convenient means of barter, in that a good or service was exchanged for another good, albeit an intermediate one, which was acceptable because of its intrinsic value as well as its value in future exchanges.

Gold and silver bullion were popular specie forms of money in the Middle Ages. They were desirable in themselves, they could be readily assayed for uniformity, they were quantifiable by weight, and they were divisible into smaller units (coins) without loss of value. Money in the form of specie, however, was not without its attendant problems. Bullion shipments were cumbersome, costly, and risky. Coins were subject to counterfeiting. In fact, coinage was in such a confused state in the Middle Ages that a given coin might be "readily accepted in one street while it was looked upon with suspicion in the other...."[1] Creation of money and the facilitation of its acceptance and exchange soon became functions of governments.

Currency, or paper money, was adopted to reduce the cumbersome aspects of exchanging specie. The earliest currencies gained acceptance because they were backed by gold or silver and simply represented claims to these specie. Such currencies were called representative money forms. Few problems were created by exchanges of these currencies, since a claim to a specific amount of gold or silver remained the common denominator.

The appearance of credit money created problems of acceptance and conversion. Currencies not backed by specific claims against gold or silver depended upon the credit of the issuing government. In other words, the general acceptance of credit-money currencies was determined by the goods and services they could claim in the country of issue. Conversion or exchange of these credit monies was also hampered, since the familiar and relatively stable standard of gold or silver was supplanted by an often nebulous and variable denominator consisting of a bundle of goods and services.

Actually, the advent of credit-money currencies brought about the effective demise of money as a common denominator. Money could hardly serve as a common denominator for goods and services when its value became dependent upon the quantity and quality of goods and services available. Money became a *circular concept.*

Gold Standards

Gold has been used in several ways, directly and indirectly, as a universal money or common denominator. Its general acceptance and relative scarcity were attributes that enabled gold to provide reasonable stability between and among the credit monies issued by governments. This stability, in turn, created a financial environment of reasonable risk, at least in the short run, for international business and the multinational corporation.

An abbreviated look at the chronological order of the gold standards employed will provide an overview of the recent past that should enable a better understanding of the present.

Gold-Bullion Standard. Under a gold-bullion standard, the central governments define or denominate their currencies (representative monies) in specific quantities of gold. The relationships between these denominations are known as *mint parities.* The central governments must also agree to redeem their currencies for the weights of gold specified upon request. This last feature, in theory at least, enabled a country's gold reserves to determine its total money supply and, as a result, the level of its internal prices as well as its external trade. In short, gold functioned as a dual standard in that it served as the common denominator for both international and national monetary systems.

The mint parities also established the ratios by which the various national currencies would be accepted in the marketplace—their exchange rates. While these exchange rates have been described as fixed in nature, some flexibility existed in the form of a narrow range or band (usually no more than one percent) around the parity rates. This band represented the costs of shipping the gold bullion—freight, handling, insurance, and the interest forgone on use of the money while in transit—and were called gold points.

The operation of the gold-bullion standard can be illustrated in two ways: first, by treating a currency as a commodity having a supply and demand; second, by examining trade imbalances.

As a commodity, the international market price of a currency (its exchange rate) tended to rise or fall dependent upon its demand and supply relative to other currencies. So long as its market price remained within the band surrounding its mint parity, a given currency was bought and sold as needed to settle international transactions. If excessive demand forced the market price of a currency above the parity band, external debtors found it cheaper to pay their debts in gold. Conversely, if insufficient demand for a currency lowered its market price below the parity band, external creditors demanded payments in gold.

From a trade standpoint, a debtor nation was one having a net deficit in its international balance of payments; that is, it owed more to other nations than was receivable from them. Consequently, the deficiencies were made up by settlements in gold.

The foregoing examples are two sides of the same coin and emphasize that, under a gold-bullion standard, trade imbalances and movements of exchange rates were inseparable.

Little further reflection is necessary to recognize that, in addition to serving as a common denominator, the gold-bullion standard also acted as an *automatic stabilizer* of national and international economies. Each country had to maintain a reasonable trade balance over time, or continuing trade deficits would drain its supply of gold reserves. In turn, lower gold reserves would reduce domestic money supplies and would lower internal price levels. Reduced domestic prices would eventually make exports of the country more attractive in international markets. Subsequent increases in exports would, in turn, produce inflows of gold. Thus, it would become a self-balancing system over time.

Since each domestic economy was tied to and affected by the international economy, governments had but to sit back and permit the free flows of gold to stabilize economies and exchange rates. These attributes of the gold-bullion standard have caused it to be described as a "passive" form of exchange stabilization.[2]

Unfortunately, the foregoing scenario is based upon several assumptions:

1. The worldwide gold supply would increase yearly in the same proportion as the net growth in the supply of goods and services and in the proper locations.
2. Each country's available gold supply would be such that trade imbalances

would bring about the necessary changes in its money supply and price level in a reasonably short time.

3. International trade and competition would be free of all artificial restrictions.

4. Scare outflows of gold (through causes such as fears of political instabilities) would not occur.

Naturally, these assumptions are not valid. The first item alone is sufficient cause for rejection of the gold-bullion standard. Production of new gold does not coincide with that of goods and services, either in amount or in location. New gold of any consequence is mined in only two or three countries, whereas goods and services are produced in all countries of the world.

Furthermore, few governments prefer passive roles, particularly where their internal economies are concerned. Yet the gold-bullion standard prevailed from about 1870 until 1914, and intermittently thereafter until 1944.

Gold-Exchange Standard. Under a gold-exchange standard, gold is relegated to a passive or secondary role as common denominator. National governments assume the roles of active stabilizers.

The various governments merely define their currencies with respect to gold. No agreement need be made to redeem any currency for gold at any time. The definitions or prices of currencies agreed upon are called *official parities.* Most agreements also specify a narrow band within which currencies may fluctuate without active government intervention. In other words, national governments simply agree to peg their respective currencies at particular levels.

As market forces (primarily trade imbalances) tend to move a given currency outside its agreed-upon band, the goverment is expected to buy or sell foreign exchange in order to keep the market rate within the given parameters. Over time, the ability of a government to intervene in the foreign-exchange markets will depend on its liquidity, or access to liquid assets, and not on gold reserves.

Upon reaching the limits of its liquidity, a government has two choices: (1) internal adjustments by monetary or fiscal actions (or both) to bring its balance of payments into line, or (2) devaluation of its currency (lowering its price relative to all others). Under the latter option, the government, after consultation with other governments, would redefine the official parity of its currency with respect to gold and, as a result, all other currencies. In effect, the government would peg the band of its currency at a new, lower level. This action would tend to make the country's exports more attractive in international markets and, in time, would improve the nation's balance of payments.

Conversely, those countries enjoying increasing trade and liquidity surpluses were expected to revalue (raise) their currencies with respect to others. In these cases, the higher relative prices of exports would act to reduce the trade surpluses and to restore international equilibrium.

Exchange rates under a gold-exchange standard are neither fixed nor flexible; rather, they could be termed rigid within adjustable bands or steps.

Also, this type of standard represents a zero-sum game in which the deficits of debtor nations are represented by the surpluses of creditor countries.

While governments prefer active roles, hindsight indicates that most are reluctant to take prompt corrective measures either internally or externally. Domestic adjustments are usually beset by political resistance or apathy. Externally, adjustments of official parities are usually delayed also. Creditor nations argue that debtor nations should devalue (depreciate) their currencies, while the debtors rebut that it is easier, therefore logical, for creditor nations to revalue (appreciate) their currencies.

Instead of frequent, nominal adjustments, such delays usually produce few but more significant changes in parities.

No Standard—Freely Floating Rates

The concept of an international monetary system without any standard or common denominator, wherein currencies rise and fall based upon the mechanisms of a totally unconstrained marketplace, is a *myth.*

Such a concept is not a system at all, since, without some form of common denominator (such as gold or another surrogate benchmark), a given currency would represent a medium of exchange only within the domestic economy of the issuer nation. Externally, all currencies would become commodities to be bartered with all other goods and services in international trade. As mentioned earlier, money in the international sense would become a *circular concept*—an indeterminate.

Also, governments will not assume spectator roles. The actions universally feared, yet rarely encountered, are those which a country would take to depreciate artificially the market rates of its currency in the short run in order to acquire competitive advantages for its exports.

Controlled Exchange

All the monetary concepts examined previously were dependent on the market system, augmented by government interferences of various kinds. A controlled exchange environment is one that is regulated in total by the government, and the market system either is nonexistent or is isolated by official controls. Under exchange control, foreign-exchange rates and transactions are regulated by government decree.

On an international basis, a totally controlled monetary system is impossible. In fact, such a situation is the antithesis of a system.

Selected countries have resorted to exchange controls in times of crises;

Germany, following World War II, is an example. Developing nations also often resort to such controls to assist and monitor internal development. Naturally, controlled economies, such as that in the USSR, embrace controlled exchange out of necessity.

The International Monetary Fund (IMF)

Variations of gold and gold-exchange standards were used with relative success until the worldwide depression of the 1930s. Britain stopped redeeming pounds for gold in 1931, and the United States devalued the dollar in 1933 (by increasing the monetary price of gold almost 70 percent, to $35 an ounce). Financial turmoil reigned until the advent of World War II.

Memories of the financial chaos preceding the war, together with the recognition that greater international cooperation was necessary (as well as possible), motivated the leading Western countries to assemble at Bretton Woods, New Hampshire, in July 1944 to devise a practicable international monetary system. The Bretton Woods agreement established the International Monetary Fund (IMF) in December 1945 and, by means of a second resolution, the International Bank for Reconstruction and Development (the World Bank).

Article I of the IMF Articles of Agreement specified the five objectives of the IMF, excerpted here:

> To promote international monetary cooperation through . . . consultation and collaboration.
>
> To facilitate the expansion and balanced growth of international trade.
>
> To promote exchange stability, . . . and to avoid competitive exchange depreciation.
>
> To assist in the establishment of a multilateral system of payments . . . and in the elimination of foreign exchange restrictions.
>
> To give confidence to members by making the Fund's resources available to them . . . , thus providing them with opportunity to correct [temporary] maladjustments in their balances of payments.

The IMF was a compromise between those who favored fixed exchange rates and those who desired flexible rates.[3]

Mechanics of the Fund were relatively simple. Par values of currencies were established in relationship to gold and were to be permitted to move within a narrow band—plus or minus one percent of parity. Fluctuations beyond that range signaled the need for corrective measures by the countries affected. Where revaluations or devaluations were necessary, those of 10 percent or less were to be implemented in consultation with the IMF. Changes greater than 10 percent required IMF advance approval.

Membership was open to any nation that would sign the articles of agreement and deposit its assigned quota with the IMF. Quotas for member nations were based upon several economic variables, including wealth, trade volumes, and the like. Quotas were deposited in two parts: 25 percent in gold and 75 percent in the country's local currency.

Thereafter, the IMF served as an international clearing house for the currencies of its members and as a source of temporary liquidity. For example, in order to meet a temporary deficit in its balance of payments, a member could borrow the currencies needed up to 25 percent of its quota (that is, its original gold deposit or gold tranche). Borrowings in excess of the gold tranche were to be charged against the member's credit tranche, required IMF approval, and were limited to twice the member's quota. Borrowings were repayable in gold or any convertible currency.

The reconstruction period following World War II was beset with a 30 percent devaluation of sterling (in 1949) and subsequent devaluations by the European nations. The European Payments Union operated from 1950 to 1958 to cope with a shortage of U.S. dollars and to help the European economies strengthen sufficiently to enable their participation in the IMF.

By 1958, the IMF effectively was operating on a gold-dollar standard, in that countries linked their currencies to the U.S. dollar, which, by that time, remained the only currency convertible into gold. Also, the majority of borrowings from the IMF by members were in dollars. Paradoxically, the liquidity essential to the IMF and its members was provided by the very condition that the IMF was pledged to prevent—a continuous maladjustment (deficit) in the U.S. balance of payments.

The 1960s may be categorized as a period of crisis management designed to support the role of the U.S. dollar as a key currency. In 1962, the Group of Ten was formed by the United States and nine other IMF members to provide interest-free currency loans to counteract crises. From 1960 to 1968, the London Gold Pool (composed of the United States and six other countries) attempted to maintain the market price of gold in line with the U.S. parity price of $35 per ounce. By 1968, the Gold Pool could no longer hold the line on the market price of gold and, when the Gold Pool was discontinued, a two-tier gold system resulted—the free-market price and the U.S. parity price of $35 per ounce.

By 1970, the international community became less willing to hold dollars as the market price of gold rose above the U.S. redemption price. Many IMF members also resented the fact that, since the dollar was a key currency, the United States could settle its debts by simply printing more dollars. To ameliorate this latter complaint, the IMF created special drawing rights (SDRs), often called paper gold, which represented borrowing power for members over and above existing limitations.

The United States faced a real dilemma. If it devalued the dollar, the United

States would impose significant losses upon those friendly nations that were willing to hold, and did hold, large amounts of U.S. dollars. If the United States chose to hold its ground and ride out the financial storm, those nations not so friendly would (and did) demand gold rather than dollars in settlement of international debts. The United States elected to ride the storm.

By August 1971, it was apparent that the storm had won. Massive gold redemptions by the United States reduced its gold reserves to such an extent that the United States was forced to cancel the gold convertibility of the dollar and to enact a 10 percent surcharge on imports as well.

To restore international monetary order, the Group of Ten enacted the Smithsonian Agreement in Washington, D.C., in December 1971. The agreement called for a reduction in the gold parity of the dollar (by nearly 8 percent), while the parities of most of the other major currencies were left unchanged or were increased. In effect, the dollar was devalued versus all other major currencies, and all exchange rates were immediately revised. The exchange parity band was also widened from the former 1 percent to plus-or-minus 2.25 percent, or a total band of 4.5 percent. The United States also agreed to remove its trade restriction (the 10 percent import surcharge).

Continued trade imbalances led the United States to unilaterally devalue the dollar by an additional 10 percent in 1973 and to cancel the gold convertibility of the dollar. The Smithsonian Agreement was thereby nullified, and the dollar was permitted to float.

The Present in Perspective

The present system could best be described as the *absence* of a system. There is no official common denominator for currencies in the international realm. Money, in the international economic sense, has become a circular concept. Unofficial or surrogate denominators exist: gold, special drawing rights (paper gold), the U.S. dollar, and, since 1973, black gold (petroleum).

The old IMF system, based upon a gold-dollar standard, was certainly not a system of fixed exchange rates. During the 1953-1972 period, most of the IMF-listed currencies (96 of 109) devalued at least once, and 69 of these devalued more often.[4] However, these fluctuations were relatively bland, in frequency and in magnitude, when compared with the oscillations that occurred between 1972 and 1976 (figure 7-1).

There is little question that the old system was less volatile than the new "system." Hindsight also indicates that fewer devaluations or revaluations occurred, because governments were reluctant to act. As a consequence, the changes in exchange rates tended to be fewer in number but larger in magnitude. Also, devaluations tended to be larger and revaluations smaller than were proved to be necessary. Thus, one shortcoming of the old system represented the lack of

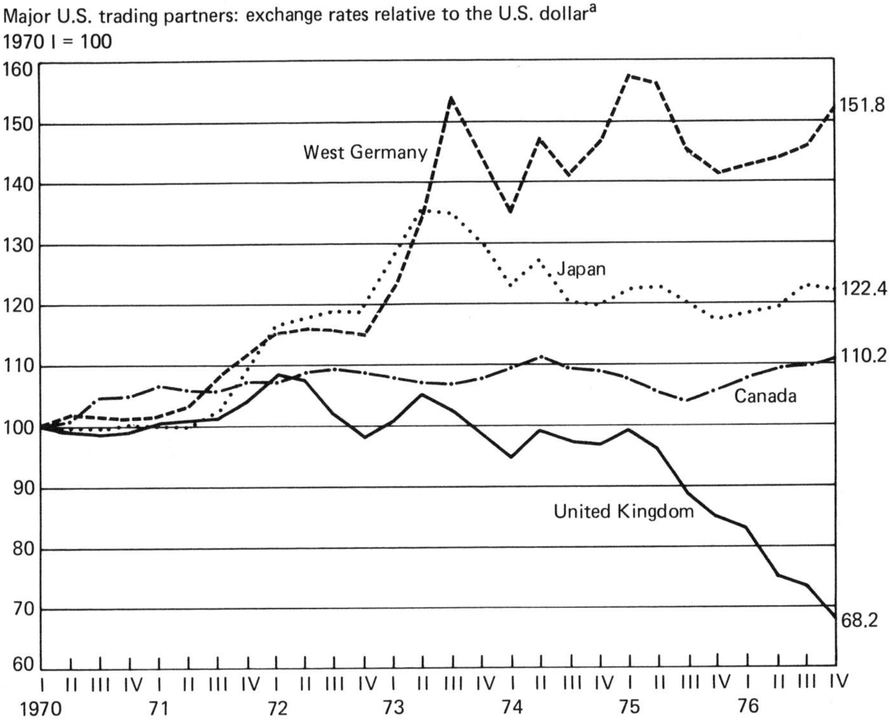

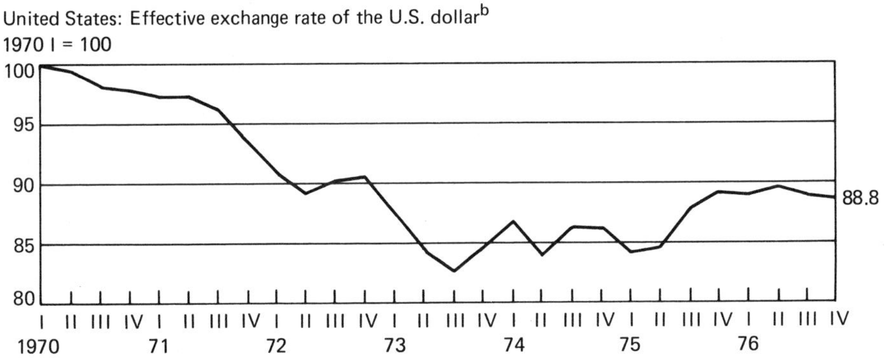

Major U.S. trading partners: exchange rates relative to the U.S. dollar[a]
1970 I = 100

United States: Effective exchange rate of the U.S. dollar[b]
1970 I = 100

Source: International Economic Report of the President, Transmitted to the Congress January 1977, p. 17.

[a]The indexes are based on the central rates except in periods of currency float where the values shown are market rates.

[b]Derived from weights based on bilateral trade with 16 major trading partners during 1974.

Figure 7-1. Comparative Exchange Rates

IMF authority to require that parity adjustments be made where and when necessary. A second defect concerned the use of the U.S. dollar as the key currency. For the U.S. dollar to supply the liquidity needed for other members of the IMF, continuous and significant payments deficits had to be maintained by the United States. These deficits created internal inflationary stresses on the dollar and, since other currencies were related to the dollar, inflation was exported to other countries indirectly. The invention of SDRs by the IMF to serve growing liquidity needs and to relieve pressure on the U.S. dollar represented an example of too little, too late. A third defect, related to the first mentioned, was the vesting of authority in politicians for decisions relating to international monetary matters.

The present situation, or system, is an international enigma composed of inflation, recession, stagflation, confused markets, and "yo-yo" exchange rates. However, fairness requires that unusual conditions be recognized.

The cancellation of the Smithsonian Agreement in 1973 and the concurrent devaluation and floating of the U.S. dollar resulted in financial turmoil—not a favorable environment in which to introduce any new system. Also, the OPEC price orgy that began in 1973 has been of such colossal proportion that the problems of reconstruction following World War II seem minuscule by comparison.[5]

Intrinsically, the present system lacks a common denominator. There are n decision makers for $n - 1$ exchange rates; therefore, the system is inconsistent. In effect, the present situation represents an attempt to employ gliding parities, with none of the parities predetermined.

A second internal defect of today's world monetary environment is an intensification of a weakness of the old system—the IMF has even less authority than before. The IMF not only has been relegated to the role of an international lending agency, but it is a rather impotent one as well. It has only two-thirds of the capital needed, and its function to control lending gives it real authority only in dealing with the financially weak or developing nations; and these are not usually the members who cause or promote stress within global financial markets. So long as surpluses of the OPEC nations remain the source of the additional capital for many borrowing nations, the IMF will remain impotent.

It has been suggested that a return to "the rule of law in international monetary affairs" can be realized by: (1) devising a new denominator, such as the SDR; (2) furnishing the IMF with sufficient authority and resources to monitor the economic actions of members; (3) removing present sources of major loan funds that are external to the IMF; and (4) establishing an effective information system by which the IMF could evaluate and regulate international lending.[6]

Some aspects of the present situation remain moot, particularly whether or not trade wars have indeed resulted from the absence of international monetary order. Economic warfare has clearly been declared by OPEC, but these strategies were founded upon natural advantages in natural economic goods. Trade wars, however, are attempts by one or more governments to create artificial advantages in international trade by various indirect means. Two common national strategies employed are dumping (the sale of a commodity at a lower equivalent price than that for which the same commodity is offered and sold in domestic markets) and deliberate currency undervaluation.

Undervaluation of a currency can be achieved by excessively devaluing or inadequately revaluing a currency. Under the old system, these results could be accomplished directly by governments, since exchange rates were determined by reserves. Under the new system, movements of exchange rates in the financial marketplace require indirect government actions.

These government interventions in international money markets have been called "dirty floats."[7] There also appears to be a consensus that government interventions in money markets have been much more frequent and massive in this period of so-called floating rates than during any phase of the old system.[8]

One thing is certain. Determination of exchange rates has switched from the public to the private sector. Along with the diminution of the IMF, the financial reins have been transferred from the central public banks to the private banks. The private banking system has been flooded with OPEC dollars and has assumed the role of a significant lender to national governments.

The key, then, is this shift of financial clout from the public to the private banking system. As in the past, parity rates may continue to be determined *in the long run*, within the *goods markets of the economic sector.* In the foreseeable future, however, unless the IMF regains the stature, resources, and influence it requires, exchange rates will be determined in the *short to medium time periods*, within the *private financial markets.*

An understanding of the current vagaries of exchange rates requires some familiarity with the vagaries of the currency markets.

Currency Markets

As mentioned earlier, the function of an exchange rate is to enable the actual exchange of one currency for another (conversion). In this respect, exchange rates are *direct* with respect to money conversions. However, direct conversions of currencies are a relatively minor part of the volume of foreign-exchange transactions, since actual conversions (money-changings) are usually limited to the tourist trade, to border dealings, and to the black market sector (where one exists).

Most other foreign-exchange transactions are *indirect*, since only claims to foreign currencies are exchanged and there is a lapse of time, however slight or great, between the exchange of these claims.

Participants in foreign currency markets are the following:

1. Sellers—those who hold claims to foreign currencies.
2. Buyers—those who owe foreign currencies.
3. Money-changers—the commercial banks that convert the claims to foreign currencies.
4. The IMF—functioning as overseer under the old system, today having no direct participation in the private market.

Market Sectors

Currencies today are commodities that are subject, at least to a degree, to supply and demand. Without predetermined starting points for parities, rates theoretically gravitate toward those points where supply equals demand, given a free market. However, there are no such things as free-floating rates or free markets.

Like most other commodity markets, foreign-exchange markets are composed of functional sectors offering specialized services:

1. Retail sector—dealings with the general public, typically through the foreign departments of local banks.
2. Wholesale sector—tradings among banking institutions and, where permitted, between large firms and brokers.[9]
3. Foreign sector—dealings between domestic and foreign banks.
4. Supranational sector—dealings among large MNCs and large private banks (singly, or as intermediaries for central national banks in some cases), usually in multiple currencies or in pseudocurrencies (Eurocurrency markets).

There are few, if any, real controls over or within the supranational sector. All other sectors are constrained by competition as well as by regulation by central banks.

Foreign Exchange Instruments

With one exception, the basic instruments of foreign exchange are the normal tools of international business:

1. *Foreign currencies*—usually limited to use by tourists and traders located at borders of countries.
2. *Bank transfers*—by cable, telegraph, or mail between a domestic and a foreign bank. Since mailing time adds a degree of risk (possible fluctuation of exchange rates), cable or telegraph transfers are the primary means used.
3. *Bills of exchange*—drafts, checks, and other negotiable instruments. Checks are less formal types of negotiable instruments and depend upon the credit

of the payer rather than a particular bank; consequently, only large firms tend to be able to transact international business using their standard checks.

4. *Letters of credit*—more readily accepted than checks, since bank credit is substituted for the credit of the importer or exporter.

5. *Foreward-exchange contracts*—unique to foreign currency transactions. They are secondary agreements drawn to minimize (hedge against) potential losses due to fluctuations of exchange rates over the time of the original contract of sale or payment. Forward-exchange contracts are usually executed between a firm and its bank, calling for delivery, at a specified future date, of a given sum of foreign currency in exchange for a specific amount of domestic currency based upon an exchange rate fixed in the contract itself.

Types of Exchange Rates

Exchange rates vary depending upon the market sector (retail, wholesale, foreign, or supranational) and the type of foreign-exchange instrument involved.

All rates are quoted in pairs, a selling rate and a buying rate, the former representing the price the bank will charge for a currency and the latter the price the bank will pay for the currency. The duality of the rates creates a zero-sum game: what one bank profits, another bank (or its client) loses.

Normally, three types of exchange rates exist: the spot rate, the forward rate, and a differential rate.

Spot rates are those quoted for immediate delivery: the same day, one day later (Canada and Mexico), or two days later (elsewhere). The basic spot rate applies to bank transfers by cable or telegraph. Rates for other bank transfers, bills of exchange, and letters of credit will begin with the spot rate and will be adjusted for the elements of time, risk, and credit stature involved. In the retail sector, additional commissions or fees are usually charged the bank's customers. In the wholesale and foreign sectors, commissions as such are rarely charged; the difference between the buying and selling rates provides the margin or profit for the servicing bank. No generalizations can be made concerning the supranational sector other than that the rates are determined by negotiation and are dependent upon the size and power of the parties, the size of the sums involved, and the currencies in question.

Forward rates are those quoted for deliveries beyond the time limits of spot rates. Forward rates are determined by a wide range of variables: comparative interest rates, the time period involved, the customer, the transaction, and the gamut of expectations concerning future market conditions for the currencies.

Differential rates are those other than the two common rates just mentioned and are limited to special markets. These markets are normally found in economies in which foreign exchange is controlled by the government. In such instances, the official government rates are often of two types: preferential rates for approved transactions; penalty rates for nonessential or unfavorable transactions. Where controlled rates differ widely from the free-market rate for a currency, black-market rates usually appear as an equalizing mechanism. Consequently, the mere existence of a black-market rate is evidence of an overvalued currency.

Determinants of Exchange Rates

Under the old monetary system, parity bands functioned much the same as price controls, except that a floor as well as a ceiling was established, at least for a period of time. Inception of the so-called floating-rate markets removed these controls. The resulting fluctuations in exchange rates directed attention to much cause-and-effect analysis. Some of the larger New York and London banks developed "scientific" computerized models to forecast currency movements and sold them to interested clients.[10]

What follows is neither a scientific (if such is at all possible) nor an all-inclusive examination of the determinants of exchange rates. Rather, a cursory look at the generally recognized variables should illustrate that exchange fluctuations, at least in the short to medium term, are the result of a veritable maze of factors that are difficult to isolate, much less to project.

1. *Supply and demand* affect floating rates of currencies much the same as for any other commodity. However, unlike most other free-market goods, the supply of and demand for currencies can change significantly in a day or two. Massive government interventions, placings of OPEC reserves, and hedgings of significant amounts can easily warp money markets. In fact, it has been postulated that hedgings of large amounts of a given currency can bring about the anticipated or feared fluctuation. Consequently, most large banks usually attempt to buy or sell large amounts of currencies in stages.

2. *Comparative interest rates* have long been used as barometers of future exchange movements and as factors in establishing rates of forward-exchange contracts. The implicit assumption is that money will flow to the location of best return.

3. *Trade deficits and surpluses* are often considered to be leading indicators of currency changes, since they will, over time, affect the supply of and demand for currencies.

4. *Inflation rates* are often erroneously and directly related to currency devaluations, much as if the two were locked in a circle from which there was no escape. The fallacy, of course, lies in the failure to recognize that not all domestic goods and services are traded in international markets. The domestic market is not directly affected by a currency devaluation if, indeed, it is at all

affected. This also lends support to the theory that currencies of developing nations tend to be undervalued, since the chief asset of most young nations—a plentiful and inexpensive labor supply—rarely is reflected in international trade.

5. *Relative economic exposure* of a given country affects its ability to manage inflation and its impact upon the exchange rate. The United Kingdom, for example, depends upon basic imports much more than the United States, and, as a result, Britain is harder pressed to ward off the importation of inflation. Significant users of foreign oil are also hard pressed.

6. *Political response to inflation* is also usually an area that is considered. Some countries, such as Germany and Switzerland, historically have earned good marks for their efforts to control rising prices. Italy, the United Kingdom, and the United States, however, have seemed reluctant to adopt the corrective measures that are considered necessary.

7. *Political stability* is a consideration normally limited to developing economies, but, where it is appropriate, it also tends to be a critical factor. Often, a change in regime also results in a change from a free-market to a controlled-exchange economy, with its unpredictable results.

8. *Future expectations*, although cited last, are certainly not the least of the determinants. Future expectations could be described as the range of opinions of subsequent events usually, but not necessarily, colored by past events.

In retrospect, the factors listed here represent an amalgam of variables: financial and economic, objective and subjective, extrinsic and intrinsic, as well as past, present, and future. Although listed separately, most are interrelated, so that the *ceteris paribus* technique of model-builders may be used only at great risk. None of the variables are static, but some are more volatile than others.

Those who choose or are forced to engage in the foreign-exchange market participate in a zero-sum game in which there is a loser for every winner. Players must rely on choosing the right moves more than half the time.

Summary

Flexible exchange rates are sometimes wrongly charged with breeding global inflation. OPEC has been the real villain since 1973. There also is a growing belief that the former system of pegged exchange rates could not have survived the OPEC price orgy.

The old system of pegged rates, while certainly not fixed in nature, did provide some measure of comfort in short-run stability. The present era of flexible exchange rates could be described as a period of short-run volatility, due, in part, to the absence of a common denominator. Money became a circular concept. Lacking a standard of reference, money is now a commodity that changes in price in response to all the vagaries inherent in the financial markets, at least in the short run.

Ideally, or theoretically at least, money should serve as a medium by which goods and services could be exchanged or their values stored for future use. In effect, money should represent a right of access to goods and services in a given economic environment or, simply stated, its *purchasing power*. The express reason for comparing two currencies should be the determination of their relative *real* values in the form of the goods and services each could claim within its domestic environment, that is, their *relative purchasing powers*. To the extent that exchange rates fail to represent surrogate measures of the relative purchasing powers of currencies, exchange rates must be recognized as deficient benchmarks, regardless of the nature of the monetary system or financial market in which the rates are determined. Shortcomings within the monetary systems or markets could only add to the initial deficiencies.

Within large, complex economies, the purchasing power of the currency varies between and among the various sectors of the country. Often, purchasing power will vary among sections of a single metropolitan area. Consequently, given the larger and more complex international economy, it is illogical to believe or expect that exchange rates mirror the relative purchasing powers of currencies at any given time.

At very best, exchange rates might be expected to reflect the general impact of inflation among countries if, and only if, the financial and goods markets, domestic and international, were free of all artificial constraints or interventions. The ratios would still be general, as stressed earlier because they would represent the comparisons of broad, dissimilar market baskets of goods and services; each would encompass the goods and services offered in international trade by a given country. Differences in exchange rates would remain blunt tools for decisions involving specific sectors or firms within national economies. Also, as mentioned earlier, the exchange rates of most of the developing countries would still tend to be understated, since their most valuable assets—plentiful, low-cost labor supplies—would not necessarily enter the realm of international trade.

Rational economic evaluations and decisions require the availability and use of *purchasing-power parity indices*, which reflect the relative commands of currencies over goods and services within their respective domestic economies at specific times. Such indices are not widely available today.

Purchasing power comparisons exist between some major industrial countries having similar market baskets of available goods and services. It would be impracticable to attempt to construct similar comparisons between a highly industrialized country (with a diverse market basket) and a developing nation (with a relatively limited market basket, often heavily impacted by only one or two commodities or services).

It may prove to be worthwhile to construct series of purchasing-power parities for similar types of economies—industrialized, newly emerging, and categories in between. Alternatively, it may prove feasible to construct indices from the bottom up; that is, to relate the domestic prices of the limited market baskets of goods and services available in developing nations to the prices of corresponding items within industrialized countries. While similar market baskets would not exist in all cases, the parities that could be developed would tend to correct the present undervaluations of currencies of many developing countries.

Purchasing-power parity indices seem to be the best tools for assessing the relative economic or real values of currencies. Until such indices become generally available, exchange rates remain the only surrogate measures. However, exchange rates and their fluctuations, when they must be used as bases for economic decisions, should be recognized for what they are and what they really measure.

Exchange rates are designed to facilitate the *actual conversions of currencies*, nothing more. Fluctuations of exchange rates represent the interpretations of all the vagaries and expectations within an imperfect international *financial* market, generally considered to be at least as fickle as the stock market. Even given a perfectly free financial market place, the financial aspect is but one dimension affecting the medium- to long-term economic or real value of any currency.

Attaching more relevance than this to exchange rates and using them as surrogate measures to evaluate past performances or future economic decisions can only be done at great risk.

Notes

1. Richard Brown (ed.), *A History of Accounting and Accountants* (Edinburgh: T.C. & E.C. Jack, 1905), pp. 111-112.

2. Franklin R. Root, *International Trade and Investment* (Cincinnati: South-Western Publishing Co., 1973), p. 163.

3. George N. Halm, *The International Monetary Fund and Flexibility of Exchange Rates*, Essays in International Finance, No. 83. (Princeton, N.J.: Princeton University Press, March 1971), 26 pp.

4. "Report of the Committee on International Accounting," *The Accounting Review, Supplement to Volume 48*, 1973, p. 130.

5. In the *International Economic Report of the President*, submitted to Congress in January 1977, the president's letter of transmittal contained the following caution: "In an interdependent world, a nation [or group of nations?] which disrupts the economies of its trading partners does so at its own eventual peril."

6. Arthur F. Burns, "The Need for Order in International Finance," *The Columbia Journal of World Business*, Spring 1977, pp. 5-12.

7. "Why the Float Gets Dirtier," *Business Week*, November 22, 1976, p. 140.

8. "Floating Exchange Rates: The Calm Before An Economic Storm," *Business Week*, October 3, 1977, p. 77.

9. In New York, "corporations are effectively barred from going to brokers to buy or sell money." Brokers cannot carry inventories of currencies and, if they attempt to charge lower rates than the banks have set, the brokers are frozen out of the exchange market. Similar practices are alleged in London and Brussels. See "The Closed Currency 'Club'," *Business Week*, October 24, 1977, p. 114.

10. Richard F. Janssen, " 'Scientific' Forecasts of Currency Trends Stir Interest as Floating Rates Boost Risks," *The Wall Street Journal*, February 9, 1976.

8

Foreign-Currency Translation

Translation of foreign monies has been a problem confronting accountants long before the days of Paciolo:

> The first important duty of the book-keeper was to convert [translate] each item in the Memorial to the monetary unit in which his accounts are kept. Having made this calculation, he transcribed the entry into the Journal. . . .[1]

In one respect it could be said that the translation of foreign currencies has returned just recently to the level of importance it had acquired in Paciolo's time. For example, Brown has postulated that, of the three books described by Paciolo—the Memorial, the Journal, and the Ledger—the Memorial was probably required because of the "confused state" of the several monies used at the time. Some form of book was needed in which every transaction could be entered, as it occurred, and translated into the local money of account prior to recording the transaction in the more official Journal.[2]

In another, more pessimistic, respect it could be argued that, given the magnitude of foreign transactions by modern-day corporations, the translation of foreign currencies has been downgraded in importance. Today, at least from the standpoint of the Financial Accounting Standards Board, the local accounts of foreign subsidiaries of U.S. multinational corporations have been relegated to the function served by the Memorial described by Paciolo—a sort of holding receptacle, nothing more.

In any respect, as more firms enter or become increasingly dependent upon transnational operations, how the results of the transactions and financial statements are translated will also assume greater importance, both internally (as a basis for managerial evaluations and decisions) and externally (as a factor used by investors, creditors, governments, and other third parties).

This chapter will consider the reasons for translating foreign currencies as well as some of the attendant problems. The various methods of translation that have been suggested and used will be reviewed, particularly the requirements of FASB *Statement No. 8 (FASB-8)*.[3] The problems remaining will then be revisited and some newly created enigmas will be examined, particularly those associated with efforts to minimize the risk of foreign-exchange exposure.

It must be emphasized that the term *exchange gains and losses* is meaningless today and should be avoided. Instead, the recorded effects of changes in exchange rates should be properly identified as:

1. Conversion gains/losses—differences *realized* upon actual settlement of transactions.
2. Translation gains/losses—those interim, *unrealized* or "accounting" differences that are reflected between the time a transaction is recorded and the settlement date. This category would include differences in exchange rates upon translation of financial statements.

Needs for Translation

Needs seem to be of higher order of importance than objectives. Within the category of needs, there is a sort of ordinal structure ranging from the desirable (nice to have) to the essential or imperative (necessity).

Objectives, on the other hand, are intentions or purposes. In a sense, objectives can be considered as intermediate steps selected to satisfy perceived needs.

Objectives of and methods for translations of foreign currencies should be judged upon their abilities to fulfill the perceived needs for the translations. Other natural considerations require that the translated information be representative (make economic sense) and practicable (worth its cost).

There are six general needs for the translation of foreign currencies. Each need presents problems that are inherent or that are encountered in producing representative results.

1. *To record transactions that are measured or denominated in a foreign currency.* A transaction is *measured* in a foreign currency if the transaction is expressed in the monetary unit of a country other than the local domicile. A transaction is *denominated* in a foreign currency if the amount to be paid or received calls for a specific sum in that foreign currency, irrespective of the exchange rates on the date of settlement.

Suppose a U.S. exporter sells to (or a U.S. importer buys from) a German firm and the invoice specifies payment on a future date of a fixed amount of German marks. For the U.S. firm, the transaction is measured *and* denominated in marks and must be translated into dollars, using some exchange rate, before it can be recorded. At the settlement date, the U.S. exporter will receive (or the U.S. importer must obtain and remit) the amount in marks specified by the invoice. If the exchange rate of dollars and marks changes during the interim, more or less than the amount originally anticipated in equivalent dollars will be received by the U.S. exporter (or paid by the U.S. importer). Some problems that arise are:

Which of the several types of exchange rates existing at the time of sale (or purchase) should be used for the translation?

If the exchange rate differs at the time of settlement, how is the difference to be treated?

If the example given is considered as *one transaction* and as incomplete until settlement is made, the selling (or purchase) price would be adjusted for the difference (the conversion gain or loss).

If the sale (or purchase) and subsequent settlement are considered to be *two transactions*, the difference would represent the result of a separate interim event—a change in the exchange rate—and a separate financial (conversion) gain or loss would be called for. The risk of a change in the exchange rate during the interim between sale (or purchase) and settlement is generally regarded as peculiar to international trade, and the result should be recognized. Also, the risk inherent in particular transactions can usually be reduced by means to be discussed later. The conversion gain or loss would represent the result of accepting the risk of a change in money prices.

Suppose a different circumstance, in which an American firm has a wholly owned subsidiary in Germany. The subsidiary acquires a long-lived asset in Germany by means of long-term debt denominated in marks. Different problems arise here because of the different domiciles of the subsidiary and the parent. The subsidiary has no translation problem, since the event would represent one transaction measured and denominated in its local currency. The parent firm is faced with problems upon translation of the subsidiary's financial statements.

From the parent's viewpoint, does the example represent one transaction or two transactions?

If it is one transaction, the exchange rate applied to the asset upon acquisition would also be used to translate the debt over a period of time, regardless of changes in rates that might occur before the debt is paid. No imbalances (gains or losses) would be reflected while the debt was held or upon payment in marks by the subsidiary. Both the asset and the debt would be *measured and denominated in the local currency* (marks) of the domicile in which the transaction occurred. Translation would simply express the amounts in their dollar equivalents existing at the time of the transaction.

If it is two transactions, the asset acquisition would be translated at a point in time, as in the case of a single transaction, but the debt would be translated over a period of time with various exchange rates. The resulting imbalances would represent translation gains and losses while the debt was held and conversion gains or losses upon settlement of the debt. This approach *measures and denominates both transactions in dollars*, the monetary unit of the parent. Both transactions would, in effect, be considered as having been conducted in the United States, by the parent, and in U.S. dollars.

2. *To prepare consolidated statements which report on the economic entity as a whole.* Only the conceptual problems related to translations of foreign-currency financial statements into dollars prior to the preparation of consolidated financial statements will be addressed here. As many problems, possibly of greater significance, arise out of the use of such statements, these will be examined in discussions of the four remaining needs for translations, which follow this discussion (and in chapters 12 and 13).

Problems common to each statement in the consolidated financial package are:

Which of the multiple exchange rates should be used?

How should the resulting imbalances, if any, be treated?

Since foreign currency statements are to be translated or *denominated* in U.S. dollars, should the underlying tranactions also be *measured* in dollars, that is, as if they had been transacted in the United States?

Should the same procedures be required of all U.S. parent firms regardless of the different particular situations possible (such as operations in countries with unstable currencies)?[4]

What is being reflected by the translation process—relative inflation rates, relative purchasing powers of currencies, vagaries of exchange markets, or some mixture of all three?

Should the relative price levels within the foreign domiciles be considered? Should price levels and foreign currency translations be considered as separate issues or as parts of one indivisible problem?

3. *To evaluate the operations of a foreign business segment.* American executives, accustomed to thinking in dollars, seem to prefer to use translated financial statements to evaluate overseas operations. Also, to further complicate matters, the evaluation process often involves comparisons with other foreign or domestic operations, many of which may have been organized to increase the equities of all stakeholders and in currencies other than dollars; to provide sources of raw materials, intermediate or finished products, or efficient access to markets for the entire multinational entity.

Similarly, external users of statements containing translated operating results attempt similar evaluations but without access to the supporting information available to management.

Problems related to the above practices are inherent as well as created:

Do financial statements lose their relevance when examined outside the context of their particular domiciles?

Do translation gains and losses reflect real changes in the economic values of foreign assets?

Can or should translation procedures attempt to make foreign operations identical to those conducted in the United States?

Can any translation procedure yield relevant data with which to evaluate multiple operating purposes?

What information should be furnished external users of financial statements containing translated results of foreign operating segments in order to enable the users to evaluate past operations and their future potentials meaningfully?

4. *To evaluate the performance of foreign management.* The use of translated financial statements to evaluate the managers of foreign operations must also be approached with caution. The range of options concerning performance evaluation (examined in chapter 10) represents an internal process. All the necessary data are assumed to be reasonably available to the parent firm; the needs of external users are not relevant.

Does the foreign manager have the opportunity and the authority to protect his segment's investment in U.S. dollars from erosion by changes in exchange rates?

Do changes in exchange rates equate with changes in local asset values and with the local impacts of inflation?

Which changes are real and must be managed? Which are illusory or beyond management control?

5. *To direct and control foreign operations.* The evolution of the multinational corporation has effectively transferred this function to the headquarters of the parent firm. If an MNC is to coordinate its global operations so as to buy, produce, market, and finance to the best advantage, decisions affecting the entire MNC must be vested at the headquarters. Changes anticipated in the market prices of currencies, exchange exposures of the various foreign segments, and decisions concerning how best to minimize the exposures, if at all, are aspects of total financial management. Information needed to assess and make these future-oriented decisions is usually available only at the headquarters location.

Translated financial statements provide retrospective information—the results of past events. Direction and similar management functions are future-oriented; financial statements can serve only as the starting point.

The crucial problem concerns recognition of the fact that gains and losses resulting from translation are merely paper gains and losses until conversion takes place; they are not real or economic gains and losses. Can a lack of understanding of the true nature of translation gains and losses on the part of management (or investors) lead to actions that result in the incurrence of real or economic losses?

6. *For the convenience of users.* Like managers, investors and other users of financial statements are accustomed to thinking in the framework of a familiar currency. Where convenience represents the primary need for the translation of

financial statements of independent entities, application of a single exchange rate (existing at the date of the statements) to all amounts in the foreign-currency statements would simply change the unit of expression, not any of the relationships depicted.

Concern has been expressed that, unless the foreign statements are also adjusted for any differences that may exist in the accounting principles employed by the two domiciles, users possibly may be misled.

> Can convenience translations of foreign-currency statements of independent entities mislead users if the translated statements indicate the domicile whose accounting standards were used to prepare the basic statements?

> What criteria should be used to assess independence of the entity?

Methods of Translation

This section will address the development of translation methods generally accepted. In appendix 8A, an annotated chronology of selected alternative methods has been furnished. Most of the alternate proposals relate currency translation to the companion problems of changing price levels and/or situational differences.

Prior to the effective date of *FASB-8* (accounting periods beginning on January 1, 1976, or later), four translation methods were well-known and employed, either in pure form or with variations:

1. current-noncurrent method;
2. monetary-nonmonetary method;
3. current-rate method;
4. temporal method.

Each of the four methods was a normative approach in that a standard or rule was established to be followed in all cases, regardless of circumstances. The several hybrid methods proposed (appendix 8A) attempted to allow for situational factors that could produce confusing (or misleading) results where normative methods were followed strictly.

Each of the normative methods will be reviewed briefly before examining *FASB-8*.

The Current-Noncurrent Method

The current-noncurrent method is the oldest translation approach officially approved for use in the United States. Originating in the 1930s, this method of translating foreign-currency statements (also called the AICPA method) emphasized conservatism and the subordinate nature of foreign operations following the depression years.

Current assets and current liabilities (working capital) were translated at the current (closing) rate. Noncurrent balance-sheet items (plant, equipment, and other assets; long-term liabilities; and equity accounts) were translated at the rates existing on the transaction dates (historic rates). Income-statement items (revenues and expenses) were translated at average rates for the period, except for depreciation, which bore the historic rates of the particular assets.

In effect, translation gains or losses were based upon the net current or working-capital position of the foreign operation. Changes in noncurrent items were not recognized, since it was assumed that the usefulness of plant and equipment was not affected as foreign currencies weakened versus the dollar—a situation common to those times. Conservatism directed that any potential gains on lower dollar-translated long-term liabilities be deferred until realized at the time of payment.

Conservatism was also reflected in several other ways. Net translation losses were to be reflected in the income for the period, whereas net gains were to be deferred and used to offset future translation losses. Also, since most foreign currencies weakened versus the dollar, translated inventories (at current rates) reflected lower, more conservative dollar costs. A third example of conservatism was apparent in the recommended treatment of foreign earnings upon consolidation: such earnings were to be taken up only when received or when they were available for repatriation without any restrictions.[5]

The current-noncurrent method mirrored the suspect nature of foreign operations and foreign currencies that prevailed until 1960.

The Monetary-Nonmonetary Method

Over time, foreign activities evolved from primarily branch operations to full-fledged subsidiaries with on-site manufacturing facilities often financed by local borrowings. Continued use of the current-noncurrent method was reexamined and challenged.

By the mid-1950s, inventories represented, on the average, upwards of one-fourth of the total assets of foreign operations. By translating inventories at current rates, the current-noncurrent method often violated the basis of historical cost in U.S. dollars. Also, where foreign currencies appreciated relative to the dollar, use of the current rate often violated the rule of lower-of-cost-or-market in dollars. It was also argued that the translation of long-term debt using historical rates only postponed the recognition of gains/losses.

Professor Samuel R. Hepworth (University of Michigan) suggested the monetary-nonmonetary method of balance-sheet translation.[6] Monetary items (those which were fixed in terms of local currency) should be translated using current (year-end) rates. Nonmonetary items were all others and should be translated using historic rates. Average rates should continue to be used for revenues and expenses, except for depreciation, which should reflect the rates existing when the assets were acquired.

Monetary items were considered to be susceptible to and immediately affected by changes in money prices. The gains or losses upon translations of net monetary items were to be reflected in the net income for the period. Nonmonetary items were not necessarily affected, based upon the premise that any changes in values could be recovered through future adjustments in selling prices, given the absence of local price controls.

Hepworth's recommendation was also advocated in a subsequent research report published by the National Association of Accountants.[7] The NAA report modified the original monetary-nonmonetary concept by suggesting that only realized gains, together with all losses, be reflected in current income. Unrealized net gains were to be deferred. This modification introduced the difficult problem of determining when translation gains or losses were realized.

Subsequent studies of actual translation practices indicated that firms were roughly divided between the official current-noncurrent method and the not-yet-approved monetary-nonmonetary method. Consequently, the Accounting Principles Board effectively authorized use of the monetary-nonmonetary method as an alternate practice by accepting the current rate for translation of long-term receivables and payables.[8]

The Current-Rate Method

Although it is not accepted in the United States (except for convenience translations), the current-rate method has long been preferred by Canadian, U.K., and European accountants. In fact, the current-rate method is often called the European method.

In its pure form, the current rate was used to translate all items except remittances actually received from foreign operations; the latter were converted (not translated) at the rates used to exchange the foreign currency. No translation gains or losses were produced; imbalances, if any, upon conversions of remittances were recorded as actual conversion gains or losses.

Modifications were necessary where foreign investments were permitted to be accounted for by the equity method. In these cases, the current rate was applied to all items except equity accounts, for which the historic rates were used. Any imbalances (translation gains and losses) were usually applied to reserves created for such purposes.

Europeans and others favored the current-rate method because it treated foreign operations as if they existed separate and apart from the parent. It was also argued that the historical cost of an item acquired with foreign currency could only be expressed in that foreign currency. Apart from theory, the current-rate method was most probably used because it was simple and inexpensive to apply. (Advocates of current-value accounting in the United States argue that, if current values were reflected in foreign statements, the current-rate method of translation could be applied appropriately and easily.)

The Temporal Method

Simply stated, the temporal method attempts to retain the aspect of time related with transactions, hence the name. The current rate is applied to items carried at present or future prices—cash, receivables, payables, and so forth. Applicable historic rates are used with all items carried at past prices, such as plant, equipment, FIFO inventories, and the like.

At first glance, the temporal method appears to be similar to the monetary-nonmonetary method, and it is, but only because U.S. accounting standards require the use of historical costs. The temporal method of translation can be applied to the statements produced by any system of accounts so long as the items carried at past, present, or future prices could be determined.

The temporal method of translation was proposed in 1972 by Leonard Lorensen[9] and was based upon the initial work of the late Samuel Hepworth.

Statement of Financial Accounting Standards No. 8 (FASB-8)

The FASB was concerned over a multitude of problems that existed when the Board undertook its study of foreign-currency translation. Multiple methods of translation were in use. Gains and losses were treated in various ways. The adequacy of disclosures was suspect, at best. A consensus did not even exist regarding the appropriate exchange rate to be used where multiple rates existed at a point in time.

Standardization of translation practices and reporting requirements represented the top priority for the FASB. The results desired were attained by selecting a normative approach—the temporal method—as the basis for translating foreign currency transactions and statements; requiring that translation gains and losses be reflected in the net income of the accounting period in which the rate changes occurred; and specifying the dividend remittance rate (for translating statements) and the spot rate (for recording transactions). The *FASB-8* rate schedule for translating statements is shown in table 8-1.

In order to have a framework with which to evaluate the various translation methods, proposals, and comments received, the FASB selected the following objective:

Table 8-1

FASB-8 **Rates Used to Translate Assets and Liabilities**

	Translation Rates	
	Current	Historical
Assets		
Cash on hand and demand and time deposits	X	
Marketable equity securities:		
Carried at cost		X
Carried at current market price	X	
Accounts and notes receivable and related		
unearned discount	X	
Allowance for doubtful accounts and notes		
receivable	X	
Inventories:		
Carried at cost		X
Carried at current replacement price or		
current selling price	X	
Carried at net realizable value	X	
Carried at contract price (produced under		
fixed price contracts)	X	
Prepaid insurance, advertising, and rent		X
Refundable deposits	X	
Advances to unconsolidated subsidiaries	X	
Property, plant, and equipment		X
Accumulated depreciation of property, plant,		
and equipment		X
Cash surrender value of life insurance	X	
Patents, trademarks, licenses, and formulas		X
Goodwill		X
Other intangible assets		X
Liabilities		
Accounts and notes payable and overdrafts	X	
Accrued expenses payable	X	
Accrued losses on firm purchase commitments	X	
Refundable deposits	X	
Deferred income		X
Bonds payable or other long-term debt	X	
Unamortized premium or discount on bonds or		
notes payable	X	
Convertible bonds payable	X	
Accrued pension obligations	X	
Obligations under warranties	X	

Source: FASB, *Statement of Financial Accounting Standards No. 8:* "Accounting for the Translation of Foreign Currency Transactions and Foreign Currency Financial Statements," October 1975, pp. 19-25. Copyright © by Financial Accounting Stàndards Board, High Ridge Park, Stamford, Connecticut 06905. Reprinted with permission. Copies of the complete document are available from the FASB.

Notes:

(1) Revenues/expenses–at average rates.

(2) Lower-of-cost-or-market rule applied in translated dollars.

(3) Equity investments and minority interests–translated before reporting method is applied.

(4) Situational factors determine rates applied to debt securities held, business combinations, preferred stock, and deferred income taxes.

... the objective of translation is to measure and express (a) in dollars and (b) in conformity with U.S. generally accepted accounting principles the assets, liabilities, revenue, or expenses that are measured or denominated in foreign currency.[10]

Whether one does or does not agree with the results produced by *FASB-8* since its effective date (January 1, 1976), the work is logically sound; perhaps it represents the best-structured analysis made by the FASB or any of its predecessors to date.

Criticism can only be directed toward the validity or the soundness of the objective upon which *FASB-8* is erected. Few would question the desirability of part (b), which calls for conformity with U.S. accounting standards; this has long been a requirement for the preparation of consolidated statements. The same comments apply to that portion of part (a) regarding expression in dollars. The real difficulty surrounds the mandate that foreign transactions be *measured* in dollars.

The different results of applying the four common translation methods to a specific situation are depicted in table 8-2. The important point is not the magnitude of the differences but that different results are produced.

Problems Revisited

There is little question that the FASB was confronted with difficult decisions concerning the translation of foreign currencies. Certainly, given the variety of alternatives, each with its group of proponents, not everyone could be pleased with *FASB-8*.

However, there is also little question that the FASB struck the narrowest gauge perspective possible to an issue of broadest scope. Holding to measurement in U.S. dollars and one-way flows of remittances in dollars has relegated accounting thought to pre-1930 branch accounting.

In an era in which half of the 100 largest economic entities in the free world are multinational corporations, and in which the annual sales of one of these multinationals, Exxon Corporation, is larger than the GNP of 106 nations, the standard-setting body of the American accounting profession has chosen to account for MNC operations using branch-accounting concepts. To require Exxon to account for operations involving more than one hundred currencies and as many countries as if they were transacted in U.S. dollars in the United States is equivalent to donning the green eye shade, pulling up the arm bands on one's sleeves, mounting the stool, and, with quill poised in hand, attempting to record Exxon's transactions one at a time in a bound journal.

On second thought, it is very possible that the process just caricatured would produce more useful results than *FASB-8*.

The Board literally ignored the needs of users of translated statements.

Table 8-2
Comparative Results of Common Translation Methods
(amounts in thousands)

	Balance Sheet 12/31/77 (in foreign currency—FC)	Balance Sheet in Translated U.S. Dollars			
		Current-Rate Method	Current/ Noncurrent Method	Monetary/ Nonmonetary Method	FASB-8 Temporal Method
Inventories—at cost (Market—FC 1,000)	FC 900	$720	$720	$ 900	$800[a]
Marketable securities	200	160	160	160	160
Other current assets	600	480	480	480	480
Noncurrent receivables	200	160	200	160	160
Plant and equipment	500	400	500	500	500
Current liabilities	(900)	(720)	(720)	(720)	(720)
Noncurrent liabilities	(500)	(400)	(500)	(400)	(400)
Equity	FC 1,000	$800	$840	$1,080	$980
Translation adjustment— gain (loss)		$(200)	$(160)	$ 80	$ (20)

Assumption: Exchange rate of FC = $1 prevailed until December 31, 1977 at which time the foreign currency was devalued to FC = $.80. Inventories are maintained at FIFO cost in foreign currency.

[a]On inventories, lower of translated market in dollars ($800 = FC 1,000 × $.80) would prevail over translated historical cost ($900 = FC 900 × $1). Without this exception, the monetary-nonmonetary and FASB-8 methods would have produced identical results.

Undoubtedly the FASB was concerned that considerations of need satisfaction would have decimated its efforts toward standardization. The two aims are not mutually exclusive.

Measurement in dollars, together with application of the temporal method (or any method other than the current rate) can lead to unreal differences between earnings measured in translated dollars and those reported by the foreign operations. This dilemma usually results because inventories and fixed assets of foreign subsidiaries are to be translated at historic rates, whereas any debt required to finance these assets will be translated at various current rates over time.

Which results are "real"? Will readers be misled, given complete financial packages? What of earnings reported out of the context of complete financial reports—for example, in *Fortune* "500" listings and in other journals? Are the results meaningful?

The FASB decided *not* "to produce an exchange gain or loss that is compatible with the expected economic effect of a rate change. . . ."[11] To do so, according to the FASB, would have required a change in the accounting standard, which specifies use of the dollar as the basis of measurement. That is a half-truth. Dollars are not involved, but rather *equivalent dollars.* Foreign assets acquired with foreign currency or debt have no direct dollar costs. Translation, by any method at any time, results in equivalent dollar costs of both assets and debt. Although the asset cannot be acquired again, nor can the debt be incurred again, the temporal method (and most others except the current rate) assigns a different value in equivalent dollars to the debt over time, producing unrealistic results. Adoption of the current-rate method at least would have retained the original relationship between the two items in equivalent dollars, which reflects objective economic sense.

It seems that use of the current-rate method could have been readily defended by the FASB. Since foreign-currency transactions have no dollar basis of measurement, the modified form of equivalent dollars could have been adopted and applied in a manner that reflected reasonable, objective economic sense. Erratic changes in reporting earnings (often called the yo-yo effect) would have been minimized while—as pleaded by FASB-member Robert E. Mays—preserving "the essence of the foreign currency statements."[12]

Under *FASB-8*, the yo-yo effect upon quarterly earnings reported by firms with significant foreign operations tends to misrepresent translation (or paper) gains and losses as economic (or real) gains and losses. Fears that external users may be misled have tempted, if not caused, managements to take irrational actions; that is, to risk or incur economic losses in order to minimize mythical losses. This represents the greatest disservice to the business community by the accounting profession since the valuation fiascos of the 1920s and 1930s.

An even greater disservice to the international community may result; only time will tell. MNCs were depicted as representing the first organized global entities that were capable and willing to manipulate their worldwide resources in order to benefit from filling perceived economic needs. Economic opportunities (and risks) are often the greatest in developing economies. Multinationals generally, at least in the past, have been willing to assume the economic risks associated with operations in developing countries in return for the benefits projected in the long run. *FASB-8* may well reduce or change the pattern of such long-term investments if MNCs become unwilling to accept the specious effects of translation losses on their quarterly earnings. It is assumed that the MNCs recognize that such losses are, like the translation method that produces them, temporal rather than real.

Exchange Risk and Protection

No examination of foreign currency translation would be complete without a brief look at what has been called exchange risk or exposure and some of the protective measures employed.

In general, exchange risk is considered as ranging from the whole of a foreign undertaking to nothing at all, and at all sorts of levels in between.

Some believe that all parts of foreign operations are equally at risk but that actual losses remain unknown until assets are voluntarily disposed of or taken over by host governments. Risks, then, are associated with the locations and magnitudes of foreign operations, and protection can best be achieved by selecting those locations having the lowest perceived risks of failure or foreign takeover. To permit assessment of assumed risks, financial statements should disclose the locations and magnitudes of overseas investments. Since the long-run view applies, only actual conversion gains or losses realized on repatriations should be recorded in accounts; other temporary fluctuations in money prices are not relevant and should be limited to footnote or similar disclosure.

Another view relates exchange exposure with the net-current-asset position of a foreign operation. Assets available for use within the next accounting period and the liabilities incurred to finance them will be affected by changes in money prices. Since gains or losses on current assets and liabilities are offsetting, the best protection is achieved by minimizing working capital by various means.

A third view relates changes in money prices with monetary assets and liabilities. Nonmonetary items represent sunk decisions that either are not at risk (such as land) or are shielded by opportunities to cover value changes by adjustments of selling prices. Protection is achieved by maintaining a zero net-monetary exposure or, where that is impracticable, by minimizing the net position that must exist. Both the net-current and net-monetary concepts are medium- to long-term in nature. Both would include conversion gains and losses in current income while reflecting translation gains and losses in reserve accounts. Both would attach little importance to consolidated statements as a means of reporting risk.

A fourth technique could be called the transaction approach. Advocates believe that risks in major transactions should be protected by hedging—attempting to limit or offset potential conversion losses by gains on separate financial transactions of various kinds. This school of thought is of a short-term or temporal nature. Exchange risk is inherent in the original foreign transaction and in the speculative transaction (the hedging action); both are considered to be normal elements of business, and changes in money prices on both should be recognized in income as they occur. Hedging is considered to be a serious and necessary game in which there is a real opportunity to win. Financial statements of any type are retrospective and merely assess past results. Value is ascribed to systems that furnish information needed to assess the future money markets by managements, foreign and domestic, that are willing to invest the necessary time.

A fifth group, at the other end of the spectrum, argues that, in the long run, there is little, if any, exchange exposure. The normal holding periods of long-term assets tend to insulate them from effects of currency fluctuations. By the same token, if the level of working capital is relatively constant over time, it should also be considered long-term in nature, and translation gains and losses are inconsequential. Firms common to this group tend to be large MNCs with foreign operations in many countries and smaller, private companies that do not have to depend upon the whims of stock markets. The former consider translation gains and losses of little consequence, either because their diverse locations should equalize paper gains and losses (a form of internal hedging), or because they have tried to second-guess money markets in the past with unsatisfactory results. The smaller companies can afford to concentrate on economic realities rather than paper gains and losses.

Many MNCs manage the total costs associated with money flows by manipulating foreign-currency supplies and demands within intercorporate settlement pools, or so-called multilateral nettings, where this is permitted by national governments. In effect, interunit payables and receivables are offset, either within the headquarters or through a financial subsidiary serving as a sort of a clearing house. Actual remittances are few and are made only to net creditors upon direction by the headquarters. Such systems of netting reduce exchange exposures, but the primary purpose is to minimize the real costs of transferring and converting multiple currencies.

Since netting arrangements are limited to the larger MNCs, smaller firms have used other routine management actions to minimize exchange risk. Common examples are:

1. *Minimizing the dollar investment.* Borrow locally to the extent permitted by available funds and interest-rate differentials. Consider the pros and cons of obtaining some local equity. Where practicable, buy materials locally and decrease reliance upon imports.

2. *Repatriating profits as soon as possible.* Where controls exist, legitimate countermeasures (such as purchasing and exporting local goods needed elsewhere) are generally more productive, in the long run, than are the shadier uses of transfer prices.

3. *Increasing local prices to compensate for the added risks and tax effects.* Where price increases are impractical or insufficient, some sales may be negotiated for payment in strong currencies, often at fixed rates.

4. *Using currency swaps.* By agreement, working-capital dollars received by a subsidiary from the U.S. parent may be swapped or exchanged for a given amount of foreign currency, with the understanding that the bank will reverse the procedure at a date set by mutual agreement.

Hedgings come in as many forms as there are risks. A common form of hedge, the forward-exchange contract, may often be advisable as a last resort to cover the risk on selected single transactions of significant amounts, such as protection for liquid assets scheduled for repatriation in the near future. In such instances, the costs of hedging by forward contract can be considered the same as the costs of insuring against any other form of loss. As a regular course of action (speculative hedging), attempts to outguess future money prices constitute a risky, specialized business. Speculative hedging can be very costly, as many large banks and MNCs can attest.

Hedging represents a zero-sum game in which the costs of protection over time will equal potential losses. Substantial currency transactions must be made in increments and, even so, if many firms act to cover exposures in a given currency, the pressure may cause the feared lower price; only the bankers and speculators gain. Executive time and talent can be employed more profitably in attending to maximizing the values of foreign operations in their local environs rather than in attempting to cope with mythical accounting losses. If local margins are stable and favorable, but translated margins are volatile, management should concentrate upon what is real.

Managements are aware of these cautions. Nonetheless, many executives are uneasy about relying upon a sophisticated market to separate the mythical from the real, where volatility in reported earnings patterns and multiples are concerned.

Summary and Recommendations

The promulgation of *FASB-8* had some favorable effects on the translation of foreign currencies: it reduced the diversity of translation, reporting, and disclosure practices; and it increased the attention of senior management upon foreign-exchange risks.

Some of the effects of *FASB-8* considered to be unfavorable are not inherent in the *Statement* itself but represent problems common to most methods of translation:

1. Exchange rates are designed to convert monies and are inappropriate for translations of currencies other than those assets earmarked for and pending repatriation.

2. Translation methods, other than the current rate, are fundamentally based upon a cash-transfer assumption.
3. The short-term vagaries of financial markets are emphasized, while the long-run determinants of the goods markets are ignored.
4. Normative methods (the current-rate method to a lesser extent) fail to allow for situational differences.

The following represent defects considered to be inherent within *FASB-8* and the potentially undesirable effects that may result.

1. The objective is inadequate and improper.
2. Procedures are conversion-oriented and, while possibly appropriate for import/export or branch operations of two decades ago, they are ill suited for today's multinational networks.
3. Taken as a whole, *FASB-8* violates the going-concern concept as well as common sense. The translated and consolidated results are valid if, and only if, the foreign operations were liquidated without loss or gain, the proceeds were remitted to the parent (while incurring conversion gains/losses only on the original monetary items), and the parent duplicated the original operation intact in the United States.
4. Cash-basis accounting results are effectively emphasized over those of accrual accounting.
5. In its deliberations, the Board either ignored or, more likely, discounted the potential impacts upon domestic capital markets.[13]
6. Managements may be inclined to incur economic losses in order to minimize paper losses.
7. Long-term investments, capital movements, and international trade may be distorted and adversely affected.
8. Floating rates may be blamed for earnings distortions, rather than translation mechanics. Governments may be pressured to increase levels of interventions to acquire artificial stability.
9. Pressures to discard historical-cost for current-value-accounting methods will increase. While translation procedures would be simplified, greater disadvantages would be introduced (in the author's opinion) in the form of subjectivity (for accounting in general) and by double-counting of the effects of inflation and changes in money prices (for translation in particular).
10. Performance evaluations of overseas operations and foreign managements may be distorted and will become more difficult to assess fairly.
11. Data storage needed for the maintenance of historical cost inventories for certain industries may exceed capacities of storage banks.

In addressing foreign-currency translation, the profession has applied pre-1930 concepts of branch accounting in an era in which multinational operations have outgrown countries. A multisituational problem has been addressed by the strict application of a single-dimensional measure within an inadequate and improper framework.

The following actions seem appropriate:

1. Encourage the FASB to reassess the objective of *FASB-8* without further clamoring. A reasonable starting point would encompass the "essentials" suggested by Robert E. Mays: preservation of the "essence" and economic sense of foreign-currency statements.

2. Since no single translation method can serve all possible needs and situations, develop criteria for matching methods and situations. Auditors should then be charged with the responsibility for assessing the logic and fairness of the selected process and the reported results.

3. Reexamine the preparation of consolidated financial statements. Preferably, one statement should consolidate all units of the enterprise, using redesigned translation methods referred to earlier. In addition, a separate schedule of all foreign operations should be furnished and should include a summary of the balance sheet and income statement of each operation, translated at the current rate. A reconciliation of the parent's foreign investments with the schedule of foreign operations should also be furnished. Problems regarding interunit transactions and allocations of common costs would be significant but not insurmountable.

4. Study the feasibility of translation factors other than exchange rates. Purchasing-power-parity ratios may represent one approach if the industrial market baskets are not generalized out of proportion. Few problems should exist in constructing ratios by industry within the industrialized countries. For developing countries, contents of market baskets might be constructed by industry, based upon items, including labor, available in the host country, then related to prices in industrialized countries for comparable items.

In this process, it may be realized that there is too much ado over consolidated statements and the unrealized gains and losses that result from translations. Quite possibly, reason would prevail and the consolidation of foreign operations would be discontinued or consolidated statements would be relegated to secondary importance. Current rates could then be applied to foreign-currency statements contained in supporting schedules to recast them into familiar dollars. The perceived effects of changing money prices on foreign operations in the short and long terms should be explained by management.

In essence, the effects of currency fluctuations, much like those of changing price levels, are much too diverse to be accounted for using normative means without the risk of misleading both management and investors. Instead, the facts and their perceived effects should be explained by management and examined by independent auditors.

By deemphasizing the mechanics of accounting and encouraging meaningful reporting and interpretation, accountancy will have taken a great stride toward coming of age as a profession.

Notes

1. The writings of Paciolo, according to Richard Brown (ed.), *A History of Accounting and Accountants* (Edinburgh: T.C. & E.C. Jack, 1905), pp. 111-112.

2. Ibid., p. 111.

3. Financial Accounting Standards Board, *Statement of Financial Accounting Standards No. 8*: "Accounting for the Translation of Foreign Currency Transactions and Foreign Currency Financial Statements," October 1975. Hereinafter referred to as *FASB-8*.

4. Mueller has suggested that a decline of 25 percent or more, for two years or more in succession, might represent a "reasonable cut-off point" in defining an unstable currency. See Gerhard G. Mueller, *International Accounting* (New York: The Macmillan Company, 1967), p. 197.

5. *Accounting Research Bulletin No. 43* (New York: AICPA, 1953), para. 4.

6. Samuel R. Hepworth, *Reporting Foreign Operations* (Ann Arbor, Mich.: University of Michigan, 1956).

7. *Management Accounting Problems in Foreign Operations*, Research Report No. 36 (New York: National Association of Accountants, 1960).

8. *Accounting Principles Board Opinion No. 6*, "Status of Accounting Research Bulletins" (New York: AICPA, 1965), para. 18.

9. Leonard Lorensen, *Accounting Research Study No. 12*, "Reporting Foreign Operations of U.S. Companies in U.S. Dollars" (New York: AICPA, 1972).

10. *FASB-8*, para. 6, p. 3. Reprinted with permission.

11. Ibid., p. 38.

12. Ibid., p. 16.

13. In May 1977, the FASB announced the initiation of two studies: one commissioned to investigate the effect of *FASB-8* on the market prices of selected stocks; a second study planned to examine the effects on the management of exchange risk. See "The CPA Letter," AICPA, May 9, 1977. Given the vagaries of cause-effect relationships common to human behavior studies, the most that the FASB can expect to learn is the degree of enmity toward *FASB-8* that exists within the business community in a structured format.

Appendix 8A:
Annotated Chronology
of Alternative Foreign-
Currency Translation
Methods

1963 *Accounting Research Study No. 6.*, "Reporting the Financial Effects of Price-Level Changes" (New York: AICPA, 1963), pp. 148-149.

    1. "Ideal" circumstances wherein changes in exchange rates reflecting changes in the purchasing power of foreign currencies "rarely exist."

    2. Recommended exchange rates be used as starting points to determine relative purchasing powers of currencies on a case-by-case basis.

1969 *Statement of the Accounting Principles Board No. 3. (APBS No. 3)*, "Financial Statements Restated for General Price-Level Changes" (New York: AICPA, June 1969).

    1. Recognized that changes in prices of foreign currencies do not necessarily represent changes in foreign purchasing power (para. 21).

    2. Declared that foreign currencies, receivables, and payables are nonmonetary items but may be translated at current rates for convenience (para. 21).

    3. Adopted translate/restate method for including statements of foreign operations in U.S. consolidations (para. 45).

    4. Ignored changes in foreign price levels.

1969 David B. Zenoff and Jack Zwick, *International Financial Management* (Englewood Cliffs, N.J.: Prentice-Hall, Inc., 1969).

    1. Agreed with *APBS No. 3* that changes in foreign purchasing power are not synonymous with changes in exchange rates.

    2. Recommended restate/translate approach:

        a. Restate foreign assets and liabilities for changes in local price levels, then translate all at current rates.

        b. Translate equity accounts using historical rates.

    3. Ignored changes in U.S. price levels in consolidations.

1970 Donald R. Mandich, "Devaluation, Revaluation—Re-Evaluation?" *Management Accounting*, August 1970.

    1. Considered hedging "unconstructive."

    2. Results of currency changes should merely be footnoted, together with a comment regarding the projected long-run effects on earnings, if any, and "in general, to what degree."

1972   Lee J. Seidler, "An Income Approach to the Translation of Foreign Currency Financial Statements," *The CPA Journal*, January 1972, pp. 26-35.

   1.   Believed foreign operations were treated as second-class activities.
   2.   Proposed use of a hybrid method:
      a.   Translate current items at current rates.
      b.   Translate fixed items at current rates when dollar declines, at historic rates when dollar appreciates.
   3.   Based upon premises of conservatism and repatriation of foreign earnings to the U.S. parent.

1972   R. MacDonald Parkinson, *Translation of Foreign Currencies* (Toronto: Canadian Institute of CPAs, 1972).

   1.   Recommended that circumstances, such as degree of independence of subsidiaries, are relevant considerations.
   2.   Suggested a "situational" approach be employed.

1972   Keith R. Schwayder, "Accounting for Exchange Rate Fluctuations," *The Accounting Review*, October 1972, pp. 747-760.

   1.   Suggested a restate/translate/restate approach:
      a.   Restate foreign nonmonetary assets for changes in local price levels.
      b.   Translate net assets at current rates and equity accounts at historic rates.
      c.   Restate U.S. statements for changes in U.S. general price levels, treating the foreign investment as a monetary asset.
   2.   Added changes in U.S. price levels to the Zenoff and Zwick proposal (1969).

1974   Arthur Andersen & Co., *Accounting Standards for Business Enterprises Throughout the World*, 1974.

   1.   Foreign-currency balance sheets should be restated using current values, then translated using current rate as of closing date.
   2.   Foreign income statements should be translated using average monthly rates.
   3.   Changes on nonmonetary items should be applied as adjustments to costs of the related items.
   4.   Changes on monetary items should be reflected as current-period gains/losses.

1974   AAA, "Report of the Committee on International Accounting," *The Accounting Review, Supplement to Volume 49*, 1974, pp. 250-269.

Recommended that purchasing-power-parity indices be constructed and used, rather than exchange rates.

1975   AAA, "Report of the Committee on International Accounting," *The Accounting Review, Supplement to Volume 50*, 1975, pp. 90-95.

1.   An "ideal" translation (directly comparable with U.S. operations) could not be achieved.
2.   Suggested balance sheets be restated for significant changes in local price levels, then translated using current rates.
3.   Foreign income statements should be translated using weighted averages of current rates.
4.   Gains/losses should be reflected on income statements.

9 Transfer Prices

Few accounting problems of multinational enterprises—possibly only those related to taxation—contain as many conflicting interrelationships as the dilemma of transfer pricing. Consequently, while many aspects of domestic and multinational accounting are similar or parallel, transfer pricing continues to represent an area of wide diversity.

In the international realm, transfer prices have been and are used to circumvent all sorts of restrictions upon the flows of resources across national boundaries. Conventional domestic practices—designed to achieve other goals within a single environment—were discarded by most firms because they were clearly inappropriate.

Multinational enterprises are still searching for transfer-pricing systems that are compatible with their needs. Since these needs are diverse and often conflicting, prospects for the development of systems (or policies) that can be employed uniformly across all segments of an enterprise are remote.

Transfer prices may represent the least understood aspect of multinational operations. Most problems seem to arise when domestic and international goals are confused. To minimize this problem, transfer-pricing concepts and practices will be examined from the domestic standpoint initially. Then the additional variables peculiar to the international environment will be introduced in order to promote recall and understanding of the issues.

Background

The subject of transfer prices arose with the movement toward decentralization of operations by large domestic firms such as General Motors and General Electric just prior to World War II. Much has been written about the subject over the past three decades, although primarily from the domestic viewpoint. Attention to international issues has increased with the evolution of multinational enterprises.

Of the many definitions of transfer prices available, perhaps the most appropriate is that suggested by Horngren (modified by the bracketed notation):

> *Transfer prices* are the monetary values [amounts] assigned to the goods and services exchanged among the subunits of an organization.[1]

The term *amounts* is preferred over *values*, since transfer prices are often arbitrary amounts applied to intracompany transactions, with no basis in value or cost.

References sometimes made to a "buying division's cost" and a "selling division's revenue" should be avoided. They may serve to portray the activity of an intracompany transfer, but the allusion that revenue is somehow earned in the process can be deceiving. A domestic firm earns no revenue by selling to itself. Regardless of the practices employed, transfer prices represent, in the end, the costs associated with the goods or services exchanged. Any amounts in excess of cost are eliminated when consolidated financial reports for the total entity are prepared in accordance with existing accounting standards. In reality, then, the transfer of a commodity from one domestic unit of an organization to another, in itself, has no more effect upon that organization than would the transfer of a commodity from one storeroom to another within a single-plant company.

Domestic Practices

It is not often remembered that transfer prices have long been used within single firms to allocate the costs of service departments (such as maintenance, power, and plant cafeteria operations) to the production departments. In these instances, however, only transfers of costs were involved, so that they might be attached to the items produced. No fictitious revenues or markups were added to muddy the waters.

In the search for expanded markets and profits by complex manufacturing firms in the United States, the process of management was changed significantly. Highly centralized firms (those that reserved all major decisions for the headquarters) were forced to delegate some authority for decision making to subunits. Local units needed such freedom if they were to react timely to local conditions. Furthermore, the state of communications during the 1930s and 1940s simply could not accommodate centralized decision making.

In truth, complex organizations never could be completely centralized— nothing could be accomplished efficiently. Similarly, total decentralization is also a myth, since some person or group must coordinate the activities of the several parts if the firm is to accomplish its objectives by other than chance. Most firms operate somewhere along the continuum.

Since decentralization remains a matter of degree, management devices must be tailored to fit the circumstances. Although data are necessarily limited, an extensive study of some 190 multidivisional companies made by the National Industrial Conference Board in 1967 simply confirmed the diversity of domestic transfer-pricing practices.[2]

Domestic Objectives

The number of divisions and the volume of transactions among these divisions grew along with decentralization. The number of decision makers also proliferated. The concerns of central management grew proportionately and in three areas: control, coordination, and evaluation.

Transfer prices were adopted by diversified domestic organizations as tools: (1) to construct a framework to control operations; (2) to motivate managers to maximize profits of the total firm in the long run; and (3) to evaluate the performance of both divisions and managers.

Problems related to *control* of the organization as a whole were usually dependent upon the degree of autonomy or independence of the various units. In other words, the more freedom granted to a unit, the greater the problems of control. Independence of the units, in turn, was usually determined by the structure of the organization.

Firms that were vertically integrated normally granted less autonomy to subunits. For example, the interdependencies that existed among units of firms in the oil and steel industries necessarily constrained the degree of freedom with which the units could make decisions without coordination.

More autonomy was possible within horizontally integrated firms. General Motors and General Foods are examples of complex organizations in which the several divisions, while operating in the same industry, strove for separate identities and niches within the total market. Each niche created was large enough to provide an economy of scale sufficient to permit the divisions to operate almost as if they were separate firms.

The conglomerate—a third general form of organization—represented a cluster of units with operations only loosely related if at all. In the normal case, the cluster grew over time by the acquisition of existing firms in order to diversify and protect future earnings from the vagaries of a single industry, as well as to increase total earnings. Units were autonomous upon acquisition and tended to remain so. In many cases, attractive long-term investment opportunities were sought rather than control of day-to-day operations.

Of course, few organizations would fall neatly within any one of the three forms mentioned without some overlapping. Therein lies part of the problem—constructing a system of transfer prices to serve as a standard framework to control operations of units having various degrees of independence. In this context, a unit is independent if, and only if, it: (1) is free to make its own decisions; (2) transacts no business with other units; (3) operates in a separate market; and (4) generates and controls its own resources. Independence, then, like decentralization, is generally a matter of degree.

Coordination of decision making is often called "goal congruence" or the process of assuring that the interests and decisions of unit managers will be compatible with the best long-run interests of the total organization. Transfer prices are attempts to acquire that assurance by motivating managers to make the right decisions without unduly limiting their freedom. The effect of transfer prices upon decisions by unit managers depends upon many variables. Some of these are the information or data base available; the elasticity of market demand; pricing policy or strategy of the unit (to penetrate or to "skim cream"); and the role of the unit within the organization (cost, profit, investment, or other responsibility center).

Evaluation, or measuring the performance of the unit and its management, can be facilitated by the use of appropriate transfer prices. Performance evaluation will be examined in chapter 10, but suffice it to say here that, in order to yield valid measures, transfer prices must be compatible with the roles of the units. Experience has proved that inappropriate roles often are assigned to subunits both prior to and during evaluation (for example, cost centers treated as profit centers). The resulting transfer-pricing practices produce a morass of worthless, if not misleading, information.

As can be gleaned from the foregoing, domestic transfer-pricing practices could hardly be approached dogmatically. Conflicts existed in the objectives themselves—to provide autonomy yet control operations with different roles. Conflicts also arose in selecting transfer prices that motivated proper decisions while providing equitable performance measures of all units.

Types of Transfer Prices

Domestic transfer prices can be classed as cost-based or market-based. Variations exist within each category, and a hybrid form (dual pricing, which combines the cost bases with other methods) is also used occasionally.

Cost-Based Methods. Dependent subunits normally use methods based upon cost. Cost-based methods are commonly applied to both vertical transfers (to successive levels of production or distribution) and horizontal transfers (to similar levels of production or distribution) by captive units (those that are not free to buy and sell as they choose). Consequently, transfers at cost tend to be favored by the more centralized firms as the basis for control, decision making, and performance evaluation. Problems arise when a division's output is sold to external customers as well as transferred within the organization.

In general, transfer prices based upon cost are simple and inexpensive. Cost data are routinely available from accounting systems, are easily understood, and often represent the only practicable choices where external markets for the goods or services either do not exist or are not realistic. Usually, cost-based prices are considered to be the only logical means to account for internal transfers from cost centers.

Four types of cost-based methods are used domestically: (1) full cost (standard or actual); (2) full cost plus; (3) variable cost (standard or actual); and (4) variable cost plus.

1. *Full-cost (standard or actual)* methods have several advantages:

Standard costs prevent normal variances from being passed on to transferees, yet permit the addition of unusual costs, such as those caused by special or rush orders.

Fixed costs are included to assist in long-run decisions.

They are easy to defend internally (less friction) and externally (to government and regulatory agencies).

They are compatible with normal cost and budget systems.

They facilitate systematic use over time.

Disadvantages of full-cost prices are:

They can be inadequate for decision making by transferees, unless variable costs are reflected separately.

Profits cannot be used as motivators for transferors, since, if intermediate transfers are based on cost, only selling units (final transferees) will record any profits.

They exclude cost of capital employed by transferors.

They are incompatible with decentralization of intermediate operations.

Actual costs pass inefficiencies along to final transferees and may adversely affect their competitive positions.

2. *Full-cost-plus* methods attempt to overcome some of the disadvantages of full cost by the addition of increments to cover costs of capital and/or to represent pseudo profits. The latter action can be used to simulate market conditions and obtain the benefits of profit as a motivator, albeit artificial. In tax cases and similar situations where pricing practices must be defended, cost-plus methods often satisfy arm's-length criteria.[3]

Full-cost-plus prices, however, only increase the inadequacies of full-cost data for decision making purposes.

3. *Variable-cost (standard or actual)* prices are advantageous insofar as control and decision making are concerned:

They enhance systematic control of relevant costs (those that tend to change with volume of activity).

They assist lowest-cost input decisions and minimize the possibilities of outside purchases at higher costs to the organization.

They facilitate cost aggregation and pricing as well as output decisions by vertically integrated firms.

They are essential for consideration of special orders, make-or-buy decisions, and distress pricing.

Valid criticisms of variable-cost methods include:

Lack of consideration of fixed expenses and capital employed may reduce long-term profitability.

Profit cannot be used to motivate or evaluate.

They can lead to dumping charges, since prices are not representative of economic substance nor arm's-length criteria.

They are furthest removed from sensibility to market factors.

Only losses can accrue to transferees if variable-cost prices are used exclusively. Losses are also possible if variable pricing is used for internal transfers and market prices are used for sales to external customers.

4. *Variable-cost-plus* methods are the least used of the four cost-based approaches. While variable costs represent powerful tools for decision making in the short run, all costs plus a reasonable economic return must be covered if the entity is to survive over time. Additives applied to variable costs, regardless of their intended purposes, serve to blunt their capacities as decision tools. Consequently, this approach tends to be reserved for the handling of special-purpose activities and usually represents the floor, or the lowest amount to be used within a schedule of possible transfer prices.

Market-Based Methods. The benefits attached to market-based transfer prices are dependent upon the assumption that a perfectly competitive external marketplace exists and functions. Stated another way, deficiencies in the marketplace produce corresponding inadequacies in market-based transfer prices. Since few perfect markets are said to exist today, transfer prices based upon market conditions continue to be sound in theory but defective in many respects when applied in practice.

Assuming that a reasonably competitive market exists, market-based transfer prices have the following advantages in domestic operations:

Units may be operated as autonomous entities.

Advantages of decentralization may be obtained while increasing productivity and market share.

Profits determined by external markets are less subject to internal manipulation and are reasonable measures of performance.

Market prices serve as ceilings for transfers when operating near full capacity, since the opportunity costs (benefits forgone on external sales) are spotlighted when internal transfers are considered.

Market factors increase management's awareness of consumer needs and encourage innovation.

Competitive market prices stimulate control of costs and encourage efficiency.

Market-based prices comply with arm's-length and other guidelines for fair business practices.

As mentioned earlier, most of the shortcomings of market-based transfer prices are the results of market imperfections:

Market-based prices are impractical where no intermediate or final market exists at the transfer point, or where the markets are ill-structured or imperfect in other respects.

They are inappropriate where list/nominal prices are only vaguely representative of real market prices.

Under normal operating conditions (at less than full capacity), decisions regarding internal transfers may not be congruent with the best interests of the total enterprise.

Overemphasis on market prices may result in lack of adequate attention to control of costs.

Market prices are susceptible to collusion if they are based upon what the market will bear.

If market prices are not adjusted for market variables (such as warehousing, distribution costs, and the like), unfair schemes, such as zone pricing, can result.

Negotiated or Bargained Prices. These represent refinements of market-based transfer prices. By definition, amounts agreed upon by negotiation between the subunits involved most closely represent arm's-length prices. Bargaining can adjust for unusual or inappropriate aspects of the marketplace and, in some cases, can simulate market conditions where none exist. Negotiations can improve use of economic resources where excess capacity exists, if both parties are open to reasonable concessions.

Problems related with negotiations in general also apply to bargained transfer prices. The process consumes expensive management time. All parties must be knowledgeable of market factors. Units must bargain from positions of similar strength; that is, each must be free to buy and sell where it chooses. Captive units are generally at a significant disadvantage in such negotiations. Finally, transfer prices that must depend upon future agreements do not lend themselves to systemization.

Dual-Pricing. These systems, which record a given transaction at two prices, are gaining acceptance for several reasons. Most complex organizations operate somewhere along the centralized-decentralized continuum. Some operating segments will be highly centralized. Other operations will have more freedom of choice. Some units or functional areas will be best suited to the cost-center approach; others will respond best to roles as profit or investment centers. Firms comprised of units with various interdependencies have adopted practices of dual pricing in order to acquire the benefits of both cost-based and market-based methods. For example, central manufacturing operations that are captive (can only ship to sister manufacturing or distribution units) can be controlled internally by standard cost and budget systems. Also, the motivation of profit can be acquired by using transfer prices containing synthetic profits (cost plus) in recording shipments from these cost centers. If the transferee is charged with only the standard cost (full or variable), decision making will be enhanced at that and subsequent levels. The differences, of course, represent interunit markups that would be eliminated upon consolidation of statements. In effect, methods of dual pricing, regardless of the variant forms employed, attempt to reconcile the objectives of control, decision making, and performance evaluation.

Even the best-intentioned and best-designed dual-pricing methods have drawbacks. The use of dual transfer prices results in some double-counting of profits; the aggregate of divisional profits would not reflect that of the enterprise as a whole. Some critics also believe that controls over costs at all levels would tend to deteriorate; but that condition would not necessarily result—it would depend upon the caliber and astuteness of management. Perhaps the strongest objection to dual pricing arises when an artificial markup is credited to the transferor rather than using the prevailing market price.

Domestic Overview

Transfer prices represent a dilemma of substantial proportions for domestic complex organizations. Organizational philosophies reflect various degrees of decentralization. Structures also vary from vertical to horizontal and all sorts of combinations in between. Units may operate as cost, profit, or investment centers or, as is often found, may actually function within a framework of variable interdependencies.

The objectives of domestic transfer pricing are as conflicting as the roles of the units themselves. To grant the autonomy necessary for decentralized operation requires that some sacrifices be made in control and decision-making abilities. Methods of evaluating the effectiveness of delegated decisions must be developed. Selected performance measures must be appropriate for the roles of subunits and must be equitable.

In sum, the *pursuit of equity* defines the critical path usually followed in selecting domestic transfer-pricing methods. The number of conflicting roles and goals necessarily dictates that some trade-offs be made. Consequently, various transfer prices will be employed between subunits of a single entity for identical transfers to various transferees, dependent upon the purposes of the transfers.

International Practices

Outside the United States, domestic transfer-pricing goals and dogma are usually discarded. Multinational enterprises are confronted by all the domestic constraints mentioned plus a number of additional hurdles peculiar to the movement of goods and services across national boundaries. Domestic operations are simplified by a single environment of American rules, controls, and laws. Multinational operations may occur in more than 100 countries, each with various opportunities and constraints.

Additional variables occur in the area of choice. It can be said that both domestic and multinational firms select operating locations that will maximize total profits by yielding the best returns on investments; providing the cheapest factors of production; producing outputs most efficiently; and offering the most profitable markets.

However, multinational enterprises simply have many more options available. Some locations will be better sources of materials or components; others will be attractive sites to assemble or produce; still others will contain the most desirable markets; while altogether different countries may be the best locations to obtain financing, to warehouse, or to organize and collect profits. Consequently, multinationals will transfer a much greater amount of goods and services between units in order to capitalize on the benefits of various locations. While data are difficult to come by, estimates cite transfers between related firms as accounting for more than half of all international trade.

Thus, practices of international transfer pricing are affected initially by the same conflicting elements as are domestic methods—autonomy, control, coordination of decision making, performance evaluation, and equity. The international milieu is further complicated by the wider options available in choices of locations, each with peculiar advantages and constraints.[4]

The advantages and problems created with various national environments create the real differences between domestic and international transfer-pricing practices.

International Objectives

Data concerning international practices of transfer pricing, even if they were available for a large number of companies, would be suspect. Transfer pricing has generally been regarded as confidential information. Where details would be made available, there would be no assurance that the described methods were actually practiced. However, common sense serves as the basis for some speculations.

At least a dozen different considerations impact international pricing decisions. These factors can be grouped under four objectives: to control or coordinate operations, to minimize taxes, to circumvent controls, and to reduce risks.

Control or Coordinate Operations. Decentralization is the antithesis of multinational enterprise. The size and flexibility of an MNC are effective assets only because they can be manipulated in the best interests of the total organization in the long run. Global resources must be controlled or allocated by the headquarters unit, and transfer-pricing mechanisms represent one of the tools used in the allocation process. Only the central headquarters generally has access to the data base needed to make resource decisions in the best long-run interests of the total firm. Often these decisions run counter to the short-run benefits of certain units or divisions. In such cases, the interest of the subunits must be subordinated to those of the total firm. *The principle of equity among units must be discarded.*

Transfer prices serve as the core of the data base used for decision making. Regardless of transfer prices reflected in transactions among subunits, reports to headquarters must reflect the relevant costs involved. Consequently, meaningful cost accumulations for internal reporting dictate that transfers of resources within the MNC be founded upon cost.

Minimize Taxes. Transfer prices are often effective means of minimizing the tax burden of the organization as a whole by controlling income to be reported in and taxed by the various host countries. High transfer prices can be used to reduce income earned in high-tax countries. Conversely, low transfer prices can divert profits to so-called tax havens—countries with no income taxes or with relatively low tax rates.

Tax reductions can also be realized by the selective use of transfer prices. Oil companies, for example, will tend to price crude-oil shipments as high as possible in order to reflect the lion's share of profit in drilling operations, which benefit from the percentage depletion allowances applicable to natural resources in U.S. tax laws. In locations that assess high withholding taxes on dividends, high transfer prices can siphon off resources long before they would be available as distributable income. Border taxes (ad valorem duties and tariffs) can also be reduced by means of assigning low transfer prices to the goods.

These examples are simplified. There are usually many pitfalls and trade-offs. Of primary importance is the fact that three parties are involved: the enterprise, the country of the transferor, and the country of the transferee. If earnings are diverted from one location, they must accrue to another. Multi-nationals operating in more than a hundred countries must be adept jugglers if they expect to gain a net advantage every time. Other more subtle trade-offs are involved also. Low transfer prices used to minimize ad valorem border taxes may result in exposure to even higher value-added taxes in some countries. The multiplicity of the taxes, their effective rates, and the variable nature of the rates themselves create a maze of no small proportions.

Circumvent Controls. Almost any control imposed by a host government can be reduced, if not circumvented, by the selective use of transfer prices.

Restrictions on the distribution of income can be nullified by high transfer prices, since flows of funds to parent firms as cost remittances cannot be effectively limited. Similarly, earnings can often be repatriated in the guise of service fees, royalties, and interest charges, although such items can be regulated to some degree by host governments.

Exchange controls can be minimized by using lower transfer prices to enable importation of a larger volume of goods within fixed levels of foreign-exchange allotments. Export quotas similarly can be influenced by the transfer prices applied.

Trade and antitrust regulations can be made tolerable by assuring that transfer prices employed range within the minimum and maximum guidelines that exist.

Reduce Risks. Transfer prices can reduce the risks associated with overseas investments. Time is one element of risk that is amenable to control in some instances. If the investment is of a short-term nature, then high transfer prices can be used to return resources to the parent firm as soon as possible.

Similar actions minimize risks associated with fluctuations of exchange rates in selected areas. Where exchange rates are soft or are expected to deteriorate, higher transfer prices can salvage more dollars immediately and thus reduce the risk of later remittances or repatriations at depressed rates.

Where the political environment is deteriorating and conditions are considered to be irreversible, higher transfer prices can reduce the exposed investment until the axe finally falls. Such use of transfer prices is itself irreversible, since the action can only further exacerbate the existing problems.

In the more typical cases, involving long-term outlooks, transfer mechanisms can improve the image of the enterprise in the host country. For example, the firm often can construct price schedules and otherwise encourage shipments from or to those countries that enjoy political favor. Transfer prices can also assure that reasonable profits are accumulated in those locations having representative numbers of indigenous shareholders. Such actions enhance the role of the multinational as a good citizen and improve local relations, which are beneficial in the long run.

Repercussions

In some respects the foregoing may connote nefarious or shady dealings. In reality, however, multinational enterprises are simply acting in their self-interests, as encouraged by Adam Smith, and responding to the opportunities and challenges existing in various free-market environments. What is fair for the multinational may or may not be considered fair by the governments concerned. Where governments have established effective regulations regarding transfer prices (and these are difficult), multinationals will adopt pricing methods that are reasonable—in an economic sense, in consistency of application, and in the generation of local earnings.

Multinationals can easily run afoul of host governments without any nefarious intent. Products or components may enter a host country from three or four supplying divisions of a single multinational. Even if fair transfer prices are employed, the different manufacturing and other costs of doing business (such as effective tax rates) in the countries of origin can easily produce different entry prices for the same item. The company is then faced with explaining the different prices to the host government or becoming vulnerable to charges of dumping or other unfair trade practices.[5]

All too often, issues such as transfer pricing are examined with only one eye open; that is, from the viewpoint of a U.S. parent firm operating in foreign host countries. The United States is also a host country for an increasing number of foreign-based multinationals that are eager to carve out their shares of American steel, auto, electronic, shoe, and chemical markets. The transfer-pricing practices of these MNCs, whether fair or not, have forced many large U.S. producers to relax their traditional methods of target pricing (margins based upon long-term umbrella prices established by industry leaders) and to adopt flexible pricing (product margins adjusted to reflect market conditions).[6]

These events in the United States illustrate the point made previously—that an MNE has only two effective challengers, another multinational or a host government. Within relatively free markets, competition between and among multinationals generally results in economic benefits for consumers.

Governments, at least those of industrialized countries, tend to serve as umpires to see that the competition remains fair. Political cries of foul play and pressures for protectionist measures most often arise from domestic industries that have permitted themselves to become archaic and can no longer compete. An excellent example is the American steel industry, which has become fossilized because it believed itself immune to real foreign competition and pocketed profits rather than modernizing plants.

Protectionism will be avoided among the industrial countries so long as the governments refrain from direct subsidizations of antiquated industries. Of course, since multinationals have effectively converted local, domestic markets into global markets, governments should adopt methods to retrain employees in affected industries similar to procedures used by the EEC countries during the period when internal trade barriers were being phased out.

Since the OECD represents all the major industrialized nations of the free world, its pronouncements presumably represent the overt intentions of its members. The OECD "code of conduct" for multinational firms and host governments, adopted on June 21, 1976, outlined the spirit and intent of "fair treatment" in business conduct. It was not at all surprising that "policies followed in respect of intra-group pricing" were particularly required to be disclosed by reporting companies. (See appendix 4A, item viii.)

Perhaps the greatest influence upon international transfer-pricing practices in the near future will be the result of the changing structures of the multinationals themselves. If the majority of the multinational enterprises mature into transnational networks (TNNs), as suggested by Perlmutter,[7] then transfer prices will tend to reflect economic sense and equity for a diverse group of stakeholders, rather than for a parent firm in a single domicile. This, in itself, would encourage systematic application based upon reasonable objectives. A second factor may well be the frustration resulting from attempts to juggle transfer prices to achieve multiple, often conflicting, objectives among hundreds of operating locations. The maze of interacting variables will defy overt manipulations of trade-offs and eventually will result in more uniform applications based upon broad policies.

Summary

The objectives of transfer pricing and the examples of particular uses were cited to stress the differences that exist between the domestic and the international realms.

Domestically, the primary objective of transfer pricing is the maintenance of equity among divisions in order to facilitate the performance evaluations required by decentralization. Secondary objectives often conflict, and the several types of divisions (cost, profit, and investment centers) preclude the adoption of a uniform system of transfer prices that can be applied to similar transactions of all units.

In the international sphere, equity among subunits is rarely given primary consideration today. The perceived best interests of the multinational enterprise as a whole are paramount. Transfer prices are used as devices to coordinate and control operations, to minimize taxes, to circumvent controls, and to reduce the risks inherent in multinational operations. As the elements within the several environments (political, legal, economic, and sociocultural) change over time, the objectives of transfer prices will also change, in either nature or relative importance, or both. Consequently, while a system of transfer pricing would facilitate the control of global resources, no standardized system could be flexible enough to achieve multiple purposes in dynamic environments.

Multinationals profess to use systems of transfer prices that they term *flexible*, or *managed*, or *creative*. What they are really saying is that multiple methods are used to serve multiple purposes. For internal reporting purposes, cost-based amounts are clearly preferable. The more sophisticated systems will further segregate costs into variable (or direct) and fixed components. Transfer prices used for interunit billings may include dual-pricing methods, but, in the end, the methods will depend upon the circumstances.

As multinational enterprises continue to evolve and mature over time, the interests of diverse stakeholders in many countries and/or the intractability of the maze of trade-offs to be considered will lead to more emphasis upon equity and consistency in transfer-pricing policies.

Notes

1. Charles T. Horngren, *Cost Accounting: A Managerial Emphasis*, 4th ed. (Englewood Cliffs, N.J.: Prentice-Hall, Inc., 1977), p. 675. Reprinted with permission.

2. *Interdivisional Transfer Pricing* (New York: The National Industrial Conference Board, 1967).

3. Section 482 of the U.S. Internal Revenue Code operates to place a controlled taxpayer on a tax parity with an uncontrolled taxpayer. The standard applied to transfer prices is "arm's length," or the amount that would have been charged in independent transactions with unrelated parties under the same or similar circumstances.

4. Itzhak Sharav, "Transfer Pricing—Diversity of Goals and Practices," *The Journal of Accountancy*, April 1974, pp. 56-62.

5. For an excellent example, see M. Edgar Barrett, "Case of the Tangled Transfer Price," *Harvard Business Review*, May-June 1977, pp. 20-22, 26, 28, 32, 36, 176, 178.

6. "Flexible Pricing," *Business Week*, December 12, 1977, pp. 78-81, 84, 88.

7. See chapter 1.

10 Performance Evaluations

Performance evaluations of the subsidiaries of multinational enterprises and their managers, like transfer prices, were products of decentralization. Also like transfer prices, performance evaluations had their domestic counterparts. Domestic practices of performance evaluations (some of which were suspect in themselves) were applied by many firms (with or without minor adjustments) to overseas operations for which they were totally inappropriate. Other firms recognized the environmental differences affecting foreign operations, were confounded by these differences, and made no formal evaluations as such. Whether it was worse to apply inappropriate measures or to apply none at all is a moot point.

Most of the fault must lie with top managements that cannot think beyond their domestic frameworks, that are determined to evaluate others exactly as they believe they are judged, or that allege that they don't have the time to do the job properly. Some of the blame must also rest with controllers, accountants, and advisers who find it most convenient to use data available routinely, or with little extra effort, from financial-accounting reports—whether or not they recognize that the yardsticks used are inappropriate. Some of the blame now must also be shared by the accounting profession itself (or at least by its official arm, the Financial Accounting Standards Board) for promulgating requirements, such as *FASB-8*, which only encourage—if not sanctify—myopic evaluations in U.S. dollars by multinational enterprises and the investing public. The infatuation with U.S. dollars that permeates *FASB-8* is an excellent example of the ethnocentric (home-country) orientation by MNEs depicted by Professor Perlmutter in chapter 1.

Domestic Practices

As decentralization became the maxim of management in the United States, certain authorities for decision making were delegated to unit managers. Periodically, those possessing the authority to make decisions had to account for the efficiency and effectiveness of their operations and their decisions. The assessments by top managements of the reported results became known as performance evaluations.

Pluralisms are stressed here, because they are crucial. Two subjects are involved—the unit and the manager. Each performs different and multiple roles.

Several criteria or measuring sticks must be used in order to measure these performances logically and fairly. Quantitative criteria include both financial and nonfinancial measures. Often, qualitative criteria are extremely important, even though they are the most difficult to assess. The standards with which the measurements should be compared are also numerous. Performance evaluations are often invalidated because top managements attempt, for whatever reasons, to use some form of single standard—usually profit or return on investment—to evaluate multiple and often conflicting objectives.[1]

Responsibility Accounting

Concepts of responsibility accounting were devised to place performance evaluations into manageable contexts. Responsibility accounting merely defined spheres of reference (responsibility centers) that had control over costs and/or revenues and to which inputs (resources) and outputs (products, services, or revenues) could be traced. These spheres or responsibility centers varied in complexity of control, structure, and purpose.

In the author's opinion, some managements have forgotten the relationship between the function of some business segments and their fair evaluation. The following is presented for recall as well as reconsideration.

Cost Centers. Insofar as controls and objectives are concerned, cost centers are the simplest spheres of reference. Control is exercised over costs incurred. Objectives normally call for the maximization of outputs, in quantity and quality, within the constraints on inputs specified by time-and-effort, standard-cost, flexible-budget, and similar systems. Structures vary from a single person, operation, or machine to the function of an entire plant. In practice, control and evaluation are enhanced by breaking down structures into the smallest components exercizing control over costs.

Responsibility reports should focus attention on costs that are controllable at the levels being addressed. Costs that are not controllable should be either separated or excluded. For example, any cost that has to be allocated arbitrarily among responsibility centers is considered to be noncontrollable. All costs, of course, are controllable at some level in the organization; the objective is to report each cost as controllable by the level exercising the authority to incur the cost.

Performance evaluations of cost centers are primarily financial and focus upon variances from predetermined standards. The better systems are based upon reasonably attainable standards, tailored to suit the responsibility centers, and revised as conditions change. Other quantitative, nonfinancial measures are often employed as well: numbers of reject products, machine breakdowns, employee turnovers, and the like. Qualitative assessments may be made by product engineers, by using surrogate measures (such as using the numbers of grievances to judge employee attitudes), or, all too often, by relegating assessments to consumers where products are concerned.

Expense Centers. Also among the simpler forms of responsibility levels are expense centers. These typically are administrative and service departments whose controllable expenditures are not attached to the cost of goods produced. In practice, these operations are often considered as cost centers. Objectives of expense centers are to provide services of acceptable quantity and quality, usually within the levels of expenses in predetermined and approved budgets.

Financial evaluation consists of relating inputs (controllable expenses incurred) with the budgeted amounts that, upon original approval, represented acceptable levels. Output evaluations are difficult. Often only subjective assessments are made, such as a lack of complaints from the activities or customers served. Sophisticated applications often examine costs per order, credit checks processed per day, orders or letters typed per hour, and the like.

Revenue Centers. By definition, revenue centers can affect output levels (revenues) in relation to the inputs (resources represented in expense budgets), but no direct control is exercised over the costs of the products or services to be sold. Motivation and control are sought by means of budgeted revenues and expenses. The twin objectives are to maximize revenues while spending within authorized levels. Sales offices are typical revenue centers, often with further segmentation into product lines, territories, salesmen, and so on.

Performance evaluation usually begins with financial comparisons of actual and budgeted levels of revenues and expenses, after variable portions of the latter have been adjusted to reflect actual activity levels. Since the costs and qualities of the items sold are not controllable, appropriate adjustments should be made for any favorable or unfavorable effects caused by changes in these factors that are not recognized by budget revisions. Nonfinancial measures are also employed, although not necessarily in a systematic fashion: market shares, changes in sales mix, repeat sales, numbers of customers, quotas, calls made by salesmen, complaints, and others. Such nonfinancial measures become increasingly important as inflation affects revenues expressed in monetary units.

Profit Centers. Units or divisions that have control over both costs and revenues are profit centers.[2] That simple definition shrouds some crucial conditions relating to independence:

1. The unit must be free to produce or purchase the trade goods and services it requires where and when it chooses. Decisions concerning investments (such as capital acquisitions and expenditures over specified amounts) are reserved for, or must be approved by, higher headquarters.

2. The unit must be free to market its outputs solely to external customers anywhere or within defined territories or regions. Selling prices and other marketing decisions must be controllable by the unit so that it may respond to the conditions in the outside marketplace.

In effect, true profit centers are independent, miniature businesses financed by a parent organization. The interdependencies that exist among units of most complex organizations preclude the existence of many true profit centers.

Performance evaluations relate outputs (revenues) with inputs (costs and expenses) by focusing on profits (revenues minus identifiable expenses). Profit is an absolute measure that, standing alone, can be assessed subjectively as representing acceptable or poor performance. Profit becomes a more meaningful measure when relative comparisons are also possible:

> With budget or plan (*if* revisions were made as conditions changed and/or the noncontrollable elements can be isolated);

> With results of prior periods (*if* circumstances remained comparable or the effects of changes can be identified); or

> With the profits of other units of the firm (*if* operating conditions are comparable).

The stressed *ifs* cannot be overemphasized.

Table 10-1 presents a simplified, general model of a controllable income statement that has many advantages when applied to bona fide profit centers. It permits evaluation of segments (where each segment possesses the attributes of a true profit center) as well as of the divisional profit center as a whole. Where the enterprise is entirely composed of divisional profit centers, a similar format could be used by the headquarters. Emphasis is placed upon revenues and expenses that are controllable by and directly traceable to the divisional profit center and its segments. Expenses that are not directly traceable to segments (that is, those which would have to be allocated arbitrarily in order to be distributed) are treated as what they really are—common expenses. Experience has proved that firms waste an inordinate amount of time and create untold amounts of ill will by useless, arbitrary allocations of common expenses. If such expenses are controllable only by the headquarters or divisional offices, they should be reflected only in performance reports addressed to those levels. No allocations of expenses should ever be made to lower levels or segments that have no voice in the approval of the expenses incurred.

There are also technical advantages connected with the controllable income statement in table 10-1. Short-term decisions are enhanced by the isolation of contribution margins. Similarly, the long-run desirabilities of segments can be assessed fairly by reference to segment margins without having to "back out"

Table 10-1
Profit-Center Controllable-Income Statement—General Example

	Total	Segments			
		A	*B*	*C*	*D*
Sales, revenues	$XXX	$XX	$XX	$XX	$XX
Less variable expenses:					
Cost of goods sold	$ XX	$ X	$ X	$ X	$ X
Selling	XX	X	X	X	X
Administrative	XX	X	X	X	X
Total variable expenses	$ XX	$ X	$ X	$ X	$ X
Contribution margin	$ XX	$ X	$ X	$ X	$ X
Less direct fixed expenses:					
Production	$ XX	$ X	$ X	$ X	$ X
Selling	XX	X	X	X	X
Administrative	XX	X	X	X	X
Total direct fixed expenses	$ XX	$ X	$ X	$ X	$ X
Segment margin	$ XX	$ X	$ X	$ X	$ X
Less common fixed expenses:					
Production	$ XX				
Selling	XX				
Administrative	XX				
Total common fixed expenses	$ XX				
Controllable operating income	$ XX				

Notes: Within a single profit center, segments may represent divisions, products, regions, and so forth. Statements based upon different classification systems could result in different classifications of the same cost as variable, direct fixed, or common. When prepared for the total enterprise, segments would represent the individual profit centers. Common expenses would primarily reflect the expenses connected with the headquarters' operation. Ratio analysis is aided by the inclusion of percentages opposite appropriate items, vertically and horizontally.

allocated expenses that would not be saved if the segments were discontinued. Also, the suggested format is compatible with the use of direct costing methods, which (1) relate changes in profits to changes in revenues rather than production; (2) eliminate transfers of fixed production costs from one period to another with changes in inventory levels; and (3) tie in with flexible budget and standard-cost data.[3]

There are equitable methods of measuring the performances of bona fide profit centers and their managers. Problems result when divisions operating with significant interdependencies are converted into artificial profit centers, usually by the imposition of transfer prices containing pseudo profits.[4] Such practices do not measure the profit performance of independent units operating in free markets, nor the abilities of their managers to act in the best long-run interests of the total enterprise—the avowed purposes. Instead, margins created by the use of transfer prices and other cost allocations that are considered to be equitable and are imposed by top managements (the evaluators) are actually measured. Also, profits can vary, favorably or unfavorably, because of a host of events not attributable to segment managers' acting in the best interests of the enterprise as a whole.

Regardless of the inherent inequities cited, two characteristics of profit—its simplicity and its power to motivate—have made it a favorite measure of the performances of operations and their managers.

Unfortunately, the fictions upon which most profit-center evaluations are based have not been taken seriously. If they were, many domestic segments would no longer be cast in ridiculous roles as profit centers. The mythical need to concoct transfer prices in order to generate pseudo profits and equitable treatment among units would also have been eliminated. Attention would have been directed to isolating real measures of performance and appropriate standards upon which evaluations could be based.

Investment Centers. Theoretically, investment centers are extensions of profit centers: control is presumed over revenues, expenses, and the levels of assets employed in generating profits. All the requisites of profit centers apply—freedom to purchase, produce, and market—plus control over capital acquisitions and expenditures. All the attendant fictions common to profit centers are encountered in practice, together with some additional myths.

Few divisions of complex organizations are bona fide investment centers. Most enterprises reserve decisions on or approvals of major capital acquisitions and expenditures (over a specified amount) for the central headquarters. Many divisions are strategic as well as financial segments of the larger enterprise. They perform work and supply services for other divisions. They are often required to use common support services furnished by the headquarters. Levels of inventories and receivables usually are affected by their strategic roles (service for other units) and often are influenced (if not effectively controlled) by the headquarters. Where such conditions are present, to consider the divisions as independent investment centers is absurd.

If the domestic investment center is a fiction, perhaps it should not be surprising that the prevailing method of performance evaluation would also be a fiction.

Return on investment (ROI), or rate of return, is a method that relates profits with the resources employed in their generation. Development of the concept is attributed to the Du Pont Company and for many years was known as the "DuPont formula." Virtually all major decentralized domestic corporations use some version of return on investment as the primary measure of the performances of divisions and their managers.

Many variations of return on investment have been used to cope with some of the shortcomings of the measure that have been pointed out over the years and to tailor the method to fit differing circumstances. Two general forms have been employed: For evaluation of the division:

$$\frac{\text{division return (segment margin)}}{\text{investment in division}} = \text{ROI}$$

For evaluation of the division manager:

$$\frac{\text{division controllable return (manager's contribution)}}{\text{controllable investment}} = \text{ROI}$$

The alleged advantages of the ROI ratio are:

1. It encompasses all the important factors in a single measure.
2. It is simple to compute from conventional financial statements.
3. It measures overall efficiency, since it relates results (operating income) with inputs (resources used).
4. It is a common denominator that can be used for comparative evaluations, both internally (with plans, other divisions, prior periods, and trends) and externally (with similar ratios for the industry, other firms, and other opportunities).
5. It is a logical motivator of managers, since, if they know they will be evaluated by ROI, they will act to maximize the ROI of their divisions.

Many of these attributes are conditional or contain internal flaws. They also may be mere fables, which, as Aesop cautioned, "can easily represent things as we wish them to be."

As a comprehensive measure, ROI contains the effects (both favorable and adverse) of elements that are not controllable by the activities and individuals to be evaluated. Where should credit or responsibility vest?

The simplicity of ROI is not really an asset. It is actually the symptom of a malady common to most models—simplex consideration of complex problems—compounded by the naive belief that conventional financial statements can depict efficiency and effectiveness. (Vancil contrasts efficiency and effectiveness: "efficiency means doing something right and effectiveness means doing the right something."[5]) Financial statements can provide insights of efficiency in the broad sense of the term, but they cannot denote effectiveness. Accounting profit is not synonymous with accomplishment.

Relating income with resources used is, conceptually, an improvement over focusing on income alone, but practical problems related to the definitions of revenues, costs, and resources must be solved. The simplified example of an investment-center report shown in table 10-2 illustrates some of the revenue and cost classifications commonly used.

Table 10-2
Example of an Investment Center Report
(in thousands)

Revenues:	
External sales	$ 700
Intracompany transfers	350
Total Revenues	$1,050
Less: Variable expenses	550
Division Contribution Margin	$ 500
Less: Controllable fixed costs	200
Manager's Contribution	$ 300
Less: Non-controllable direct costs	80
Division Segment Margin	$ 220
Less: Allocated home office costs	60
Division Net Income	$ 160
Less: Capital charge (10 percent)	148
Residual Income	$ 12

Assets employed:		
Controllable by manager	$ 625	
Total investment in division	1,480	
Return on investment:		
For evaluation of manager ($300 ÷ $625)		48%
For evaluation of division ($220 ÷ $1,480)		14.86%
Residual income:		
For evaluation of manager ($300 less capital charge of 10 percent applied to $625 controllable investment)		$237,500
For evaluation of current divisional performance ($220 – $148)		$ 72,000
For evaluation of corporate decision to make original investment		$ 12,000

Intracompany transfers are of critical importance. As discussed in the preceding chapter, if divisions perform significant work for other units, and if transfer prices are established by the headquarters, then the headquarters is determining a portion of the income levels used to evaluate divisions and their managers. What and who are really being evaluated? Segregation of costs into controllable, noncontrollable, and allocated categories is often troublesome but does not present nearly the number of problems associated with transfer prices.

All sorts of difficulties are encountered in defining the resources used (the asset base). The definitions always bias the resulting measures in one way or another. While the asset bases of divisions are usually circumstantial, they are often forced to conform to a single mold in order to acquire the subsequent benefits of alleged comparability. Some measures of assets used are more susceptible than others to manipulation by management.

What assets are traceable to the division? Which assets represent sunk decisions, and which are controllable by the manager? What about those headquarters assets that are considered common to the support of all divisions? Should the asset base be determined at the beginning or at the end of the year—or at a simple, moving, or weighted average?

Should assets be reflected at original cost (gross) or book value (net of recorded depreciation), or by some other method? Original cost is favored by some because: (1) it is routinely available; (2) it is not affected by multiple methods of depreciation accounting used by the various divisions; (3) it serves to offset the increases in replacement costs in times of inflation; (4) it prevents the upward bias in ROI rates as well as the favored treatment of older divisions resulting from the use of net-asset bases; and (5) according to studies, it is used by many of the respected industrial giants.

The use of ROI as a common denominator for comparative evaluations, internally and externally, is subject to all the same ifs previously mentioned regarding the use of profit as a relative measure. Comparability of operating conditions must exist in fact, or reasonable adjustments must be made for differences, before ROI can be a valid yardstick. Also, it should be recognized that ROI represents a composite measure of an assortment or mix of various assets and investments having various risks. Use of ROI as a common denominator would attach the same risk, on the average, to all investments. Finally, someone must determine what a reasonable ROI objective should be and whether it should be a specific ratio or an acceptable range or band. The temporal nature of most operations, particularly new and developing ventures, must be taken into account. Some time often is required to generate returns on many investments, and the focus of ROI is upon short-term results.

Instead of encouraging management to make economic decisions in the best long-run interests of the enterprise, return on investment can actually discourage the adoption of profitable opportunities—and by the more profitable divisions. For example, suppose a division has been generating an average ROI of 25 percent. What motivation would exist for the manager to submit a project that is expected to yield only 20 percent, thereby lowering his average performance (and probably his bonus)? However, if the average returns of the other divisions range from only 10 to 15 percent, the enterprise as a whole will have missed a desirable opportunity. In short, ROI depicts profit as a percentage, whereas profit should also be considered in dollars, since only dollars can be deposited in the bank.

A refinement of the ROI approach—residual income—can be used to remedy this defect and to consider profit in dollars as well as percentages. As shown in table 10-2, expressing incomes in dollars, less charges for imputed interest (or benchmark ROI rates) applied to the resources employed, focuses upon dollar incomes in excess of the selected threshold rate. Threshold rates can be adjusted to reflect the varying degrees of risk associated with the operations of different divisions. This measure tends to encourage submission of projects that are expected to yield returns above threshold rates. Residual income is considered by many firms to be more effective (as a motivator) and valid (as an evaluator) than ROI. Logic alone indicates that residual income is a better motivator. However, residual-income approaches are constructed upon a foundation weakened by most of the basic problems of definition and measurement that are related to return on investment. Consequently, residual income has no more validity or equity as an ex-post, macro measure of overall performance than any other single measurement.

Domestic Overview

Decentralization of domestic operations required concurrent delegations of authority and development of methods to assess the efficiency and effectiveness of the subunits and their managers.

Responsibility accounting conceptualized the roles of the various subunits as cost, expense, revenue, profit, or investment centers, depending on the operating decisions over which the subunit had effective control. The autonomy of the units ranged from very little control (for captive units) to almost complete control (miniature, separate businesses).

Methods of performance evaluation were devised for compatibility with the roles of the units. Benchmarks included standard-cost and master-budget goals, profit, return on investment, and residual income.

Where interdependencies existed or evolved (where some units did work for others), the roles of the various domestic units became blurred if not multiple. Executives in corporate headquarters either were not aware of these facts or, more likely, they believed (or were convinced) that profit recognized the effect of all important variables; was a great equalizer of differences; was an easy common denominator to calculate and use; and was a powerful motivator. (After all, they, themselves, were evaluated by profits and returns on investments. If such measures were fair for them, why not for others? Everyone is on the same team.) Profit in absolute or relative terms became *the* criterion for performance evaluations of domestic operations and their managers.

Several important facts were ignored or dismissed. In most centralized firms, few individuals below the chief executive officers are responsible for profits. Where transfer prices were prescribed to produce equitable pseudo profits for subunits, both equity and profitability were determined by the evaluators at the headquarters rather than by those who performed and were to be evaluated. Most units, even in the domestic economy, serve multiple roles, and no single criterion could possibly assess the efficiency and effectiveness of the units and their managers.

Over time, critics recurringly pointed out that profit-based measures, such as return on investment, were misleading, destructive, and obsolete for use as the primary measures of performance.[6] Little change resulted, since most executives acknowledged the deficiencies inherent in ROI as a measure yet insisted that it was the best available. This is nonsense.

Many better measures exist; that is, measures that represent valid assessments of efficiency and effectiveness and can be selected to fit the particular circumstances, whatever they might be. These will be addressed in the following section, which introduces the additional operating variables peculiar to the international arena. Methods that are valid measures of international operations with a much larger variety of interdependencies should also be manageable for less complex domestic operations.

For alternate methods to gain acceptance, at home or abroad, executives will have to divorce themselves from virtual dependence upon data in financial reports designed for external users. In this regard, perhaps the greatest contribution of responsibility accounting (apart from role clarification) is represented by contribution-income statements; at least a different structuring of revenues and expenses is imposed for internal uses.

Additional effort is required to identify and select better measures. This requires time. However, division managers normally invest a year's time in producing the results to be evaluated. Chief executives can surely invest more time than is required to peruse return-on-investment charts in order to evaluate performances.

International Practices

For many of today's multinational enterprises, the 1960s witnessed the evolution of the overseas subsidiary from "stepchild"[7] to strategic link. Initial overseas investments were usually made only after extensive analyses of foreign markets and environments. Even then, the chief concerns were competing and existing. Once begun, operations were virtually controlled and managed from the corporate headquarters. Domestic methods that had proved to be of value were transplanted. As the foreign subsidiaries became established, it was natural that concern would begin to gravitate from continued existence to performance evaluation.

Surveys and Opinions

An early (1969) study of the larger multinationals[8] indicated that primary concern was still being placed upon the safety of the capital at risk in the relatively new foreign operations. Parent firms literally managed the units overseas. Since the soundness of the parent's decisions to make the foreign investments was paramount, performance evaluations paralleled domestic practices and focused upon profit. Emphasis upon ROI appeared to be increasing but had not yet gained widespread acceptance.

The study also reported that corporations recognized the shortcomings inherent in "any system of figures," not to mention the added pecularities of foreign operations. A few firms participating in the study conducted annual evaluation proceedings that would rival any conducted today by the Pentagon.

In a 1973 report,[9] the AAA Committee on International Accounting confirmed the predominance of the profit-center concept in performance evaluations of domestic operations. Similar use of profit was considered to be inappropriate for foreign operations, since they had strategic objectives as well; many big decisions were made by corporate headquarters; and the multiple objectives of international transfer prices invalidated profit measures. Performance appraisals of foreign operations were described as limited, with a growing tendency toward reliance upon budget variances. The need to maintain a *duality* in foreign appraisals was considered essential; that is, knowing how efficiently the subsidiary used its resources and the ability or effectiveness of the local manager. Subsidiaries were most often evaluated by the use of conventional financial measures, with mental revisions to allow for circumstances.[10] Local managers were reportedly not appraised at all or were appraised merely by "personal impressions." Recommended improvements were the use of quantitative criteria other than financial data; audits of performance; and "point systems."[11]

The opinions expressed in the report of a subsequent AAA committee[12] indicated that performance evaluations by MNEs represented a mixture of subjective appraisals, absolute measures (such as profit or ROI), and comparative assessments (with other foreign units, prior period results, and/or operating budgets). Each of the evaluation methods then in use was cited for the failure to maintain the necessary separation between subsidiary and manager performance. A critical need was also said to exist for the development of new, more valid approaches to performance evaluation by MNEs.[13]

The most provocative criticism of the methods used to evaluate foreign operations was authored by Robbins and Stobaugh in 1973.[14] Their article was based upon the findings of an extensive study of the evaluation practices of all the major U.S. MNEs (189) at that time. Evaluation methods in use were considered to be confusing, misunderstood, and unsound. Almost without exception, the multinationals admitted using the same measures to evaluate overseas and domestic operations. Return on investment was the criterion applied in virtually all cases, even to evaluate those subsidiaries that were captive cost centers; that is, those units that produced goods entirely for distribution to sister units and for which the transfer prices (and pseudo profits) were determined by the parent firm.[15]

Robbins and Stobaugh suggested that ROI—the "bent measuring stick"—be discarded. Thereby, the need to create fictitious profits by means of synthetic transfer prices would also be avoided. Instead, budgets tailored to fit the real objectives and peculiar circumstances of the foreign subsidiaries were recommended.[16]

Revaluation

Often, when one attempts to deal with a problem, the most difficult aspect involves obtaining recognition that the problem exists. The exposure given the articles mentioned in the last section should have created an awareness. It is also understandable that, given an awareness that unrealistic measures are being employed, chief executives would remain reluctant to give up the familiar financial criteria by which their performances are evaluated—profits and returns on investment. However, in every enterprise there are few executives who are actually responsible for profits. If realistic performance measures are to exist for the others, changes in thinking are necessary. The initiative for change can only come from those top executives who evaluate—not from those being evaluated.

The literature is replete with suggestions for alternative performance measures. However, just as no single measure can be expected to produce valid assessments of a complex of roles, neither can a fixed set of measures. What is necessary is a zero-base, total revaluation of the process by which the performances of segments and their managers are to be assessed within decentralized firms, domestic as well as multinational.

Realistic Evaluations

Parochial emphasis upon the fictions of profit and ROI in performance evaluations can be eliminated by focusing upon realities (domestic and international) in the following process:

1. Define the objectives of the unit.
2. Determine the roles of the unit and its manager.
3. Select the criteria to measure performances.
4. Select the standards to evaluate performances.
5. Select the timing of evaluations.
6. Determine the process for communicating the results.

The objectives of the unit can be defined by asking why the unit was (or is to be) established. What markets are served—local, export, or both? Is the unit an outlet for goods produced elsewhere—in the United States or by another foreign unit? Is local assembly or manufacturing involved? Are components or products sold externally, transferred internally, or both? What strategic purposes are concerned: acquisition of a market foothold; protection of technology; preemption of competition; maintenance of a vertically integrated structure; protection or diversion of earnings generated elsewhere? These and similar probings help to identify the major purposes of the unit and the general results that are expected—increased market shares, competitive costs, a new product life cycle in a new environment, new export markets, outlets to provide economy-of-scale for the parent or sister units, tax shields (U.S. and/or foreign), profits, and the like.

Role definition relates the determined objectives with the functions that are controllable at the unit level by its manager. If manufacturing or assembly is involved, controllable costs are of initial importance, regardless of where or by whom the products are to be marketed. Appropriate cost centers should be designated. For marketing functions, segments that control expenses and/or revenues should be identified. Few profit centers will tend to be found, for, to be valid, each must represent a separate business in miniature, free of intracompany transfers and free to control all aspects of operations other than capital sources and expenditures. Investment centers must evidence all the freedoms mentioned as well as control over investment decisions. In most instances, only the corporate headquarters will qualify as a legitimate investment center. Analyses such as those described should satisfy all but the most stubborn that the myriad decisions orchestrated by corporate headquarters invalidate most profit and ROI applications.

The next two steps—selection of criteria and standards—are relatively straightforward once objectives and roles have been established. Standard costs (based upon reasonably attainable standards) and budgets will be most appropriate for manufacturing operations. Budgets will also be logical methods for most expense and revenue centers.

In fact, budgets will be recognized as the most flexible of all criteria and standards. They can be tailored to recognize all the peculiar factors of the various environments—legal, political, and socioeconomic (and these are vital elements in the conduct of most international operations). Budgets can project all sorts of measures—financial, nonfinancial, and qualitative—and, once approved, also can serve as tailored standards. Budgets are not perfect standards, since they reflect the optimism and pessimism of the humans preparing them. Still, inflated or deflated budgets (those that are not realistically based upon all known circumstances) can and should be adjusted by headquarters to conform with reasonable expectations. In other words, submitted budgets must be justified, and, once approved (as submitted or revised), they should represent acceptable levels of performance. Since budgets are projections, revisions must be required whenever circumstances upon which the budgets are based change over time. Budgeting systems are often maligned, but experience has proved that in virtually all such cases the budgeting process was not taken seriously by top management. Since the cornerstone of realistic performance evaluations rests upon valid objectives, management of, by, and for these objectives becomes essential. Budgets are the key instruments.

Where units produce for other units as well as marketing for their own accounts, temptations to attach arbitrary profits to the intracompany transfers must be resisted. The contributions of these internal transfers can be recognized and validated by various means—comparative costs, volumes, service, quality, availability, and many similar yardsticks. Profit should be defined as occurring only as a result of a bona fide sale to an unrelated entity. This would put to rest the fable of most profit and investment centers.

The foregoing remarks may be accepted insofar as transfers among totally owned subsidiaries are concerned. What of those units that have minority interests owned by outsiders? Can "profits" be eliminated in those situations? The answer is no insofar as conventional financial accounting is concerned, but yes where managerial reporting applies—and only the latter is relevant when performance evaluations of managers are made. So long as majority control exists, dual transfer prices should be prescribed (cost-based for internal uses, market-based or cost-plus for financial purposes), since reasonable profits will be expected by minority interests—and their governments—on all transactions, internal and external.

One additional factor must be addressed in relation to criteria and standards—foreign currencies. Should the financial measures of budgeted and actual performance be made in the local (foreign) currencies or in U.S. dollars? The unequivocal answer is "It all depends!" In practice, it is practical for evaluations of investments in an initial foreign unit, as well as those in short-term ventures intended to generate one-way flows of profits to the U.S. parent, to be couched in terms of dollars. There is no valid, overriding reason to evaluate any other foreign units in dollars. (Translations of foreign-currency statements are still required for financial reporting, but these translated data need not and should not be used to assess the merits of foreign operations that are going concerns.)

Translated dollars have even less validity in the evaluations of foreign managers. As discussed in chapters 7 and 8, currencies fluctuate for numerous reasons beyond the control of foreign managers. As one currency appreciates or depreciates today, it does so in relationship to many others, not just one or two. For most multinationals, translating operating results of a global network of interdependent divisions into dollars can easily misrepresent economic realities. For example, the local currency of subsidiary A may depreciate and reflect unfavorably in translated statements. Yet that very event may make the outputs of subsidiary A more competitive when marketed by sister units B and C, thereby favorably affecting their volumes and profits. In this scenario, the manager of A not only would be penalized, he would receive no credit for the added profits accruing to B and C. In other cases, a local manager may undertake ventures that produce significant profits in his local currency but involve comparatively small translation losses. The profits are commingled with all other profits; the increase in translation losses is segregated for all to see. As money prices change, performance evaluations of units and managers in translated dollars cannot be justified.

Evaluations in local currencies are also deceptive (since the results are the products of physical units multiplied by "rubber units" of money), but to a lesser degree. The problem here is to segregate the uncontrollable effects (changes in money prices) from the controllable effects (efficiency and effectiveness). Valid assessments will most often consist of comparisons between such budgeted and actual nonfinancial criteria as volumes of goods and services produced and exchanged; qualities of the outputs; reliability of shipments; or use and efficiency of plant. Also, as money prices change, evaluators will be forced to introduce a great deal more subjectivity into their proceedings. While this is generally disliked by those who evaluate, it seems desirable to interject judgments before operating statements are translated—when attention can be focused upon the factors that may have caused the currency fluctuations. Applying after-the-fact mental adjustments to translated dollar figures only obscures the important factors and their possible impacts upon the future.

The timing of performance evaluations of established foreign operations generally follows the domestic pattern of informal monthly or quarterly assessments, with a more comprehensive, formal annual appraisal. The improvements in communication technologies have reduced the lag-time of overseas reportings and have enabled concurrent evaluations of foreign and domestic operations.

Informal, short-term reviews normally involve the exchange of strategic information and the appraisal of changes within the local environments, and provide opportunities to update budgeted projections, if necessary.

Annual evaluations should consist of an intensive analysis of the contributions of the units (both past and future) and the abilities of the local managers. As has been discussed, the two are separate actions. The first attempts to assess the past and potential worth of each foreign unit as a strategic part of the global enterprise. This judgment concerns past decisions made by the corporate headquarters, evaluated by subsequent events and colored by future expectations. Subjectivity cannot be avoided. The second purpose, evaluation of local managers, is appropriate each year, if for no other reason than to reinforce the fact that each manager has a strategic role to play. All sorts of valid measures have been presented that emphasize controllable operating criteria. Changes in money prices will invalidate many of the traditional financial measures applied. Suggestions that the annual period of evaluation be extended[17] would decrease the effects of short-term currency fluctuations. However, in the process, emphasis would tend to be placed upon the ex-post results of a currency cycle on the operations of a subsidiary rather than upon the ongoing management actions that could be taken to benefit the total enterprise (such as reserve production from an Italian plant for shipment to Britain if the lira retained the most favorable relationship with the pound sterling).

For operations in the developing stages, annual evaluations will have less meaning and merely will represent interim reports of progress toward anticipated objectives.

Communication of performance evaluations must be a two-way process. Whether the process occurs at the corporate headquarters or on site at the foreign subsidiary is immaterial; each approach has its peculiar benefits. Since the process is a dialogue, experience has proved that much can be gained by each party if the site is alternated from time to time. The cost in management time is generally more than offset by firsthand exposures to people, places, and conditions that cannot be captured by written narratives or figures. This annual association is also an excellent opportunity for headquarters executives to inform local managers of the so-called big picture. Experience has also proved that this added effort helps the local manager understand the strategic relationship of his unit—that it functions as part of a global system and that it is not out there all alone.

Summary

Perhaps evaluation of the performance or worth of a foreign subsidiary may best be summarized by use of an analogy. Suppose that the worth of a single diamond in a multistone dinner ring were to be assessed. If the diamond were standing alone and unmounted, various criteria could be applied: size, shape, weight, color, brilliance, and the like. Based upon these criteria, the marketplace would establish a value for the stone. With the stone placed in a setting, however, the aforementioned criteria lose much of their significance and, at best, become relative measures. A stone possessing all the most desirable features can look out of place among others with different hues and features. On the other hand, a stone with an impurity giving it a particular color is generally the most desirable in a setting with similar stones. The structure of the mounting can detract from as well as enhance the appearance of the several stones. Finally, the placement and mounting skills of the artisan will affect the visibility and brilliance of the particular stones as well. To be sure, the marketplace will attach a value to the ring as a whole, but a wide variety of determinants will be involved—objective, subjective, past, present, and future.

No analogy is necessary where manager evaluation is concerned. Surrogate measures are required, since the worth of the human organism, per se, is not in question. Contributions of individuals represent composite impressions of a mélange of circumstances, stimuli, and actions. The task of evaluation involves determining whether credit or admonishment appears due. Until someone invents a valid single measure to accomplish the task, various yardsticks will have to be used, depending on the objectives, roles, and activities within the purview of the managers. Budgets, standard costs, and responsibility reports are financial measures that can be tailored to fit most circumstances. Nonfinancial measures become increasingly important as monies lose their abilities to serve as common denominators, alone or in translation.

Comprehensive financial measures, such as profit and return on investment, are constructed upon foundations containing flawed assumptions. They should be used with caution even in the best of circumstances and should only serve as starting points for other more valid examinations. They have no validity, standing alone, as evaluations of strategic segments or their managers.

Notes

1. Richard F. Vancil, "What Kind of Management Control Do You Need?", *Harvard Business Review*, March-April 1973, p. 76.

2. The use of profit-center concepts is attributed to General Motors Corporation. See Alfred D. Chandler, Jr., *Strategy and Structure* (Cambridge, Mass.: MIT Press, 1962).

3. For a concise description of direct costing and contribution approaches to income measurement, see Ray H. Garrison, *Managerial Accounting: Concepts for Planning, Control, Decision Making* (Dallas: Business Publications, Inc., 1976), pp. 216-228.

4. Billy E. Goetz, "Transfer Prices: An Exercise in Relevancy and Goal Congruence," *The Accounting Review*, July 1967, p. 437.

5. Vancil, "What Kind of Management Control," p. 82.

6. John Dearden, Professor at Harvard Business School, dissected the ROI concept and its problems in the following series of articles appearing in the *Harvard Business Review* (references denote starting pages and problem areas examined): "Problem in Decentralized Profit Responsibility," May-June 1960, p. 79 (investment in fixed assets); "Problem in Decentralized Financial Control," May-June 1961, p. 72 (current asset base); "Limits on Decentralized Profit Responsibility," July-August 1962, p. 81 (differing profit goals); "Mirage of Profit Decentralization," November-December 1962, p. 140 (responsibility levels); "New System for Divisional Control" (with Bruce D. Henderson), September-October 1966, p. 144 (transfer prices); "Appraising Profit Center Managers," May-June 1968, p. 80 (performance evaluations); and "The Case Against ROI Control," May-June 1969, p. 124 (summary of problem areas).

7. David Zenoff, "Profitable, Fast Growing, but Still the Stepchild," *Columbia Journal of World Business*, July-August 1967, pp. 51-56.

8. John J. Mauriel, "Evaluation and Control of Overseas Operations," *Management Accounting*, May 1969, pp. 35-39, 52.

9. "Report of the Committee on International Accounting," *The Accounting Review, Supplement to Volume 48*, 1973, pp. 120-167.

10. Ibid., p. 158.

11. Ibid., p. 159.

12. "Report of the Committee on International Accounting," *The Accounting Review, Supplement to Volume 49*, 1974, pp. 250-269.

13. Ibid., p. 253.

14. Sidney M. Robbins and Robert B. Stobaugh, "The Bent Measuring Stick for Foreign Subsidiaries," *Harvard Business Review*, September-October 1973, pp. 80-88.

15. Ibid., p. 82.

16. Ibid., p. 88.

17. Ibid., pp. 85-86.

11 Information Systems

Information refers to perceptions, facts, and data that increase knowledge and understanding. A system is usually defined as a collection of procedures designed to serve a particular purpose. Within the business context, an information system should furnish the right information, to the right people, at the right time. A good information system will do this at the lowest possible cost.

Computers have erroneously been equated with information systems. However, the electronic computer is no more an information system than was the quill, pen, typewriter, abacus, adding machine, or mechanical calculator that preceded it. All are data-processing tools. Human beings and their ability to harness the attributes of these tools to serve their needs are the requisites of a system.

The electronic computer is a powerful instrument. Without it there would be few multinational enterprises today. Those that would exist probably would be smaller in scope and certainly would be much less efficient. Stated another way, the advent of the computer made the multinational enterprise manageable and, therefore, possible.

Evolution of Multinational Information Systems

The information systems of multinational enterprises evolved much the same as did the firms themselves. As mentioned in chapter 1, the early overseas ventures of U.S. firms consisted of branch operations, which usually were marketing arms. The information needs of the branches (and the home offices) were minimal. Conformance with legal and other reporting requirements imposed upon branch operations by host governments were new factors that had to be coped with, but these were rarely significant. The accounting and reporting systems used by these overseas branch activities were basically the same as those employed by branches in Chicago or New Orleans.

Often the only assets at risk overseas were imprest working funds to defray routine local costs. Such working funds were operated as large petty-cash funds. A fixed amount was assigned to the branch for deposit in a local bank. An accounting was made of the total fund each time a replenishment was requested from the home office, usually monthly or quarterly.

As international business changed from branch operations to on-site assembly and manufacturing subsidiaries, the demands for information mushroomed.

In most cases, the parent attempted to export and implant its domestic information and control systems. These methods were usually not compatible with the accounting, reporting, and tax requirements imposed by the host countries in which the subsidiaries were domiciled. Adaptations were introduced and multiple records systems were employed where necessary, but, as a whole, the information system was usually "characterized as a bastardized version of its domestic counterpart."[1]

The subsequent transformation of a series of disjointed overseas subsidiaries into an integrated, strategic, multinational network of operations increased and transformed the needs for information. Conventional financial reporting mechanisms either were ill suited for strategic decisions or were simply not timely enough to coordinate operations. Further improvisations were made to existing systems. Reports increased in numbers but not necessarily in usefulness. Local managements often spent more time managing information systems than they did managing their businesses.

The redundancy found in many present-day multinational information systems reflects their evolutionary development by the piecemeal approach.

If the objectives of multinational enterprise networks differ substantially from those of their domestic counterparts—and the evidence indicates that this is true—then the need for different information networks is also indicated. In some cases a fresh start using a systems approach[2] will be troublesome but necessary.

Types of Information Systems

At the risk of compounding the cardinal fallacy of looking at an information system as a collection of separate systems, the following interrelated segments are discussed to establish the necessary context.

Accounting Information Systems (AIS)

Accounting, as the language of business, represented *the* business information system for centuries. Accounting data still represent the core of the information system used by business today.

Accounting contains the basic elements required of any information system: recording, classifying, summarizing, and reporting. Primarily by means of self-regulation, the accounting profession developed standards and procedures that, over time, provided a reasonable degree of reliability, timeliness, clarity, and uniformity to accounting reports. This self-regulation also enabled the profession to adapt to the evolving needs of business and to keep the costs of accounting services within reasonable limits.

In the author's opinion, accountancy benefited most from the fact that financial-accounting systems were designed from the top down.[3] That is, a process similar to the following was employed, although often not consciously:

1. Purposes or objectives were defined (internal controls and outputs in the forms of statements and reports).
2. Component parts and functions were determined (ledgers, journals, and accounts).
3. Procedures or duties were described (recording, classifying, summarizing, reporting, and divisions of duties).
4. Information and processing needs were established (inputs of data, financial and otherwise, and their manipulation).

This approach produced a high degree of integration. It can also be said that much of the logical flow or coordination evidenced in financial-accounting systems resulted from the standards and guidelines promulgated by the profession and by the SEC.

Until the 1960s, the business information system was effectively the domain of the accountant. Data were processed manually (pen and ink), mechanically (by bookkeeping and punched-card machines), and, within the largest firms, electronically (by early versions of business computers). In most colleges and universities, a course entitled "Accounting Systems" represented the required exposure to information systems in accounting curricula. The typical course was a senior-level, capstone requirement for accounting majors and involved the design or revision of an entire accounting information system.

Financial Information System (FIS)

Most of the earliest electronic computers were placed in accounting departments under the purview of the controller. The machines were considered to be best suited for the routine processing of the mountains of mundane yet essential data related to payrolls, inventories, receivables, payables, and the like. Even the earliest versions of electronic computers were underutilized, or even misused, by accounting departments. The greatest power of the computer is its ability to make iterative (repetitive) calculations rapidly. However, the first accounting applications primarily used the computer system as a giant (and expensive) sorter and printer; its computational abilities were not taxed at all. Even today, the major business uses of the computer involve data storage, retrieval, and updating.

Many of the special needs of the treasurer were subsequently incorporated into the conventional accounting system, and this new product became known as the financial information system.

Management Information System (MIS)

New generations of computers, including the minicomputer, enabled more data to be processed faster and at less cost. The methods by which man communicated with the computer—programs or software—multiplied, were simplified, and, for some functions, were standardized or packaged. Methods by which computers could communicate with computers were also developed.

The technological advances in the electronics and communications industries produced what has been called an information explosion and significant changes in the business information system.

Probably as much out of necessity as by design, the growth of most large, domestic corporations came about by decentralization. Distances, time frames, communications, and sheer volumes of data required that some decisions had to be delegated to subunits. The computer and communication technologies afforded complex organizations a wider range of choice. Certain operating decisions could be pushed even farther down the organizational structure and could be supported by better information at all levels. Strategic decisions and those that had a potentially significant impact on the organization as a whole could still be reserved for the central headquarters. Thus, the computer changed the emphasis on decentralization to one permitting centralized control of important decisions.

Managerial accounting, formerly constrained by the inability to apply conceptual developments, became a practical and influential force in the conduct of business affairs. Concepts of responsibility accounting were able to be applied to the smallest as well as the largest segments of an organization. Budgeting and standard-cost systems were made easier to prepare and update as conditions warranted; consequently, their inherent values as performance evaluators and guides for decision making were not only realized but enhanced.

The mathematical manipulations of operations researchers (often incorrectly referred to as management scientists) were also made practicable by the computer. Models, simulations, and linear-programming applications not only became operable techniques but benefited from the prestige and aura of exactness associated with applied mathematics. Scientific management soon became the catchword within and among business schools.

Some business schools reinstated a required course in "production." Although the production function has always been a required exposure in the curricula of accredited schools, most had long since deleted the course and covered the business-oriented content routinely in other courses, such as cost or managerial accounting, statistics or operations research, and, to a lesser extent, in economics offerings. There was little question that production was an essential business function. However, in the industrial world, the production activities are usually managed by engineers. How much immersion into the mechanistic aspects should be required of business students when only general concepts would be retained and used?

Before long, the quantitative and behavioral specialists in management argued between themselves whether the goal should be to optimize (choose the best solution) or to satisfice (select a satisfactory solution). The pressures from various schools of management led to what one noted author called "the management theory jungle."[4] The surge of developments within management, the interest of managerial accountants, and the power of the computer led to a new concept called the management information system.

The advent of the computer also created an immediate need for the skilled technicians who make it work: electronics technicians, programmers, operators, and systems analysts. The former course in accounting systems was replaced by one in computer systems in many schools of business. Accountants tried to absorb the conventional body of knowledge required by their profession as well as to become computer experts. Most failed, either because there was too much to absorb, or because accountants and computer experts require different natures and breadth, or both.

Computer experts didn't fare much better in attempting to master the entry requirements of accountancy. In public accountancy, rewards are most lucrative at the partner level. Only CPAs are eligible to become partners according to most state laws. The literature recurringly has cited complaints that the progression of computer experts was limited to the principal level (something less than that of a partner) because of their inability (for whatever reasons) to pass the entrance requirements of the profession. Since CPA firms need computer experts, and since there are few CPA-computer experts, the laws will be bent before long.

Total Information System (TIS)

The computer expert is generally credited with suggesting the development of the total information system. This contrivance would encompass all the information management could ask for—both internal and external—and would be totally integrated; that is, information would be input only once and would be processed, stored, and recalled as necessary. Some firms profess to have total information systems. However, naming a system is one thing; what it really is can be quite another. Every system is necessarily limited, since it is, by nature, only a part of a larger universe.

Systems as Ways of Thinking

Four "ways of thinking" were developed by Churchman.[5] These are characterized by:

1. *The efficiency experts*—a system should identify inefficiencies and eliminate them.

2. *The scientists*—mathematicians, modelers, and some behaviorists who sub-scribe to the objective treatment of all systems as if they were branches of physics.
3. *The humanists*—in systems composed of people, emphasis must be placed upon human values; systems should not impose upon or intervene in the free expression of these values.
4. *The antiplanners*—a system is not an elaborate scheme that can be planned or modeled; the experience gained by living within the system is the essential key to business management.

Another way of placing systems into context is depicted in figure 11-1. The diagram illustrates the scope of the various segments of the business information

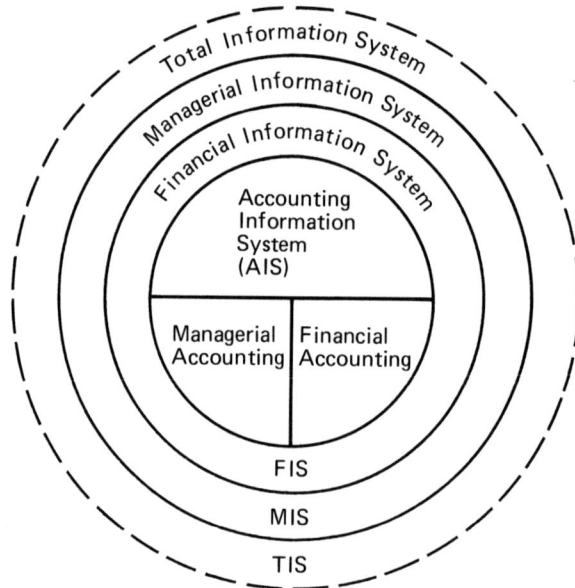

Notes:
(1) The total information system (TIS) is circumscribed by a broken line to represent the infinite nature of the environmental data involved.
(2) The MIS includes all essential internal data plus some information regarding the external environment; for example, industry, competitor, and GNP data, as well as projections.
(3) The FIS represents the conventional accounting information system augmented by internal and external data peculiar to the financial-management function of the treasurer.

Figure 11-1. The Scope of Information Systems.

system. In practice, the lines of separation become blurred by the overlappings that naturally occur. The total information system is depicted as existing in concept only. In most of the business systems in operation today, many of the procedures and data banks comprising the accounting system also serve as the core around which other systems are constructed.

Several cogent generalizations can be made regarding the nature, structure, and use of a business information system:

1. It is a man-machine system: the machine processes data and furnishes reports; man makes the decisions.
2. Data in reports becomes more concentrated in progression up the managerial hierarchy.
3. The necessary integration can best be obtained by design from the top down; the bottom-up approach tends toward the loose construction of an inverted pyramid, which often topples of its own weight.
4. Computers and operations-research methods are well suited for applications dealing with functions that can be objectively defined; that is, operational planning, controlling, and decision making. Machines and mechanistic approaches are ill suited for tactical and strategic planning and the related decision making.[6]

Information systems are, much like beauty, dependent upon the eye of the beholder. There are many "ways of thinking," each with its peculiar advantages and limitations. Regardless of the opinions of the author and other bystanders, the ultimate measure of the worth of a given system will depend entirely upon the user's perceived worth of the information.

Coordination Needs of Multinationals

Unlike the several possible objectives of domestic information systems, the purpose of information for multinational enterprises points to a single need—coordination.

As discussed earlier, decentralization is the antithesis of the multinational enterprise. It cannot buy, produce, assemble, market, and finance to best advantage if its segments are free to act as each believes best. The role of each segment must be coordinated. Thus, coordination is the management function of multinational enterprise and is dependent upon an efficient information system.

Coordination by MNE headquarters consists of three parts: policy making, planning, and adapting. The first part provides guidelines and establishes the limits within which local managers may function. The second involves the examination of conditions (internal and external) within the global environment upon which operating strategies are to be based. The third function includes various catalytic actions designed to activate, monitor, react, and adapt.

Although the headquarters of the MNE normally serves as the coordinator, this does not mean that the subunits play passive roles. On the contrary, if adequate information is to be available upon which the headquarters can base decisions, much of the information must be supplied by the subunits, and in a timely fashion. Also, where significant lateral interdependencies exist among subunits, each will be expected to furnish information to the sister units with which it cooperates.

While there are exceptions to most generalizations, the information process-ing performed by the headquarters can be characterized as the manipulation of a large volume of similar, but not necessarily identical, information from hundreds of sources and, due to communication lag-times, almost on a constant basis. Subunits are usually less affected by volume, but they must be extremely sensitive to changes in external environments and responsive in time.

External Financial Reporting

Of the various components of information and reporting systems used by MNEs, those supporting external financial reporting are usually the most structured, the best defined, and the least appreciated. Differences between the financial-reporting requirements of parent and host countries are usually (and eventually) overcome by the maintenance of multiple sets of records: the official set required by the host country, the set specified by the headquarters, and, where applicable, a third set maintained in accordance with local tax regulations. The time frames of external reportings normally create periodic, rather than continuous, pressures (although there is little difference for MNEs that perform complete monthly consolidations).

The many different external reporting requirements present serious prob-lems to outside users who must search out and adjust for the pitfalls contained in financial reports. To the MNE, external financial reportings are (and have been) generally viewed as bothersome nuisances—merely compliance reports having little, if any, value to the firm. As a result, managements usually regard external-reporting procedures as externally imposed appendages to their internal systems networks.

Probably the greatest headache surrounds the reporting of interests in firms that are not legally (or effectively) controlled. Information must be requested rather than demanded. Most foreigners, not accustomed to the disclosure requirements imposed upon U.S. firms, generally believe that we create "much ado about nothing," and consequently, they are seldom in any hurry to cooperate.

Reporting Internal Operations

The internal reporting of routine operating data is complicated by problems of volume, time, environment, and privacy.

The effects of volume can be tempered by computerization, data compression, standardized format, and coding. (The last action, although it increases the possibility of error, is extremely important to protect the confidentiality of information that must be transmitted over public channels.)

Time frames have been reduced and privacy increased by the use of coded Telex transmissions and leased lines linking computers. Mails are too slow for most communications, are subject to loss, and are accessible to unauthorized individuals, including competitors. The audit trail (hard copies of inputs) is usually retained by the reporting locations.

Environmental effects upon internal communications concern problems of language, culture, control, and compatibility of systems. Language problems can be lessened by the use of standardized reporting formats (supported by preparation instructions in the local and parent-country languages). Where the parent's language is not commonly used, language programs (motivated by wage increases for levels of proficiency attained) are wise investments, but they require time. Cultural differences often present humorous, yet difficult, problems. Many indigenous staff personnel wonder why Americans are always in such a hurry. Experience has proved that "late" is a single time dimension to many local employees; that is, if a report was due yesterday, it is already late and there is no need to hurry, for whether the work is completed tomorrow or next week, it will still be late. As with external reporting, if an MNE does not effectively control a subsidiary, then management information must be obtained by negotiation rather than by fiat. Last, but not least, the compatibility of parent and subsidiary information systems can vary widely. It may be necessary to process interim (other than annual) reportings of some units out of cycle with the others. In many cases, peculiarities in local operating conditions are such that a fourth set of records is required for local decision making.

Internal reporting also includes feedback to the subunits and the lateral flow of information among them. These information flows have been the least responsive to need. Subunits lack the "big picture" available to the headquarters. Consequently, local decisions must be based upon policy guidelines and the most recent plans approved by the parent. As events change the validity of available guidelines, local managers are often forced to take no action (and pass up attractive opportunities) or to act in ignorance.

Strategic Reporting

Strategic reportings of changes in the local external environments, either actual or anticipated, are often of greatest value to the parent. These reports also present the most difficulty. Some economic data can be structured; that is, specific or general responses can be required concerning factors such as price levels, balance-of-payments data, interest rates, hedging costs, exchange controls, competitor information, and the like. Information pertaining to the political and social realms depends more upon the astuteness of local management than upon the structure of reports. Recognition of events affecting local laws, regulations, government policies, expropriations, nationalizations, labor/union relations, and consumer tastes depends upon the abilities of local management to sense change. Also, the occurrence of such events will not usually coincide with the timing of internal reportings and should be reported out-of-cycle (flash reports).

Cautions, Trends, and Innovations

Neither the foregoing sections nor the following attempt to address the mechanics of information systems; these are the domain of technicians. Managers must specify what information they want as well as how and when they want it.

Cautions

Total uniformity among the information segments of a multinational enterprise is neither practicable nor desirable. Rather, the systems should be harmonized so that they can work in unison toward filling the information needs of management. Coordination of the global operations of the firm is the central objective of the information system.

Managers are also well advised to remember the caution that information is a self-generating organism that reproduces without urging.[7] It can easily engulf those who equate quality with the quantity of information. All too often, new hardware only speeds up the replication of deficiencies inherent in existing systems.

In the design of new systems or the revision of present ones, modelings and similar quantitative techniques should be relegated to problems that are structured and readily quantifiable. Most often, such problems will lie within operational and control areas. Rarely are such methods appropriate for strategic and other decisions at executive levels.

Since the ultimate value of information is its worth to the user, selectivity by users is essential. Managements, not computer technicians, must determine the outputs desired from information systems. Unless managements specify their information needs precisely, the information or systems analyst will provide what he believes management wants. The two are rarely the same. (The author has a particular aversion to codings in reports. Valuable executive time can be wasted in unnecessary decodings, whereas, if technicians are properly instructed, the computer can print the information in English faster than most individuals can read.)

It would be nice to develop new global information systems by using the "fresh-start" approach. Ongoing operations usually preclude this option. Instead, the best that can be expected in the foreseeable future is revision and/or refinement of selected portions of the information system. Compatibility of the several systems components will present a significant but not insurmountable problem. A second concern will relate to the trade-off of additional present costs of redesign versus the future benefits of more responsive information.

Trends

Fortunately, trends reflect increasing use of the computer in areas in which it has the greatest potential—improving controls. Many large multinationals have reportedly used the computer and improved communications technologies to enhance the control and use of cash. In cooperation with commercial banks, multinational enterprises have established electronic funds transfer systems, which have, in part, enabled the firms to accumulate vast hordes of cash and marketable securities at the close of 1977: IBM, over $5 billion; Exxon, over $4 billion; Ford and General Motors, over $3 billion; and 16 others from $600 million to almost $2 billion.[8]

Concern over the effects of currency-translation gains and losses (occasioned by *FASB-8*) may well have been one reason for MNEs to implement computerized cash-monitoring systems, either internally or by means of purchased services from the commercial banks. A second reason—possibly more plausible—concerns the general uncertainties related with international investments. Most corporations can earn much better returns from operations than from short-term investments. Cash build-ups often reflect wait-and-see attitudes. Such conditions do not bode well for international expansion and economic growth in the short run.

A second trend—long overdue—reflects executive realization that the computer is not a system but a tool, albeit a powerful one. Smarting from the monies wasted on false starts, many large firms now refuse to design systems or revisions without the personal participation of the managers concerned. The projections of computerized models are less frequently being regarded as facts rather than as the products of assumptions about tomorrow. Last, but not least, data-processing centers are being informed that the multinational enterprise exists to serve the needs of its markets, not the whims of systems designers.[9]

Innovations

Improvements in information systems will be in the realm of communication, both internal and external.

Internally, communication of man with the computer will have to be improved before it will be useful to and therefore appreciated by top executives.

When this will happen is uncertain, but it will come to pass. Unfortunately, the author is much less optimistic concerning improvements in the internal communications of man with man (or persons with persons). The aspiring young executive with the ability to consolidate meaningfully a sheaf of reports and supply a concise narrative explanation on a single page has his or her future assured.

Externally, satellite systems that enable instantaneous two-way communications will simplify multinational coordination in the immediate future. Experimental systems using NASA's communications technology satellite reportedly enable long-distance participants to communicate as easily as if they were sitting at the same table. In addition to two-way visual and audio contact, users can display and exchange hard copies of all types of reports and similar documents.[10]

Such systems not only will revolutionize information systems but may alter travel practices and organization structures, and very possibly may enable the multinational enterprise (or the transnational network foreseen by Perlmutter) to achieve its full potential as a coordinator of global resources to the benefit of an interdependent world community and itself.

Notes

1. "Report of the Committee on International Accounting," *The Accounting Review, Supplement to Volume 48*, 1973, p. 159.

2. C. West Churchman, *The Systems Approach* (New York: Dell Publishing Co., Inc., 1968). Churchman describes the systems approach as "simply a way of thinking about these total systems and their components" (p. 11).

3. See Gordon B. Davis, *Management Information Systems: Conceptual Foundations, Structure, and Development* (New York: McGraw-Hill Book Company, 1974), pp. 403-409.

4. Harold Koontz, "The Management Theory Jungle," *Journal of the Academy of Management* 4, No. 3, December 1961, pp. 174-188.

5. Churchman, *The Systems Approach,* pp. 13-14.

6. This latter point has been thoroughly delineated by Robert N. Anthony, *Planning and Control Systems: A Framework for Analysis* (Boston: Harvard Business School Division of Research, 1965).

7. Churchman, *The Systems Approach*, pp. 127-128.

8. "Cash Management: The Art of Wringing More Profit From Corporate Funds," *Business Week*, March 13, 1976, p. 63.

9. "A Corporate Viewpoint," an interview with Walter Wriston, Chairman of Citicorp, by Randolph L. Denosowicz, in *The Columbia Journal of World Business*, Fall 1977, pp. 125-128.

10. William P. Moore, "Satellites May Revolutionize American Business Methods," *St. Louis Post-Dispatch*, January 10, 1978, p. 4D.

12 Consolidated Financial Reporting

Few subjects (other than possibly statistics) cause accounting students more anguish than their exposure to consolidated financial statements. Problems are long, complicated, and tedious, with working papers to match. Yet the two or three entities and locations involved in most classroom problems are a far cry from the hundred or more firms and scores of countries making up today's multinational networks. Computers have helped in the collection and initial processing of the data, but the adjustments and eliminations are determined, for the most part, as they were in the classroom—manually, by human data processors.

Consolidated financial statements (hereinafter referred to as consolidations) are as simple or as complex as the entities being consolidated. That rather bland cliché points out two facts that are not so readily apparent. First, consolidations have completed their full circle of usefulness insofar as the financial reporting of large, multinational enterprises is concerned. The complexities inherent in the entities themselves permit consolidations to conceal more than they reveal. Second, the language of business is an adaptive art. When methods outlive their usefulness in certain contexts, the accounting profession is stimulated (from within and without) to develop reasonable alternatives.

This chapter will review the state of the art of consolidated reporting. The chapter that follows will examine segmented reporting, a supplementary (or complementary?) form of disclosure.

Background

In the United States, the 1950s could be described as the era of combinations; the 1960s, the rise of conglomerates; the 1970s, the age of multinationals. While these statements—like those made by modelers—represent simplex views, they are representative of growth patterns that developed in response to conditions in the environments of the times.

Business combinations occur "when a corporation and one or more incorporated or unincorporated businesses are brought together into one accounting entity."[1] Combinations usually are classed as one of two types— mergers or consolidations. Both are legal definitions and depend upon the nature of the surviving entity. For example, in a merger of firms A and B, either A or B would continue to exist and would conduct the combined operations; the other would cease to exist as a legal entity. On the other hand, consolidation of firms A and B would result in the creation of a new legal entity, firm C, which would conduct the total operation; both A and B would cease to exist in law. The following diagram illustrates both processes:

Merger: $A + B \rightarrow$ either A or B as sole legal survivor.

Consolidation: $A + B \rightarrow$ creation of C as new legal survivor.

Legal aspects aside, the economic effects are similar in both forms—a larger economic entity, often with synergistic attributes, is created.

Growth in market shares and earnings has been the prime motivator. Growth by external combinations was usually much faster and more appealing than the process of expansion by internal means.

There were other reasons, of course. Horizontal combinations in the same industry often reduced competition. Vertical combinations helped assure steady flows of materials or component parts at favorable prices. Acquisitions of needed technologies, management skills, and economies of scale also were often cited. In some cases, income-tax advantages were obvious reasons as well. For example, a tax loss carry-forward—of little real value to a firm with poor aspects for future earnings—could be "cashed in" as the result of an appropriate combination with another firm that is producing significant earnings.

Combinations of firms within the same industry soon ran into headlong confrontation with the Justice Department's Antitrust Division and the Federal Trade Commission, who jointly enforced the Clayton Act, Section 7 of which states in part:

> ... no corporation engaged in commerce shall acquire, directly or indirectly, the whole or any part of the *stock* or other share capital [acquisitions] and no corporation subject to the jurisdiction of the Federal Trade Commission shall acquire the whole or any part of the *assets* of another corporation [combinations] engaged also in commerce, where in any line of commerce in any section of the country the effect of such acquisition may be substantially to lessen competition or to tend to create a monopoly. (Emphasis and inserts added.)

As a result, the 1960s witnessed a trend toward the conglomerate, or diversification by combinations of firms in unrelated areas of trade and industry. All of the benefits afforded by horizontal and vertical combinations applied, plus two more. Diversification hedged against the diminution of profits in a single industry. Also, while the Clayton Act still applied, violations were much more difficult for the government to identify and prove.

Combinations lost favor to parent-subsidiary associations, resulting from the acquisition by one firm (the parent) of a controlling interest in the voting stock of another (the subsidiary). (Although there are exceptions, the general rule presumes and defines control to vest in ownership of more than 50 percent of the voting stock of a corporation). No legal changes occurred either in ownership of assets or in the continued existence of either company. Nonetheless, acquisitions of control generally accomplished the same strategic and economic effects as combinations and often presented some additional advantages. Acquisition of a controlling interest required less investment than a total purchase. Also, in those cases in which the capital of a subsidiary included fixed-return securities (bonds or nonparticipating preferred shares), the parent could realize leverage in earnings. (Earnings leverage or gearing occurs whenever a firm can acquire capital at fixed rates lower than the rate of earnings generated by operations. The excess accrues to the common shareholders, thus increasing the earnings rate of their equity.) Finally, while acquisitions were regulated by the Clayton Act, open-market stock acquisitions were difficult to monitor, since all sorts of devious means (including straw parties and holding companies) could be improvised.

Growing numbers of divestiture and other antitrust actions motivated domestic corporations to look overseas for expansion. No other country regulates cartels, monopolies, or trusts to anywhere near the degree prevalent in the United States. Ironically, restraints imposed upon domestic growth mechanisms of U.S. corporations encouraged them to seek greener pastures overseas. The number of foreign subsidiaries of U.S. corporations nearly tripled from 1957 to 1972 (see chapter 1), and the multinational enterprise became a fixture in the jargon of business.

The foregoing describes the general pattern of corporate growth by external combinations and acquisitions. Not every multinational followed this exact pattern, of course. As a consequence, the procedures governing the preparation of consolidated statements retained their domestic orientations until the era of the multinational

Purpose of Consolidated Reporting

Consolidated statements provide an overall financial view of a group of companies without forcing statement users to piece together reports of the separate subsidiaries. Consequently, it is necessary to understand what constitutes (1) the group and (2) the user's needs.

In reference to the group, it is important to distinguish between a legal entity and the concept of an economic entity.

A consolidated group is composed of legal entities—the parent company and its subsidiaries. Each is a *separate legal entity* in that each has its own articles of incorporation in accordance with the laws of the state or foreign domicile in which it was chartered. From the legal standpoint, each entity is autonomous.

For consolidation purposes, these autonomous legal entities subsume the role of a *single economic entity*. The case of an automobile manufacturer that has vertically integrated may serve as an example. For a variety of reasons, the firm may form new subsidiaries or acquire existing companies with such product lines as metal, paint, glass, parts, and rubber. While each subunit is an individual entity, together they have a common business objective—automobile manufacturing. The entire corporate group is an economic entity. A shareholder in the parent firm has, at once, an interest in each and every subsidiary making up the group.

User needs served as guides to consolidation theory and practice. Since, as legal entities, the individual subsidiaries were required to issue financial reports in the locales in which they were domiciled, emphasis in consolidated reporting was placed upon the needs of investors and creditors of the parent company. The general guidelines for consolidations stipulated that the reports should be "meaningful" and "suitable" to user needs without "unnecessary detail."[2] These guidelines exerted a powerful influence upon consolidated reporting by multinational enterprises with U.S. parents.

Criteria for Consolidations

Consolidated reporting evolved much like all of accounting. The uncertainties existing following World Wars I and II were reflected in concerns over the legitimacy of consolidating foreign operations. "Especial care" was recommended to be used in including earnings and assets of foreign subsidiaries, and the significance of such inclusions was to be disclosed.[3] Given the extent of the uncertainties that existed, the very propriety of consolidating foreign operations was often considered suspect. Alternatives suggested in *Accounting Research Bulletin No. 43*, chapter 12, paragraph 9 were:

1. Consolidate domestic subsidiaries only and furnish a suitable summary of foreign operations as a supplement.
2. Furnish two consolidations: one for the total enterprise, one for domestic operations only.
3. Furnish a complete consolidation, supplemented by statements of the parent company only, summaries of domestic operations, and summaries of foreign operations.

By 1959, foreign operations had outlived suspicion, and consolidated statements were considered necessary contents of financial reportings. *Accounting Research Bulletin No. 51*, issued in August 1959, expressed in paragraph 1 the "presumption" that consolidated results were relevant and necessary for fair reporting.

Consequently, for U.S. parent firms, the need to report on the entire group became generally accepted. Attention was then directed to the clarification of criteria for consolidations. Reasonable uniformity was desired in determining which subsidiaries should or should not be consolidated and, if not consolidated, how they should be accounted for in the financial-statement package.

Effective control and commonality of operations were the fundamental criteria for consolidation presented in *ARB No. 51* and reinforced by the SEC in Rules 4-01 through 4-09 of *Regulation SX*. Effective control was usually defined as ownership of a majority voting interest, either directly or indirectly through connecting affiliates. Commonality of operations presented few difficulties, since the express purpose of this criterion was to assure that only similar accounts would be combined and not, for example, the dissimilar attributes of leasing, banking, and manufacturing operations. (Charges of off-balance-sheet financing are forcing reconsideration of the exclusion of financial subsidiaries.)

Ample room for judgment remained, however, since emphasis was placed upon meaningfulness to users. Separate statements or statements for selected groups of subsidiaries were recommended where they were considered to be more informative.

Generally, subsidiaries that were not consolidated were reported in the consolidated statements as a one-liner—"investments in unconsolidated subsidiaries." These investments were to be reflected using either the cost or equity method, according to *ARB No. 51*, paragraph 19, although the equity method was "preferred." Subsequently, *Accounting Principles Board Opinion No. 10* (1966) stipulated that the equity method should normally be applied.[4]

Under the cost method, the initial investment is recorded by the parent at cost; income is taken up by the parent only as dividends are received from the subsidiary.

The equity method also reflects the initial investment at cost but equates the investment with the percentage of equity acquired. Thereafter, the parent changes the investment account as its equity changes: increases for the parent's share of earnings reported; decreases for the parent's share of losses reported or dividends received. In short, the equity method reflects the parent's share of the book value of the subsidiary as it changes over time.

In 1971, *APB Opinion No. 18* not only reaffirmed preference of the equity method but provided working guidelines for its application. Basically, unless evidence existed to support the contrary, ownership ratios of voting stock determined how investments in affiliated companies were to be accounted for and reported:

1. More than 50 percent—the equity method will be applied, and consolidation is required (assuming homogeneity exists).
2. From 20 to 50 percent—the equity method will be applied since "significant influence" is presumed.

3. Less than 20 percent—the cost method may be used, since significant influence cannot be presumed to exist.
4. Joint ventures—the equity method should be used, since it best presents the "underlying nature" of the investments.[5]

All the pronouncements cited stipulated that the consolidation policy followed by the parent firm should be adequately disclosed.

The Mechanics of Consolidation

Once the consolidated group has been defined and identified, the method of consolidating financial statements is easy to describe but rather cumbersome and time-consuming to apply in practice. The actual process resembles a decision tree having many branches denoting possible situations, each with a multitude of twigs representing the alternative procedures permitted.

The following steps represent the process, highly simplified, that would be employed by the home office of a U.S. parent company with foreign and domestic subsidiaries having common business objectives:

1. Obtain the adjusted trial balances of the parent company and the subsidiaries. Data for the foreign subsidiaries would be stated in their national currencies. (Many multinationals have qualified personnel available overseas and provide them with guidance concerning translation procedures and rates. In such cases, trial balances received by the parent would be restated in accordance with U.S. accounting standards and in dollars. The parent would then be involved only in steps 5 through 8.)

2. Adjust (restate) the statements of foreign subsidiaries (those which reflect accounting practices of the country of domicile) to conform with generally accepted U.S. accounting standards. (Foreign statements would still be expressed in their national currencies.)

3. Translate all foreign currency amounts into U.S. dollars in accordance with *FASB-8* (see chapter 8 of this book).

4. Determine translation gains or losses as specified by *FASB-8*. Since no location is specified for the disclosures, the author recommends that the gain or loss be shown below operating income in the section listing financial income and expense. Also, it is good accounting (and common sense) to separate the aggregate gain or loss into its two components—conversion (actual) and translation (paper) gains and losses.

5. Eliminate the effects of all intercompany transactions (those within the walls of the economic entity); for example, intercompany receivables, payables, sales, purchases, and profits. (This step and the one to follow minimize double-counting as well as the recognition of income before it is earned.)

6. Eliminate the investments in subsidiaries recorded in the parent accounts

under the equity method and the corresponding portion of the shareholder equities of the subsidiaries. If the subsidiaries are not totally owned, the portions not owned are reflected as minority interests.

7. Consolidate the financial statements by grouping similar accounts of the individual entities together into general accounting classifications in the consolidated reports.

8. Prepare full and adequate disclosures of the consolidation policy employed and the supplementary information considered necessary in the circumstances.

As stated, this process has been highly simplified; the mechanical complexities involved in actual practice lie outside the scope of this work.[6]

Myths, Facts, and Abuses

There are a few myths and many facts connected with consolidations. Problems arise when the two become confused. Abuses result when fictions are knowingly represented as facts.

Myths

The illusion that is created of a legal entity existing in parallel with the economic entity is a myth.

The generalized "presumption that consolidated statements are more meaningful than separate statements"[7] and the assumption that usefulness and, therefore, user demand "has been amply demonstrated by the widespread acceptance ... "[8] are also myths. The facts that follow shortly demonstrate limited usefulness. The "acceptance" cited may more properly reflect the preferences of issuers rather than users.

Some asset classifications, primarily inventories, are fictions. Where operations are interdependent, very often the finished products of some units represent raw-material inputs for others.

Perhaps the most damaging of all fictions imposed upon consolidated statements was the treatment of gains and losses on currency translations by *FASB-8*. When paper gains and losses that may never occur are knowingly treated as realized economic gains and losses, then accountants have crossed the threshold between fact and fancy. Then again, the imposition of this latest myth may, of its own weight, dissipate much of the aura of acceptance ascribed to users and may lead to the more meaningful disclosures that are necessary.

Facts

Consolidated financial statements are *single-purpose* reports. Their sole purpose is to provide stockholders of the parent company with limited macroinformation on the entire economic entity, which would otherwise not be available. They serve no other express purpose. Charges that consolidated statements conceal more than they reveal (which is a fact) normally reflect frustrations resulting from attempts to use them for purposes that they were never intended to serve.

Investors, both parent and minority, are furnished little information of value. The process of aggregation commingles the operations of profitable and unprofitable units. Similarly, units that may be in financial straits are combined with those that are fiscally sound. The relative significance of interdependencies and internal volumes cannot be determined. Whether growth in activity of the economic unit resulted from internal accomplishment or by the acquisition of more subsidiaries is hidden.

Creditors of the parent and the subsidiaries may be misled and should look elsewhere for information. The aggregate pools of assets are not available proportionately to satisfy existing obligations. Furthermore, the parent often has no legal liability for the obligations of its subsidiaries. Lien disclosures and conformances with bond and/or loan agreements become difficult to decipher.

Analysts and other sophisticated users are frustrated rather than assisted by consolidated statements. The reported cash assets are a hodgepodge of currencies, some of which are extremely volatile, stated at the composite of their temporal values relative to the reporting currency. Computed ratios are meaningless, since they are affected by the elimination of interunit transactions and they are group averages, not necessarily representative of any or all of the individual parts. Other than for the most general of purposes (for example, to denote relative overall magnitude or size), consolidated statements are not intended to be used to compare multinational enterprises; the myriad differences in compositions of firms, industries, and locations render such comparisons meaningless.

The foregoing comments are not criticisms of consolidated statements; they are simply statements of fact. Consolidated financial statements represent the sole area within accounting for multinational enterprises in which it is more important to understand what is not purported to exist than what is.

Abuses

Over time, and for several probable reasons, the reporting practices of U.S. conglomerates and multinationals have changed from selective consolidation to consolidation of almost everything.[9] In the process, single-purpose consolidated statements have effectively supplanted the general-purpose statements relied upon by investors, creditors, and other users for information upon which to base decisions. Given the attributes and shortcomings of consolidated statements, actions knowingly taken (and condoned) that enabled consolidations to become the primary—and often only—financial statements represent abuses of the standard of fairness.

It is not reasonable to assume that managements are overly concerned about fairness in financial reporting. In fact, it could be said that the caution in *ARB No. 51* that the user "should not be burdened with unnecessary detail"[10] has been literally and liberally interpreted by managements.

Public accountants, on the other hand, purport to be concerned with fairness in financial reports; some derivative of fairness is required to appear in every written opinion issued on audited statements.

Granted, users and their respective needs have evolved over time as well. The small investor, for a variety of reasons, has disassociated himself from the stock markets. His void has been filled to a great extent by mutual funds and similar groups acting on behalf of themselves as well as the accounts of their new clients, the smaller investors. Such organizations are sophisticated analysts of information, and their needs are much more diverse.

Here again, managements would normally be reluctant to lower the corporate veil erected by consolidated reports. The disclosure of unprofitable subsidiaries or the presence of significant operations in unstable environments might result in the selling of large blocks of shares and thus have an adverse effect on market prices.

Accountants should have been aware not only of the evolving changes in user needs but also that consolidated reportings, standing alone, did not furnish suitable information.

The International Milieu

Circumstances in the international realm, initially at least, were in stark contrast to those described in the United States. Relatively few other countries stressed or required consolidated financial statements. In some environs, such as Germany, the relationships existing between and among companies were often considered to be confidences too sensitive to be divulged, much less detailed in reports.

Accountants International Study Group (AISG)

Among the earliest comparative studies of consolidation practices was that of the Accountants International Study Group, published in 1973.[11] More similarities than differences were found to exist in the practices employed within the United States, Canada, and the United Kingdom.

However, the study reported that firms in the United Kingdom were required to file much more information than their Canadian or American counterparts. In the United Kingdom, firms were required to file financial statements of all companies—subsidiaries, parent, and consolidated—with the Registrar of Companies. These statements were then available for the use of creditors and investors of both the parent and subsidiary units. Furthermore, annual reports in the United Kingdom included statements of the parent company in addition to the consolidated financial package.

Similar requirements did not exist in either the United States or Canada. In fact, not even the names of subsidiary firms were required to be reported, although the study indicated that such affiliations were common disclosures in practice. The study also mentioned that, in the United States, parent companies were required to submit to the SEC (in annual Form 10-K reports) a "list or diagram" of all subunits and the portions of voting equity owned by their parents.

The AISG study contained rather vague suggestions for improvement. Disclosures of the names and relationships of the companies were suggested where "appropriate." Also, where the investments in and operations of related companies were "material" (without definition), supplementary statements or schedules were recommended.[12]

The Organization for Economic Cooperation and Development (OECD)

In the wake of its examinations of multinational corporations, the OECD adopted its "Declaration on International Investment and Multinational Enterprises" on June 21, 1976. The set of guidelines contained in the Declaration represented a voluntary code of conduct for companies and countries.

Prominent among the seven areas addressed by the guidelines in the Declaration was that devoted to disclosure of information by multinational enterprises. Many of the 24 OECD member-nations had voiced concern over the lack of adequate information on the MNEs operating within their borders.

Government agencies have basically the same needs for financial information (and face the same frustrations) as do private investors. Governments, however, can demand; private users can only complain. The OECD members (except Turkey, which abstained) agreed that it would be expedient and fair as well if general needs were set forth in a guideline that would apply to all MNEs operating within OECD-member countries. This approach prevented each of the participating member-nations from having to deal with individual situations and companies on a piecemeal basis. It also avoided possible complaints from firms that certain countries required more information than others.

Governments, as statement users, need aggregate as well as segmented information. The guideline specified both forms. (Segmented or disaggregated information is addressed in chapter 13.)

The information to be disclosed for the enterprise as a whole included: the composition of the total entity; sales and operating results; significant new capital and research-and-development expenditures; a funds statement; and policies on transfer pricing and accounting–including consolidation practices. (The guideline on disclosure is presented in chapter 4, appendix 4A.)

Although voluntary by design, the guideline effectively supplemented the accounting and reporting requirements of OECD-member countries. Few additional requirements for consolidated information were placed upon parent firms headquartered in the United States and some of the other industrial nations. Other MNEs, however, faced disclosure of consolidated information for the first time. (Presumably, every MNE collected and summarized aggregate information for internal use but did not necessarily disclose the results unless required to do so.)

For United States-owned multinationals in particular, the bulk of the information (both consolidated and segmented) called for in the OECD guideline was being disclosed in annual reports to shareholders; in Form 10-K reports to the SEC; and/or to the federal government in compliance with Public Law 94-472 (International Investment Survey Act).

The only new aggregate disclosure required of United States-owned MNEs by the guideline concerned "the policies followed in respect of intra-group pricing."

The European Economic Community (EEC)

In April 1976, the Commission of the European Economic Community (Common Market) issued its proposed seventh directive regarding consolidated accounts. In typical European understatement, the proposed directive was described as "often controversial." When and if the directive is approved, significant changes will be required, not only in the national reporting practices of most EEC members, but in the existing company laws of the states as well.

Naturally, disagreements abound in both reporting and legal aspects. Some believe that the project to harmonize company laws in the EEC (the Wurdinger proposal) should be considered jointly with the directive on consolidated accounts, since the two necessarily overlap. Historically, the EEC has favored a piecemeal approach that addresses parts of a major dilemma at a time rather than attempting to obtain an improbable consensus on a complex problem. From a different viewpoint, passage of the seventh directive will make harmonization of company laws much easier.

Reporting controversies are significant but not crucial. Some disagree with the inclusion of all companies within the existing proposal; that is, not only the large, limited companies but the smaller, private, and family groups as well. It seems likely that only limited companies (corporations) will be subject to the final directive.

There is also some concern over the technical problems surrounding the proposed requirement that foreign (non-EEC parent) multinational enterprises prepare a consolidated report on EEC operations as well as one for the MNE as a whole. Since the existing directive stipulates that intracompany transactions would not be eliminated from the Community consolidation, the apparent aim is to disclose the overall volume of activity conducted in the Community by the MNE. Such information could best be disclosed by supplemental reports; although they would not be integrated with the consolidated statements for the total entity, neither would the Community consolidation. Few real technical difficulties and little cost would surround the mere line-by-line combination of the unadjusted statements of EEC subsidiaries (although theorists would surely cringe). In this issue, the pragmatists should prevail, since the resulting information is considered useful and necessary notwithstanding the theoretical oversights.

One reporting issue is at once commingled with legal overtones. Vertically integrated firms are required by the directive to prepare and submit separate multilevel consolidated reports for each subgroup (units within a single EEC nation). Due to the differences in the company laws of the EEC nations, subgroups tend to exist simply because they represent the most convenient manner to organize and operate a vertically integrated enterprise in Europe. Therefore, if information regarding the total operations of an MNE within a given EEC country is the objective, it could be satisfied by requiring supplemental data to be segmented by geographic area. Such a requirement would also be compatible with Item ii of the OECD guideline (presented in chapter 4, appendix 4A).

The remaining issue concerns the law; it is an excellent example of what Britishers call a "sticky wicket." Should the enterprise be defined as the legal or the economic entity? Europeans are familiar with, and tend to feel more comfortable with, the legal concept of the firm. As mentioned previously, when company laws within the EEC are harmonized, the diminution of legal differences would tend to make the acceptance of the concept of the economic entity somewhat more palatable. The EEC Council of Ministers approved the fourth directive regarding annual accounts of limited companies on June 27, 1978. The provisions will likely apply to statements for fiscal years ending in 1982.

In the author's opinion, given the diverse natures of the EEC partners—in cultures, outlooks, languages, customs, and laws—the EEC has tackled and resolved issues that would have confounded unions of peoples having much more commonality of background and purpose. There is little reason to doubt eventual acceptance of the seventh directive.

In fact, to venture a bit further out on the same limb, the extent of future international harmonization of accounting and reporting standards will depend more upon the ability of the EEC partners to create agreement out of discord—not only among themselves but within their spheres of influence—than upon the initiatives of the accounting profession and/or the business community.

The International Accounting Standards Committee (IASC)

On June 29, 1973, the national professional societies of nine countries (Australia, Canada, France, Germany, Japan, Mexico, the Netherlands, the United Kingdom, and the United States) organized the International Accounting Standards Committee. Sometimes referred to as the London Group because of its headquarters' site, the IASC now boasts some 50 associate members and is pledged: (1) to improve financial disclosures and (2) to harmonize worldwide accounting standards.

The IASC lacks the supranational impact of the EEC and the political leverage of the OECD. Members merely agreed to use their "best efforts" to have IASC pronouncements adopted by the standard-setting bodies in their respective countries. It is also plausible that some of the direct influence of the IASC was lessened when, in its first year of existence, the standard-setting authority of its largest member (the AICPA) was surrendered to the FASB. Thereafter, the AICPA could function only as an intermediary rather than as a member with the authority to implement approved IASC standards.

To date, the nine standards issued by the IASC have purposely been limited to broad, general, and conventional topics. Another half-dozen or so are in various stages of development. The more controversial issues have been reserved for attention after the IASC becomes more authoritative via international acceptance.

Of relevance here, *International Accounting Standard No. 3* "Consolidated Financial Statements,"[13] was approved in March 1976, was published in June 1976, and became effective for reports covering periods "beginning on or after 1 January 1977." The *Standard* generally paralleled consolidation practices accepted in the United States except for (1) the express stipulation that the needs of some users are best served by separate statements of the subunits and the parent (paragraph 7); and (2) recommended disclosures concerning composition of the group and the "geographical distribution of assets and liabilities" (paragraph 33).

The IASC *Standard* was directed toward (and had the greatest impact upon) those countries in which consolidated statements and the equity method of accounting for investments were not accepted practices. For example, Japan moved to require consolidated statements in April 1977. Prior to that time, American businessmen alleged that some Japanese companies gained a competitive advantage by "burying" losses in the accounts of nonconsolidated subsidiaries. Since such losses did not lower the earnings of parent firms, the parent firms could maintain abnormally low selling prices in international markets.

Selected International Practices

In October 1975, Price Waterhouse International published *A Survey in 46 Countries: Accounting Principles and Reporting Practices*, which represented an expanded, second edition of its 1973 *Survey* of 38 countries. An impressive total of 246 topics was covered in the 1975 edition (as compared with 233 in the 1973 publication), including a total of 38 relating to consolidation practices. The 1975 *Survey* contains a wealth of information on international accounting and reporting practices, in a convenient form that would not otherwise be available for reference.

Criteria for consolidated reportings[14] indicated that firms in most of the countries surveyed (28 of 46) tend to include all subsidiaries, foreign and domestic. Among these, the majority (18) defined control as ownership of more than 50 percent of voting equity, while effective control was also recognized by 7 others. Among the 14 industrial nations in the 46 countries surveyed, the same pattern was reflected, except that Australia was the only nation in which effective control, rather than majority ownership, was the criterion for consolidation.

The category of disclosures in the *Survey*[15] presented some interesting points. In 6 of the 46 nations surveyed, only consolidated statements were issued to parent stockholders. Of the 14 industrial countries, only in Canada and the United States were consolidated statements issued alone; this practice had been prohibited by 10 of the others. At the other end of the reporting continuum, in 18 of 46 countries, only parent company statements were issued, and 5 of the 18 represented industrial countries.

Based upon the foregoing, firms in the nations at both ends of the reporting continuum are out of step. Those furnishing only consolidated financial statements evidence the need for the OECD guideline and other emphases upon segmented reporting (see chapter 13). Similarly, those locations in which only parent-company statements were customary will be affected by the OECD guideline and by IASC *Standard No. 3*, requiring consolidated statements.

Summary

The absence of consolidated financial statements has been a deficiency in some countries other than the United States. This problem has been tackled by the IASC, the EEC, and the OECD. The last organization has elected (and wisely so) to require essential segmented data and other information as well.

For users of financial statements of United States-based MNCs, a different problem exists; the usefulness of consolidated financial statements, standing alone, has gone full-circle. The complexities of multinational operations (and those of domestic conglomerates as well) permit consolidated statements to conceal more than they reveal. Whether this is intentional or accidental is irrelevant. The fact remains that most consolidated financial statements have evolved into single-purpose statements of limited usefulness to any user group. Consequently, the "acceptance" often ascribed to consolidated statements in the literature probably reflects the opinions of issuers rather than users.

Consolidated financial statements do provide a macro glimpse of the total economic entity—and this is necessary. However, consolidated reports serving as the only disclosures are threaded with aggregate information that tends to obscure and blunt their use as decision tools. Consolidated information must be accompanied by adequate disclosures of components in order to permit interested parties to examine the weft and the warp as well as the entire fabric.

Notes

Note: In these references, APB denotes the Accounting Principles Board and ARB represents Accounting Research Bulletin.

1. *APB Opinion No. 16*, "Business Combinations" (New York: AICPA, 1970), p. 281.

2. *ARB No. 51*, "Consolidated Financial Statements" (New York: AICPA, 1959), para. 3.

3. *ARB No. 43*, "Restatement and Revision of Accounting Research Bulletins" (New York: AICPA, 1953), chapter 12, paras. 4-6.

4. *APB Opinion No. 10*, "Omnibus Opinion—1966" (New York: AICPA, December 1966), para. 3.

5. *APB Opinion No. 18*, "The Equity Method of Accounting for Investments in Common Stock" (New York: AICPA, March 1971), paras. 14-17.

6. For a thorough treatment of the details of consolidations, see James A. Gentry, Jr., and Glenn J. Johnson, *Finney and Miller's Principles of Accounting: Advanced*, 6th ed. (Englewood Cliffs, N.J.: Prentice-Hall, Inc., 1971), chapters 5 through 12.

7. *ARB No. 51*, para. 1.

8. *APB Opinion No. 10*, para. 2.

9. Albert P. Ameiss, "Two Decades of Change in Foreign Subsidiary Accounting and United States Consolidation Practices," *International Journal of Accounting Education and Research*, Spring 1972, pp. 1-23.

10. *ARB No. 51*, para. 3.

11. *Consolidated Financial Statements* (New York: Accountants International Study Group, 1973). The AISG consists of the professional accounting organizations in the United States, Canada, and the United Kingdom.

12. Ibid., para. 73.

13. *International Accounting Standard No. 3*, "Consolidated Financial

Statements" (London: International Accounting Standards Committee, June 1976), 17 pp. This and all other IASC *Standards* can be obtained from the AICPA in New York.

14. *A Survey in 46 Countries: Accounting Principles and Reporting Practices* (Canada: Price Waterhouse International, 1975), items 207-209.

15. Ibid., items 210-214.

13 Segmented Reporting

Much of the setting underlying demands for segmented reporting was established in the preceding chapter. The eras of the conglomerates and the multinationals brought the process of consolidated financial reporting full-circle. Consolidated statements of diversified enterprises became essentially single-purpose reports serving an important yet rather limited purpose. By the mid-1960s, investors, analysts, credit granters, and regulatory agencies of governments were forced to make decisions in virtual ignorance of what business diversified firms were engaged in, much less the scope and profitability of the various activities.[1]

This chapter will address the major actions that have taken place (and continue to evolve) to lift the consolidated veil.

What Is a Business Segment?

Basically, a segment of a business is broadly defined as any reporting subunit of a larger enterprise. Unlike most definitions, this one expands rather than limits the parameters of consideration, since it includes not only the smaller, typical activities (such as lines-of-business, products, market areas, and divisions) but the larger, legally separate entities as well (such as domestic and foreign subsidiaries).

Definition and selection of segments for reporting purposes have been the root causes of most of the resistance to segmented reporting by the business community. In general, businessmen prefer to retain as much aggregation as possible for a variety of reasons. Users in the private sector want information that is useful in making assessments and decisions. Most regulatory agencies need data that are comparable and, therefore, more specific and uniform in context.

To some extent, regulatory agencies can demand the inputs required. Private users must depend upon voluntary disclosures by business or, failing that, upon help from the regulatory agencies and/or the accounting profession. Like most areas of financial-reporting practices today, the state of the art of segmented reporting is the result of events in both the public and private sectors. Refinements will occur primarily through trial and error.

Role of the Securities and Exchange Commission

The Securities and Exchange Commission has obtained various types of line-of-business (LOB) information for some time. In 1969, registrants were required to provide LOB data in their statements. This requirement was subsequently extended to include all annual Form 10-K reports (in 1970) and annual reports to stockholders of listed firms (in 1974).

In general, the SEC rules evolved to require disclosures of (1) those lines of business which represented 10 percent or more of total revenues or earnings and (2) those products which comprised 10 percent or more of revenues for the most recent five years. (For companies with revenues of less than $50 million in either of their last two fiscal years, both criteria have been 15 percent.) Additional information in narrative form was required in filings with the SEC (but not in shareholder reports) and covered such factors as competition, sales backlogs, major customers, raw material sources, and the like.

Since the SEC disclosures have been brought into general agreement with those promulgated by the FASB, the specific requirements of both will be examined in a later section devoted to the FASB.

The SEC has earned the reputation of initiator in the area of segmented reporting. The SEC requirements have also served as sounding boards for opinion and experimentation, which undoubtedly assisted the FASB in its deliberations.

Role of the Federal Trade Commission

The Federal Trade Commission has been involved since 1974 in what is often described as an "uphill struggle" to obtain financial information on a product-line basis from major industrial firms. One-third of the 345 large manufacturers asked by the FTC to provide initial line-of-business reports in 1974 (on 1973 data) refused to comply. Subsequent FTC requests met with similar, if not increasing, resistance from the business community. The FTC subsequently filed suits to obtain compliance. Countersuits were filed by some 170 firms, challenging the FTC's authority and the product-line reporting program.

The Federal Trade Commission, created in 1914, was designed to complement the activities of the Justice Department in implementing the antitrust provisions of the Sherman and Clayton Acts. As a quasi-judicial agency, the FTC's primary purpose concerned surveillance of the structure of U.S. industries in order to maintain competition.

The growth of conglomerates represented the initial challenge for the FTC. Almost concurrently, the spread of the multinationals added another frustration (since foreign operations of U.S. corporations are subject to U.S. antitrust laws if they affect U.S. commerce in prohibited ways). In order to perform its function, the FTC designed its product-line or line-of-business report based upon the economic activity codes of the *Standard Industrial Classification Manual* (SIC) published by the Office of Management and Budget.

Part of the resistance to the FTC's line-of-business reporting centered around the codes used. Not only were the SIC codes selected by the FTC cumbersome (four classification levels representing a standard set of 275 industry categories), but enterprise accounting systems rarely, if ever, collected data corresponding with the SIC code classifications. Burdensome additional costs and/or dictated revisions to existing accounting systems were the charges levied by business. Naturally, the balance of resistance constituted (1) the reluctance of businesses to furnish information upon which their competitive activities were to be assessed, and (2) fear that the FTC would make the information public.

After more than three years of litigation, the Federal Appeals Court upheld the FTC line-of-business program and ordered the dissident firms to comply by August 9, 1978.

The role of the FTC is significant because it illustrates the different segmented information required to assess conformity with proscriptive laws. The FTC needed uniform reporting based upon industrial operations (production functions, materials, or finished products). Segmented information required by the SEC and the FASB (as will be discussed) is organized around the markets of enterprises and dovetails much better with accounting systems.

So long as the FTC requires segmented information according to SIC codes, the reporting process will not be compatible with those of the SEC and the FASB. An acceptable alternative would involve acceptance by the FTC of segmented reports constructed in accordance with FASB requirements supplemented by segmentation of revenues only by the SIC codes specified. Allocations of costs and expenses either could be performed by the FTC or could be prescribed by them. Such allocations would seem to be no more nor less arbitrary than the methods reporting firms must now devise.

Role of the Financial Accounting
Standards Board

Consideration of segmented reporting by the FASB began in April 1973 and culminated in the release of its *Statement of Financial Accounting Standards No. 14*, "Financial Reporting for Segments of a Business Enterprise," in December 1976 (hereinafter referred to as *FASB-14*).

The FASB sought to provide users of financial statements with information concerning the nature of the major activities of enterprises as well as a basis to assess their "past performance and future prospects."[2] The FASB cautioned, however, that the segmented data would have "limited usefulness" in comparing segments of different enterprises because of the inherent differences between and among firms.

In sum, *FASB-14* required that annual financial statements for fiscal years beginning after December 15, 1976, contain segmented information concerning (1) operations by industries or markets; (2) foreign operations and export sales by geographic area; and (3) major customers.[3]

Initially, segmented disclosures were also required in complete (as opposed to condensed) interim financial statements. This requirement was retroactively rescinded by *FASB-18* "Financial Reporting for Segments of a Business Enterprise–Interim Financial Statements," issued in November 1977.

All enterprises originally were subject to *FASB-14.* The effect on most nonprofit enterprises would only involve disclosures concerning major customers. Single-line firms could have to report data on foreign operations, export sales, and major customers.

Segment Selection

A reportable segment was broadly described in *FASB-14* as a product or service, provided primarily to unaffiliated (outside) customers, which constitutes a significant component of the enterprise as a whole–accounting for 10 percent or more of combined revenues, profits, losses, or identifiable assets. (*FASB-14* used two bases for segment selection: combined and consolidated aggregates. The former refers to the amounts prior to the eliminations of intracompany transactions in the consolidation process.)

Reportable segments were to be selected by management based upon the inherent nature and organization of the enterprise, together with the following:

1. *Nature of the product*–related products or services having similar uses, profitabilities, risks, and opportunities for growth.
2. *Nature of production*–items sharing common facilities, using similar raw materials, or having like measures of capital/labor-intensiveness.
3. *Marketing process*–commonalities such as geographic market areas, sales forces, customer types, or supply/demand sensitivities.
4. *Responsibility centers*–existing cost, profit, investment, and similar responsibility centers, if and only if all the preceding attributes are satisfied as well. (Naturally, reporting can be simplified to a great extent if existing organizational segments satisfy the other criteria cited. Consideration is certainly recommended.)

Vertically integrated operations (those furnishing products or services primarily to affiliated units) were not required to be disaggregated. However, intersegment "sales" and transfers between geographic areas were to be reflected in segmented information in order to provide more meaningful insights concerning the true magnitude of operations within industries and geographic areas. (In consolidated reporting, such intraunit transactions are eliminated, thus netting the levels of overall activities.)

Industry Segment Reporting

For each industry segment identified, the following information is to be presented by segment:

1. *Revenue information*—sales to outside customers and intraunit transfers to be disclosed separately (existing transfer prices are to be used for the latter, and the method of accounting is to be disclosed).

2. *Operating profit or loss*—or segment margin, defined as revenues minus all directly traceable costs and expenses. Provision is made for the allocations of certain costs on a "reasonable basis." However, in the author's opinion, such actions normally serve no purposes worthy of the effort and cost involved. Certain common items may not be allocated, such as general corporate revenues and expenses, interest and tax expenses, incomes or losses from unconsolidated subsidiaries, extraordinary items, and the like.

3. *Identifiable assets*—both tangible and intangible assets traceable to a segment, as well as allocations of assets used jointly by more than one segment. Excluded assets are intersegment loans or advances, general corporate assets, and investments in unconsolidated subsidiaries.

4. *Other disclosures*—each industry segment to report gross amounts of depreciation, depletion, amortization, and capital expenditures.

Foreign Operations and Export Sales

Multinational enterprises are required to disclose foreign and domestic operations separately. Segmentation of foreign operations depends upon the number of geographic areas in which the enterprise conducts significant operations. (Significance in this context is defined as sales to outsiders or identifiable assets representing 10 percent or more of consolidated amounts; that is, after interunit eliminations.)

Much like industry segments, geographic-area segments should be identified by combining countries meaningfully. Suggested criteria are economic affinity, similarity of business environments, extent to which operations are related, proximity, and others.

Geographic-Area Reporting

Each identified geographic area will disclose the following information:

1. *Revenue information*—the same as for industry segments.
2. *Profitability*—a common measure to be applied to all areas. Operating profit

is preferred where foreign tax structures do not render the information misleading.

3. *Identifiable assets*—the same as for industry segments.
4. *Export sales*—required of domestic firms whether or not the firm must report on operations in geographic areas if sales to outside foreign customers total 10 percent or more of consolidated revenues.
5. *Major customers*—to be disclosed if 10 percent or more of total revenues are represented by sales to a single customer, or to domestic or foreign governments in the aggregate. Amounts and facts (except names) must be disclosed.

Presentation Methods

FASB-14 stipulates that amounts be expressed in dollars and be reconciled to the appropriate amounts in the consolidated financial statements. Presentations may be in the form of footnotes, as integral parts of the financial statements, or in separate schedules properly indexed in annual reports.

Sample disclosure formats appearing in *FASB-14* are shown in tables 13-1 and 13-2.

A *Statement on Auditing Standards No. 21*, "Segment Information," was issued in December 1977 by the AICPA to provide guidance to independent auditors in examining financial statements containing disclosures required by *FASB-14*. In short, the *Statement* specified that auditors should have a "reasonable basis" for assessing whether the segmented information conforms to *FASB-14* "in relation to the financial statements as a whole."

As of April 30, 1978, the FASB, in its *Statement of Financial Accounting Standards No. 21,*[4] retroactively rescinded the applicability of *FASB-14* to nonpublic enterprises. Over time, additional refinements can be expected.

Comparison of U.S. Requirements

As mentioned earlier, the SEC revised its line-of-business reporting to conform generally to *FASB-14*, as amended, on December 23, 1977, in ASR-236. At the same time, the SEC devised a new integrated disclosure form, Form S-K, which incorporates segmented disclosures as well as others that were common to more than one SEC reporting form.

The SEC requirements, as revised, go beyond those in *FASB-14* in four areas:

1. Additional information is required on intersegment transfers: identities of segments making and receiving the transfers; comparisons of transfer prices and outside selling prices.

Table 13-1
Segmented Reporting by Industry

	Industry A	Industry B	Industry C	Other Industries	Adjustments and Eliminations	Consolidated
Sales to unaffiliated customers	$1,000	$2,000	$1,500	$ 200		$ 4,700
Intersegment sales	200		500		$(700)	
Total revenue	$1,200	$2,000	$2,000	$ 200	$(700)	$ 4,700
Operating profit	$ 200	$ 290	$ 600	$ 50	$ (40)	$ 1,100
Equity in net income of Z Co.						100
General corporate expenses						(100)
Interest expense						(200)
Income from continuing operations before income taxes						$ 900
Identifiable assets at December 31, 1977	$2,000	$4,050	$6,000	$1,000	$ (50)	$13,000
Investment in net assets of Z Co.						400
Corporate assets						1,600
Total assets at December 31, 1977						$15,000

See accompanying note.

Source: *Statement of Financial Accounting Standards No. 14,* "Financial Reporting for Segments of a Business Enterprise." Copyright © by Financial Accounting Standards Board, High Ridge Park, Stamford, Connecticut 06905, pp. 54-56. Reprinted with permission. Copies of the complete document are available from the FASB.

Note (not provided here) would furnish a narrative description of the industries; types of products or services; bases of accounting for intersegment sales; definition and components of operating profit; description of items excluded from operating profits of segments; amounts of depreciation and capital expenditures by industry; and other disclosures relating to identifiable assets, government contract sales, and the like, where applicable.

Table 13-2
Segmented Reporting by Geographic Area

	United States	Geographic Area A	Geographic Area B	Adjustments and Eliminations	Consolidated
Sales to unaffiliated customers	$3,000	$1,000	$ 700		$ 4,700
Transfers between geographic areas	1,000			$(1,000)	
Total revenue	$4,000	$1,000	$ 700	$(1,000)	$ 4,700
Operating profit	$ 800	$ 400	$ 100	$ (200)	$ 1,100
Equity in net income of Z Co.					100
General corporate expenses					(100)
Interest expense					(200)
Income from continuing operations before income taxes					$ 900
Identifiable assets at December 31, 1977	$7,300	$3,400	$2,450	$ (150)	$13,000
Investment in net assets of Z Co.					400
Corporate assets					1,600
Total assets at December 31, 9777					$15,000

See accompanying note.

Note (not provided here) would furnish narrative descriptions of the basis of accounting for transfers; definition and components of operating profit, including those items not reflected therein; descriptions of identifiable assets; information on export sales (if any) from the U.S. area; and details concerning any extraordinary items.

2. Disclosures are required of material changes in operations of a dominant industry segment (one representing 90 percent or more of revenues, profits, or assets).
3. The names of major customers who are material in relation to a segment rather than to the enterprise as a whole are required.
4. Information is required for the last five years (although this will only be a temporal difference).

On the other hand, the SEC information does not necessarily have to be audited, whereas CPAs must attest to the reasonableness of requirements levied by *FASB-14*.

While differences exist between the amended requirements of *FASB-14* and those of the SEC, the two are generally compatible from a reporting standpoint. It is also reasonable to surmise that, over time, experience and amendments will bring about even greater compatibility.

The FTC rules are quite a different matter. On the one hand, the FTC requirements are less inclusive in that they apply only to domestic operations of selected large manufacturers and do not relate to major customers, export sales, geographic areas, and capital expenditures. On the other hand, the degree of specificity connected with the SIC reporting codes, and the requirement for developing operating profits for each reporting code used, differentiate the FTC system entirely. Since the FTC segment codes are the most specific, their use would presumably satisfy both FASB and SEC requirements. Business would adopt the FTC method of segment definition for all reportings—if for no reason other than efficiency—were it practicable to maintain ongoing accountings (or even after-the-fact analyses) of operations structured around the applicable SIC codes. Business and the accounting profession would be well advised to assist (rather than resist) the FTC in harmonizing its reporting requirements with those of the FASB and the SEC while obtaining the information necessary to perform its regulatory functions.

The International Realm

Internationally, there is an increasing awareness of the disparities in both accounting and disclosure standards. Professional societies, business groups, and international organizations have realized that it is in their best interests to join together in efforts to reduce the differences in accounting practices. Since this goal is necessarily one of a long-term nature, current efforts have surrounded improvements, particularly greater consistency, in disclosure requirements.

The Organization for Economic
Cooperation and Development

The "Declaration on International Investment and Multinational Enterprises" adopted by the OECD in June 1976 featured a guideline on corporate conduct (see chapter 4, appendix 4A). The primary thrust of the guideline focused upon disclosures of operating results for the multinational enterprise as a whole and segmented disclosures by geographic area as well as by major lines of business. Although the guideline preceded *FASB-14* by some six months, the OECD partners worked closely with both the SEC and the FASB in the construction of their guideline.

The guideline imposed few new disclosures upon United States-based multinationals operating in OECD countries: policies governing transfer prices and numbers of employees by geographic areas. Certainly, enterprises in those countries lacking the comprehensive disclosure standards of the United States were stimulated to provide much additional information for public disclosure. There is little doubt that, over time, such disclosures will be ingrained within the various national accounting and reporting practices.

Parenthetically, the U.S. government implemented the OECD guideline requirements—and in considerably more detail—in Public Law 94-472, the International Investment Survey Act. More than 7,500 U.S. business firms, owning 10 percent or more of a foreign firm, have thus far been required to submit the disclosures to the Bureau of Economic Analysis (BEA), on Form BE-10, under a staggered deadline: May 31, 1978 (for firms with fewer than 20 foreign investments); June 30, 1978 (for those with 20 to 99); and July 31, 1978 (for firms having 100 or more such foreign affiliations). Quite naturally the U.S. business community is becoming increasingly incensed, and justly so, over the substantial cost burdens created by the redundancies in disclosure requirements.

It is high time for the U.S. government to take an inward look and to require its various agencies and commissions to talk to one another. The establishment of a central repository for business disclosures, preferably the SEC, must be seriously examined. A single, consolidated reporting form could then be constructed to eliminate the redundancies in both costs and reportings. In turn, the SEC should be charged with disseminating the appropriate information to the other monitoring agencies, not only in the United States but, ideally, in other governments and groups, such as the OECD and EEC. The U.S. government needs a single-base repository for disclosures as sorely as it needs an effective zero-base budgeting system.

The European Economic Community

On the heels of the OECD guideline (which is voluntary), the European Parliament passed a resolution calling for the adoption of "binding rules" within the EEC to provide the weight of law to the guideline. The resolution, while only advisory, added further impetus to the EEC proceedings on the approved fourth directive (on annual accounts of corporations) and the proposed seventh directive (on consolidated accounts). Both directives are aimed at narrowing the divergent accounting practices and providing additional disclosures relating to data as well as to accounting policies.

Among the additional disclosures required by the proposed directives are the net turnovers (sales) segmented by product or activity and by geographical areas; the net contributions (profits) of each segment or market; and segmented personnel data, in numbers of employees and in cost amounts.

The opposition encountered thus far by both directives is understandable, since, in one fell swoop, they are collectively attempting to harmonize the various national company laws as well as to upgrade accounting and reporting practices of almost all EEC members.

The OECD guideline, as well as the programs implemented by the SEC and the FASB, will surely result in refinements of both directives and will assist eventual adoption. Since EEC member-states have as much as 18 months after adoption in which to conform their existing laws, the directives would probably not take effect until two years following adoption.

Here again, it would behoove the EEC to establish a central repository for the required reportings or, in lieu thereof, task the member-states with furnishing the respective EEC commissions with copies of the reports received.

The International Accounting
Standards Committee

Since its inception in 1973, IASC membership has grown from the professional societies in the nine founding countries to more than 50, counting associate-member societies. As mentioned in chapter 12, the IASC concerned itself initially with the less-controversial issues related to international standards. Consequently, one of the earlier standards, *IAS-3*, strove to increase the number of countries in which consolidated accounts were being made available. In addition, *IAS-3* recommended the disclosure of selected reports and information on a less-than-aggregate basis (see chapter 12).

Although improvements in disclosures have been part and parcel of all the IASC standards issued to date, the topic of segmented reporting has apparently been avoided as being much too controversial as yet. This is understandable, since the young IASC has had to struggle—not only to achieve the essential level of general acceptance, but to overcome onslaughts by some of the large U.S. public accounting firms, not to mention the envies of recent International Congresses of Accountants and Coordination Committees (which reportedly were primarily social groups). Fortunately, the IASC has retained its function of issuing pronouncements on international accounting standards.

The IASC holds, in the author's opinion, the real future promise of obtaining harmonized (not uniform) accounting and reporting standards throughout the free world. By assimilation (as well as by the motivation to participate in desirable ventures covered by IASC participants) the IASC pronouncements will also impact and assist the development of accounting in the controlled economies.

The International Federation of Accountants

A relative newcomer, the International Federation of Accountants (IFAC), was established by the 11th International Congress of Accountants, meeting in Munich in October 1977. The germination of the IFAC represented a compromise between two factions: those who believed that International Congresses were much too unwieldy ever to be effective standard-setters, and those who were concerned that the IASC was too small to represent adequately the collective opinions of the larger member-societies.

Fortunately, the International Congress recognized the wisdom in retaining the standard-setting authority within the IASC. The new IFAC will concern itself with the development of regional associations and guidelines for the international upgrading of educational, ethical, and technical (auditing) practices.

The United Nations

In mid-1977, the United Nations Group of Experts on International Standards of Accounting and Reporting presented its recommendations for the items, at minimum, that should be included in general-purpose financial reports. The recommendations were subsequently forwarded through U.N. channels to the U.N. Economic and Social Council for approval.

The Secretary-General of the United Nations, Kurt Waldheim, appended an additional recommendation that an "intergovernmental group" of experts be established to work with professional accounting societies—national and international—in order to secure an eventual agreement among U.N. members regarding international accounting and reporting standards.

The old adage that too many cooks may spoil the broth seems to have relevance here, particularly given the fact that the expertise of the United Nations lies in areas other than accounting. Consequently, the most practical solution would be for the new group of experts to consult and work with the IASC in upgrading and harmonizing accounting and reporting standards. The group of experts could then be free to pursue other problems concerning multinational enterprises.

Summary

The past decade of controversy over segmented reporting in the United States has led, in the main, to reasoned solutions. Much of the resistance within the business community was recognized as self-serving. Arguments that disclosures might benefit foreign competitors not subject to similar requirements were reduced by the OECD guideline. Conformance of SEC and FASB reporting requirements was an initial yet essential step in reducing the redundancy in reports. Similar conformity, or creation of a single government repository agency, should be considered immediately to minimize the burdens of FTC and BEA reports.

In the international vein, the cooperation of professional societies, as particularly evidenced by the IASC, has resulted in a reduction of the maze of divergent reporting practices and has significantly increased the disclosures presented. The OECD acted responsively to fill the voids existing in segmented-reporting requirements of multinationals, thereby applying the same levies upon all firms. This is particularly significant since the OECD countries host most of the MNEs, account for three-fourths of the world's trade, and produce two-thirds of the gross world product.

Overall, segmented reportings that lift the consolidated veil should prove to benefit all sectors. It is reasonable to surmise that frank disclosures, both good and bad, will increase the credibility of all firms and the willingness of individuals to make investments.

It has also been said that the rules determine how the game is played. If the rules conceal, then the game may or may not be played fairly—one cannot tell. If the rules reveal, then the results—whether favorable or unfavorable—will help protect the competitive environment by exposing restrictive and unethical conduct.

As with most progress, growing pains should be expected. In March 1978, the SEC warned some industries in *ASR-244* that segmented disclosures for 1977 appeared to be deficient. The SEC further warned that amended financial reports may be required of firms submitting inadequate disclosures for 1978. Trial, error, experience, and cooperation will lead to refinements in reporting and acceptance by the business community.

Notes

1. Countless studies were made by every major professional and business association. Examples are Robert K. Mautz, *Financial Reporting by Diversified Companies* (New York: Financial Executives Research Foundation, 1968); Morton Backer and Walter B. McFarland, *External Reporting for Segments of a Business* (New York: National Association of Accountants, 1968); Alfred

Rappaport and Eugene M. Lerner, *Framework for Reporting by Diversified Companies* (New York: National Association of Accountants, 1969).

2. *FASB-14*, para. 5.

3. Ibid., para. 3.

4. *Statement of Financial Accounting Standards No. 21*, "Suspension of the Reporting of Earnings per Share and Segment Information by Nonpublic Enterprises," (Stamford, Conn.: FASB, 1968).

14 Taxation

Taxation is a process that overlays sectors of accounting, economics, law, and politics. Yet few practitioners in these areas profess to be experts. Small wonder, then, that the subject of taxation, whether domestic or international, represents an insoluble maze to most businessmen, even though taxes take a heavy bite out of profits earned.

Since U.S. tax laws are more complicated than those of other nations, this chapter will concentrate upon the U.S. tax aspects of foreign operations. Comparisons, where appropriate, will be made with the tax systems of other countries.

One caution is in order. Few individuals can lift, much less comprehend, the estimated 50,000 pages making up the current manuals of the U.S. Internal Revenue Service alone, not to mention the regulations of other countries. A single chapter can only serve to place current dilemmas into a meaningful context in which the issues and the proposed solutions can be examined.

Philosophies of Taxation

In 1776, Adam Smith developed a philosophical structure for taxation. Rules to be applied were equality, certainty, convenience, and economy. Specific taxes should be judged based upon their inherent qualities of equity, efficiency, and enforceability. Two principles were also suggested upon which to base the incidence or ultimate impact of taxes: (1) those who benefit (from use taxes, for example); and (2) those with the ability to pay.

In the simpler times of Adam Smith (and perhaps even today), the foregoing philosophies could serve as adequate guides for taxes levied to raise revenues. However, in the United States the Congress, over time, has infused taxation with policies aimed at allocation of resources and income redistribution (or "social engineering"). Even the best-intentioned policies created benefits or vested interests for individuals and businesses that tended to remain long after the original needs ceased to exist and might, in fact, have been forgotten. Today, few individuals or businessmen will deny that taxation in the United States has become a veritable maze, which is unclear and uncertain, if not arbitrary. Individuals, particularly, since they truly have little voice in taxation policies, have good reason to believe that they are again threatened by taxation without representation.

241

Compared with the uncertainties of U.S. domestic philosophies, those of the international domain, oddly enough, are easier to comprehend. The essential aim of the taxation of transnational business is neutrality. In other words, investment decisions should be made based upon their inherent attributes; tax aspects should have no effect. Such is not the case, however.

International tax neutrality for business has two sides. *Capital-export neutrality* requires that the total effective corporate tax rate be the same on foreign and domestic profits. For example, if a British subsidiary of a U.S. parent paid a tax of 40 percent of its current profits to Britain, and if the U.S. tax rate were 48 percent, the United States should levy a current 8-percent tax on the foreign profits. American firms and capital would be indifferent to locations of operations insofar as taxes would be concerned. *Capital-import neutrality*, on the other hand, requires that all firms, foreign or domestic, operating in the same industry in a given country pay the same total corporate tax rate on earnings. The competitive effects of taxes would be neutralized within a given industry and country.

The taxation of foreign-source income by the United States is guided by no single philosophy. Events over time have resulted in a hodgepodge combining capital-export neutrality, capital-import neutrality, protectionism, incentives, and clauses to protect against the erosion of domestic tax revenues. Consequently, neutrality has not been achieved, however it may be defined. Foreign investments (or capital exports) are generally favored because of (1) deferrals of U.S. taxes until repatriation, and (2) tax credits (as opposed to deductions from income) for foreign subnational taxes paid.

Of particular relevance in international taxation is recognition of the fact that the total corporate tax paid (the effective tax) is the product of a statutory rate applied to a taxable base. While statutory rates vary among countries, what is taxable varies even more. As a result, until the *effective* tax rates of countries are equalized, the philosophy of tax neutrality will remain a nebulous concept.

Types of Taxes

Types of taxes would normally be irrelevant where corporate income-tax considerations are concerned. This is not so in the international realm.

Foreign operations of U.S. firms are subject to many alien types of taxes, some of which can result in larger out-of-pocket costs than income taxes. Common types are border, turnover, value-added, net worth, and remittance taxes. From the standpoint of incidence, all but the last two are indirect forms of taxation and can be easily overlooked (at least in planning).

Some of these taxes are proportional (fixed-rate), some may be progressive (rate increases as base increases), and others may be regressive (rate decreases as base increases).

Border taxes (tariffs and duties) represent the most prevalent form of major international tax. Developing nations, in particular, rely upon border taxes rather than those on income or sales. The base is larger, rates can be changed at will (for political and other reasons in addition to revenue), and administration is relatively simple.

A variety of taxes on purchases and sales exist. Purchase taxes may be imposed at completion of production (Canada), upon sale by the wholesaler (as formerly done in the United Kingdom), or upon sale by the retailer (United States). The incidence and the rate of tax may affect where multinationals buy, produce, and sell.

Turnover and value-added taxes are relatives of the sales tax. These indirect taxes are popular in Europe. They generate significant amounts of revenues, which enable lower effective levels of corporate and individual income taxes.

The turnover form of sales tax was the first used. It was applied and collected at all levels of production, intermediate and final. It produced a pyramiding or compounding effect, which was disliked. Furthermore, since turnover taxes on exports were usually refundable, governments had difficulty relating the refunds due to producers at the various stages of manufacture.

The value-added tax (VAT) deserves more than cursory mention since it is not encountered in the United States.[1] The VAT (or TVA—*Taxe Sur la Valeur Adjoutee*—as it is known in Europe) replaced the turnover tax in France in stages (1936-1954), was required of all EEC countries in January 1970, and was finally implemented by all members in 1973. The VAT was preferred over the turnover tax for several reasons (some of which were peculiar to France). By taxing only the value added (the tax was applied to a firm's gross sales with a credit for the taxes paid on intermediate goods purchased), the compounding effect of the turnover tax was avoided. Also, the VAT applied to activity rather than to profits; firms incurring net losses normally still paid a VAT (this appealed to France and Italy, where cheating the income-tax collector had become the national pastime). Vertically integrated firms were affected the same as all others. The VAT was an effective tool in national planning, since different rates could be applied to different goods. Refunds of VAT on exports (by France and Germany) were much easier to administer. Industrial investment, selective or otherwise, could be encouraged by exempting capital goods from the VAT. The collection process was pay-as-you-go, was reportable monthly, policed itself, and encouraged honesty in income-tax returns. (Since receipts had to accompany deductions for VAT paid on intermediate goods, the intermediate sellers were less apt to cheat on the reporting of total sales.)

The VAT in Europe is at least as important as the income tax, if not more so. Consequently, the goal of the EEC has been to harmonize the rates used. Many exceptions to the common rate schedule exist, since, although deviations must be requested and justified, few requests are disapproved.

The VAT can readily affect the multinational in other ways as well. Many countries relate border taxes with the VAT; commonly, the former are reduced or eliminated if a certain percentage of value added to the product occurs within the particular country. The use of transfer prices to minimize (or evade) border taxes must be approached with caution. Also, the VAT is not an income tax; it cannot be applied as a credit against any U.S. income taxes due.

Operations in the EEC can be favorably affected in two ways: first, since the VAT applies only to the value added, efficient firms pay less tax; second, the exemption of exports helps their competitive status. This last feature is permissible under trade-convention (GATT) rules, since the VAT is not an income tax.

Some countries levy *taxes on net worth or undistributed earnings*. The latter form is more prevalent (and will be addressed in the section on systems to follow), although neither tax is widely used since governments have found more effective and responsive means of influencing capital accumulation.

Remittance taxes on currencies passing between nations are common and may represent significant factors to contend with. Remittances of dividends, interest, and royalties are favorite targets. Where tax treaties exist, rates vary from zero to 15 percent. Outside treaty areas, statutory rates on dividends can be substantial: from 30 percent (Sweden) to 60 percent (Iran). Taxes on remittances represent the last line of defense for those nations interested in controlling flows of funds from multinationals operating in their domains. For the multinational, taxes on remittances, particularly on dividends, can result in a foreign tax rate greater than that of the United States and possible unused tax credits—not to mention the time value of money.

Tax-Administration Systems

Three international systems of tax administration exist.[2]

The *classical system* (used by the United States) is the most prevalent; it taxes incomes of corporations and the dividends paid to their shareholders separately.

Under a *split-rate system*, profits retained are taxed at a substantially higher rate than those distributed as dividends. Countries using the split-rate system as of January 1978, and the rates in effect were: Germany (56 percent and 36 percent); Japan (40 percent and 30 percent); and Norway (50.8 percent and 23 percent).[3] The split-rate system is also called a "partially integrated system."

The third system, *tax credit or imputation*, imputes or credits the shareholder for part of the taxes paid or deemed paid by the corporation. This is also a form of partially integrated system employed by countries such as the United Kingdom, France, and Italy.

A fourth possible system—*the fully integrated or assimilated system*—has yet to emerge. Total integration of corporation income and shareholder dividend taxes has been proposed in many countries with no success (Canada, Germany, and the United States are examples). Greece is the only country known to the author that levies no corporate tax on income distributed to shareholders. Fully integrated systems will remain rarities so long as countries (such as the United States) furnish sweetenings to shareholders (such as dividend exclusions) that are not afforded indirect investors—those whose interest earnings are fully taxed.

The major dilemma in international taxation, at least for U.S. firms, concerns *tax domains*. Three practices coexist:

1. National sovereignty—all nations exercize the right to tax income from operations within their borders.
2. Territorial—nations tax incomes earned solely within their borders.
3. Worldwide—incomes of residents and domiciled corporations are taxed wherever earned.

The United States seems out of step with other industrialized nations in that the United States exercizes its worldwide or global taxing authority. The United States also taxes capital gains; few other developed countries do.

Apparently the United States believes that exercise of its worldwide taxing authority would (or will) result in increased revenues. If the effective tax rates of other nations are (or become) similar to those of the United States, this belief may prove to be myopic. On the other hand, adherents to the territorial concept evidently expect to attract additional capital. Naturally, so long as a major potential source of this capital (the United States) exercises its global taxing authority, favorable territorial tax rates alone will not represent an inducement.

The actual administration of taxing systems also varies widely in approach, if not in quality. In some countries, tax rates can be established by negotiation prior to the time an investment is actually made. In other nations, tax liabilities are determined in lengthy annual negotiations between firms and the government. In still others, firms merely submit financial statements to the taxing authorities, who calculate the appropriate taxes due. At the other end of the spectrum are locations such as Mexico and the United Kingdom, in which the tax liabilities reflected in statements attested by independent auditors are accepted without question by the taxing authorities.

A final aspect of tax-administration systems that is unfamiliar to most Americans (at least to date) is indexation for inflation. Various forms of taxes have been indexed by Brazil, Denmark, France, the Netherlands, and Switzerland since the late 1960s. While such systems appear to be favorable at face value, they most often contain index (escalator) clauses for wages and other costs as well. The net effect upon a given firm will depend upon many variables.

Foreign Tax Credits

Where income earned and taxed in one country is remitted to investors in other countries, the income may be subject to multiple taxation. This is a particular, but not peculiar, problem to U.S. investors, since the United States follows the worldwide concept of taxation.

Two common approaches are used to avoid multiple taxation: foreign tax credits (the subject of this section) and tax treaties (examined in the following section).

A foreign tax credit is a *unilateral* action by one country that permits the income taxes normally due to be reduced by the amount of foreign income taxes paid. It represents an attempt to achieve the capital-export neutrality mentioned earlier, and it is the keystone of the U.S. approach.

Creditable Taxes

According to the U.S. Internal Revenue Code, Section 33, only taxes paid to a foreign government on *income* are creditable. Several nuances are hidden here. A favorable factor is that income-based taxes paid to any level of foreign government (national and subnational) are creditable. On the domestic scene, subnational income taxes may be deducted only as expenses, not as credits to federal taxes due. Second, practical determination of whether a foreign tax is or is not levied upon income is often moot; reference to precedent cases or competent tax advice is advisable. Third, qualifying taxes are creditable, which means that the taxpayer may elect to apply qualifying foreign taxes as credits against U.S. taxes due or to deduct them as expenses. For business firms, a tax credit is usually more beneficial. The exception would be a year in which a net operating loss would otherwise be reported in the United States; a credit against a zero tax liability is of no benefit, whereas a deduction would further increase current losses, which could be carried back.

The foregoing comments relate to foreign income taxes that are actually paid. In some cases U.S. corporations may claim credit for foreign income taxes that are considered to have been indirectly or *deemed paid* by them through second and third tiers of related foreign corporations. Existing requirements may be illustrated by example. The U.S. firm must own at least 10 percent of the voting stock of foreign corporation A (the first tier); A must own a similar portion of foreign firm B (the second tier); B, in turn, must own a like interest in C (the third tier). In addition, the U.S. firm must directly own at least 5 percent of the voting stock of both B and C. In such cases, the U.S. parent may claim as deemed-paid foreign tax credits its share (based upon ownership) of the foreign income taxes paid by all three tiers (Section 902 does not permit deemed-paid credits below the third tier).

Limitations

Currently, the amount of creditable or deemed-paid foreign taxes for a given year must be related to the amount of earnings or profits (restated in accordance with U.S. tax rules) remaining after foreign taxes for that given year—or, in tax jargon, the dividends received must be "grossed-up":

$$\frac{\text{dividend received}}{\text{after-tax earnings and profits}} \quad X \quad \begin{array}{c}\text{creditable} \\ \text{foreign} \\ \text{taxes}\end{array} \quad = \quad \begin{array}{c}\text{limit on} \\ \text{deemed-paid} \\ \text{credit}\end{array}$$

Where the dividend received exceeds the earnings and profits for that year, the excess is related to the earnings and profits of prior years on a LIFO basis, or the latest years first. (Prior to January 1978, dividends from the less-developed countries were favored in that they were not grossed-up; however, the denominator used in the example was before taxes, thereby decreasing the deemed-paid credit limitation.)

Deemed-paid credits, calculated as shown, are limited to the total U.S. tax due in a given year on combined domestic and grossed-up foreign income. This feature (Section 904) serves to limit the effective rates of creditable foreign taxes to the effective U.S. rate. Stated another way, it prevents higher effective tax rates of foreign countries from eroding domestic tax revenues. Excess credits from a given year may be carried back two years and forward five years so long as the foreign tax credit remains within the limitations in the recomputed carryover years.

For tax years prior to 1976, either of two methods of calculating the foreign-tax-credit limitation could be elected: per-country or overall.[4] The methods were similar in that each related the maximum credit allowable to the ratio of foreign-source to total taxable income:

$$\frac{\begin{array}{c}\text{foreign taxable income} \\ \text{(by country)}\end{array}}{\text{total taxable income}} \quad X \quad \begin{array}{c}\text{total} \\ \text{U.S. income} \\ \text{tax}\end{array} \quad = \quad \begin{array}{c}\text{per-country} \\ \text{limitation}\end{array}$$

$$\frac{\begin{array}{c}\text{foreign taxable income} \\ \text{(all countries)}\end{array}}{\text{total taxable income}} \quad X \quad \begin{array}{c}\text{total} \\ \text{U.S. income} \\ \text{tax}\end{array} \quad = \quad \begin{array}{c}\text{overall} \\ \text{limitation}\end{array}$$

Differences in the limits depended upon the circumstances. The per-country approach produced larger limits where some foreign operations reflected losses. The overall method offset high and low foreign tax rates, thereby minimizing excess foreign tax carryovers.

A potential method of minimizing U.S. taxes of related domestic firms with foreign operations is the consolidated tax return permitted by Section 1501. The consolidated return treats the group as a single economic entity for tax purposes. The larger total income base enables what could otherwise be excess credits of one affiliate to be offset, in full or in part, against others whose limits have not been reached. On the other hand, while losses of some affiliates will offset the taxable incomes of others, such losses also tend to lower the foreign-tax-credit limitation as just computed. Consolidated returns may or may not be favorable, depending upon the particular circumstances.[5]

Abuses

Before leaving this topic, at least temporarily, it should be pointed out that foreign tax credits were originally devised to prevent the inequities of multiple taxation of income. As with most similar, well-intentioned tax measures, over time they collectively earn disrepute because of abuses by one or a few business sectors. The oil industry and the U.S. government must share condemnation for abuses. Credits for taxes paid by oil companies to certain nations (notably Saudi Arabia and Libya) were finally disallowed by the U.S. Treasury, effective June 30, 1978.[6] Any reasonable person, not necessarily a tax expert, would have realized that the bases of the payments clearly made them royalties (claimable as deductions) rather than levies upon income (creditable to U.S. taxes). There is also little doubt that, given the "awakened" ruling, the countries in question (at the urging of the oil firms) will cosmetically revise the assessment methods to reinstate the payments as creditable taxes.

In fairness to the oil industry, it must be remembered that the dubious nature of the royalty payments was overlooked in the past, because the various best interests of the United States were served by encouraging inflows of foreign oil. Also, with oil at some two dollars or so a barrel, neither the absolute nor relative amounts were as significant as in recent times. However, since 1973, American oil firms have been cast in the roles of partners of the "bad guys." Revelations that foreign tax credits (oil firms account for almost 50 percent of the total) and percentage-depletion allowances have enabled the oil giants to escape with only 1 to 6 percent of their worldwide incomes subject to U.S. income taxes have generated demands that the rules of the game be restructured so that the oil firms pay their fair shares.

The oil industry has not been singled out for crucifixion, but rather to illustrate the chameleonic nature of U.S. tax programs. Changing times and events alter the colors of past reasonings.

On the other hand, the current arguments by American multinationals that foreign tax credits are not business incentives have little foundation. Foreign tax credits were not intended to reduce the effective levies of foreign income taxes. Business also fails to mention that foreign operating (as opposed to passive) incomes are not subject to U.S. taxation until they are received by the U.S. parent. Since money has a time value, deferrals of foreign incomes represent a distinct incentive wherever the effective tax rates of foreign domiciles are less than that of the United States. The large multinationals, particularly, have discretionary control over the timing of repatriations; they can be deferred indefinitely and used to finance expansions of foreign operations or until such time as changes in effective U.S. rates make repatriations more favorable.

Paradoxically, business has obliquely acknowledged the deferral benefits inherent in foreign tax credits by arguing for their retention as vital to their firms' ability to compete with foreign firms. So long as foreign and domestic firms operating in the same domicile overseas are taxed on equal footings, the arguments are mere rhetoric.

Tax Treaties

More than 900 tax treaties between some 150 nations exist today. What follows is necessarily an overview of treaties in general, those of the United States, and the Model Treaty proposed by the OECD.

Bilateral Forms

Tax treaties are usually bilateral agreements between countries that are intended to avoid double taxation; reduce tax harassment; prevent tax avoidance, and encourage certain forms of trade.

The first purpose cited is often necessary to obtain equity where existing methods of foreign tax credits are inadequate for avoiding double taxation.

Treaties also serve to clarify ambiguities in taxing systems that could (or do) result in so-called tax harassment of foreign firms and individuals. Usual topics relate to nondiscrimination clauses (equal tax treatment of foreign and domestic firms and individuals) and clarifications of the primary tax domains (often referred to as source-of-income rules). For enterprises, the source-of-income rules usually require the existence of a permanent establishment, which, in turn, normally depends upon (1) the type of facility and (2) the scope of authority vested in local agents. For individuals, the tax domain is usually established by residence of 183 days or more (the period for teachers is normally two years).[7]

Prevention of tax avoidance usually is approached by simple agreements to exchange tax, earnings, and related payment information. (In the author's opinion, disclosures complying with the spirit and intent of such agreements would do much to reduce the so-called questionable-payments scandals.)

While not openly admitted objectives, many tax treaties reflect the mutual concessions made on hidden agenda items that encourage trade in various goods between the nations involved.

As of April 1976, the United States had tax treaties in force with 37 nations; 4 others awaited ratification, and 11 more were in various stages of negotiation.[8] The only honest statement that can be made relative to existing

U.S. tax treaties is that they vary. Benefits can often accrue, particularly in respect to tax deferrals, by considered revisions in operating locations and structures in order to take advantage of treaty provisions.[9] Other beneficial attributes of U.S. treaties are that they are usually much clearer than U.S. and foreign tax laws; that they supersede those laws; and that they are not as easily amended as the laws and thus are more dependable bases for long-range planning.

Most tax treaties negotiated by the United States have been with industrialized countries. The conspicuous absence of less-developed countries may be reasonably conjectured. Many LDCs offer various investment incentives (usually preferential tax rates or tax holidays—periods free of taxation) to attract needed foreign capital. Consequently, such countries have asked that tax-sparing provisions be included in U.S. treaties in order that the United States would not realize windfall tax benefits as a result of taxes foregone by the LDCs.

Prior to 1970, tax-sparing clauses were included in treaties submitted to the U.S. Senate with six nations (Brazil, India, Israel, Pakistan, Thailand, and the United Arab Republic). During the same period, United States-sponsored initiatives to encourage the development of the LDCs (such as the Western Hemisphere Trade Corporation and the non-gross-up of dividends) were nullified by increases in tax rates by some LDCs, particularly those in Latin America. Smarting from these and other events, the Senate did not approve any of the six treaties.

Tax-sparing provisos are no longer included in treaty negotiations as a matter of U.S. policy. The United States argues, and rightly so, that its deferral provision prevents erosion of tax incentives of other countries so long as the foreign earnings of U.S. subsidiaries are retained or reinvested abroad. What is often glossed over by this argument is the fact that the ability to keep foreign earnings abroad is generally enjoyed only by large U.S. parent firms. Smaller companies that may be more compatible with the needs and desires of the LDCs can rarely afford long-term deferrals.

Multilateral Proposals

In 1963, the Organization for Economic Cooperation and Development (OECD) drafted a model tax treaty that has served as a guide for bilateral negotiations. The need for more uniformity in bilateral treaties has become increasingly important since the value added by foreign subsidiaries of MNEs surpasses that of domestic export sectors. Revisions of the model treaty, suggested by the OECD in 1974,[10] have not met with widespread approval for several reasons—some obvious, some conjectural.

The objectives of the OECD model treaty are basically the same as those of bilateral treaties listed earlier. The problems preventing general adoption merely reflect the greater difficulty involved in obtaining the agreement of a large group of countries rather than two. The tax neutrality goal of the revised OECD model treaty, due to the diversity of tax laws in member-states, can only be achieved by assuring that all countries have the same total effective rate applied to incomes. That requires consideration, if not harmonization, of taxes on corporate income, remittances, withholdings, and individuals—both foreign and domestic. The diverse needs of countries, as reflected by varying emphases on the different taxes, do not bode well for general agreement in the foreseeable future. Another roadblock that exists is the continued insistence by the LDCs that tax-sparing provisions be included.[11]

Foreign Tax Incentives

Many forms of tax incentives are offered by foreign countries in order to achieve a multitude of purposes. Incentives that are relatively permanent and nondiscriminatory in nature will be examined under the label of tax havens. Others that are limited in time or selective in nature will be discussed as tax holidays. Overlappings naturally exist. This crude division has been selected because the two categories are perceived differently by the IRS and have different implications for businessmen.

Tax Havens

Countries such as Bermuda and the Bahamas, that levy no income taxes of any kind, or only trivial amounts relative to those of another country, are typical tax havens.

Prior to 1962, U.S. corporations made extensive use of tax havens as collection and redistribution points for foreign earnings. The receptacle most often used was a sham or foreign-base company—one with little or no substance. Various mechanisms were used; transfer prices, chain invoicings, fictitious or exorbitant fees, and the like, shifted incomes from high-tax countries. Dividend distributions to bases in tax havens (instead of the U.S. parent) were attempts at permanent deferrals of U.S. taxes.

Instead of ending deferrals, the Revenue Act of 1962 added Subpart F, designed to tax concurrently the sham transactions of a controlled foreign corporation (CFC). Subpart F and subsequent revisions consider the following incomes from *transactions between related parties* as distributions of earnings taxable to the U.S. parent:

1. Foreign-personal-holding-company income—"passive" incomes such as dividends, interest, royalties, rents, gains on sales of securities, and the like.
2. Foreign-base-company-sales income—from sales or exchanges of personal property.

3. Foreign-base-company-services income—fees for management, research and development, and similar services.
4. Foreign-base-company-shipping income—excluded by the 1962 Act but covered in the 1975 revision. This is a unique industry, with rules to match.[12]
5. Earnings reinvested in U.S. property.
6. Earnings from insurance of U.S. risks.
7. Withdrawals of incomes from investments in previously excluded (favored) areas, such as LDC and shipping operations (in the 1975 revision).
8. Income from participation in international boycotts, distributions of shares of controlled foreign corporations, and illegal payments (bribes to foreign government officials), added in the 1976 Act.

Businessmen, accountants, and tax attorneys get grey hair (but often get rich, as well) because tax regulations do not say what they mean or mean what they say. Nuances, escape clauses, and relief provisions serve to nullify the avowed purposes of much tax legislation.

Subpart F is a typical example. Control of a foreign corporation rests upon ownership of more than 50 percent of voting power rather than upon effective control. However, only those who own at least a 10 percent interest are counted in determining control. Under the 10-70 rule (formerly 30-70), if 10 percent or less of the gross income of a CFC is Subpart F-type, it is not a deemed distribution; if the amount exceeds 70 percent, then all the income of the CFC is treated as a Subpart F distribution. Finally, no penalties other than concurrent taxation are effectively assessed against Subpart F incomes, since they are eligible for offset by direct or deemed-paid foreign tax credits.

Little, if any, additional U.S. tax revenue resulted from the enactment of Subpart F regulations. Multinationals revised their operating structures to shelter incomes by means of the escape and relief provisions. Deferrals (and the relating plannings and accountings) merely became more bothersome and costly.

Tax Holidays

Selective or otherwise limited tax concessions made by foreign countries—often called tax holidays—are generally considered less nefarious than tax havens, although the end results—deferrals of U.S. taxation—are identical.

Many forms of tax holidays exist: no taxation of foreign earnings at all or, in some cases, on those reinvested in the country; exemptions for relatively short or long time periods; lower rates for selected investments; and attractive depreciation or amortization privileges. Since these concessions are aboveboard (as opposed to covert), the policy of the U.S. Treasury has been to defer potential U.S. taxation so long as the operations were of substance and the earnings remained invested in the particular country in question. Very few compensating or tax-sparing features have been included in U.S. tax treaties with tax-holiday countries. (Exceptions, of course, relate to incentives initiated by the United States for operations in the Western Hemisphere as well as U.S. possessions and dependent states. These U.S. incentives are examined in the next section.)

The Republic of Ireland is a good example. It offers the benefits of being an insider in the Common Market. Irish tax legislation leaves profits on exports of Irish-manufactured goods free of all taxes until 1990. A special corporate tax rate (25 percent instead of 45 percent) can be earned by manufacturers in selected sectors if specified statutory growth rates are attained within given time periods. Total first-year depreciation is also allowed by Irish tax law.[13] Additional nontax incentives are also made available to tax-exempt companies: cash grants for up to half the investment in plant and equipment; attractive tax-lease financing on the balance (low rates from lessor banks that can take advantage of the first-year depreciation feature, which is of no value to tax-exempt companies); and preference-share financing (acceptance by Irish banks of tax-free, redeemable preference shares of tax-exempt companies at lower rates than, and in lieu of, customary note instruments).[14]

Cautions for business fall in two areas at least: (1) the uncertain tax climate following expirations of the tax concessions and (2) the effects upon government services and infrastructures as a result of tax holidays.

Surveillance Methods

As the intricacies of deferral mechanisms multiply for companies, so do the surveillance methods and authorities of the IRS. The most well known of these methods are:[15]

Subpart F—to tax currently covert distributions of earnings, as mentioned earlier.

Section 482—to monitor transfer prices and allocate incomes and deductions in foreign transactions between related taxpayers.

Section 367—to prevent the evasion of taxes on gains derived from the transfer and sale of appreciated assets, or from reorganizations of foreign affiliates.

Section 861—to establish geographic source-of-income rules to identify and allocate foreign-source incomes and deductions.

U.S. Tax Incentives

The incentives for foreign investment provided by U.S. laws are technically called "tax expenditures." Some sectors consider them to be tax preferences or loopholes. Business generally regards them as necessary, but insufficient, to compete internationally with foreign firms.

Incentives available to U.S. corporations are capsuled here, together with their estimated costs in 1974 tax revenues, and their current status:

1. Foreign subsidiaries:
    a. Deferral of earnings, $600 million; made more difficult, but not significantly reduced, by revisions to Subpart F requirements.
    b. Non-gross-up of dividends from developing countries, $55 million; eliminated as of January 1, 1978.
2. Foreign branches:
    a. Additional deferrals for Domestic International Sales Corporations (DISCs), dollar impact unknown; qualifications for continued deferrals made more stringent for large firms by 1975 and subsequent acts.
    b. Reduced rates for Western Hemisphere Trade Corporations (WHTCs), $50 million; phased out by 1980.
    c. Nonrecapture of branch losses initially deducted from parent's return, $150 million; 1976 Act required recapture of losses in subsequent years.
    d. Treatments of oil depletion allowances and development costs, $140 million; reduced or virtually eliminated by 1975 Act.
3. General: Treatment of subnational foreign income taxes as credits rather than as deductions for U.S. tax purposes, $230 million; no effective changes made.

In addition to those listed, incentives are also afforded U.S. corporations to encourage development of U.S. possessions and dependent states (notably Puerto Rico).

Further discussion is warranted on the DISC, WHTC, and Puerto Rican incentives.

Domestic International Sales
Corporation (DISC)

The DISC was authorized in 1971 to encourage the export of U.S. goods and services and to enhance their abilities to compete in international markets. DISCs were primarily organized as export sales arms of U.S. manufacturers. So long as the DISC met the statutory requirements each year, the income of the DISC was taxed to the parent corporation at a maximum effective rate of 24 percent. (Half of the DISC income was deferred; the remaining half was taxed to the parent at the 48 percent corporate rate.) If the DISC failed to meet the requirements in a given year, the accumulated income deferred would be taxable to the parent, payable evenly over a period the lesser of twice the term the DISC quallified or ten years.

In short, the DISC was not taxed. Only the parent firm was taxed on half the DISC income; the remainder was deferred so long as status was maintained. An additional 11-month deferral was possible where the fiscal year of the DISC fell one month after that of the parent. Given the stringent annual qualifications, which follow, most DISCs faced eventual loss of status and elimination of accumulated deferrals. The ultimate benefits of the DISC to the parent and the costs to the U.S. government represented the time value of money (interest).

Requirements for DISC status were 95 percent of gross receipts from sales of export property (products produced or grown in the United States having less than 50 percent of value represented by imported components); and 95 percent of assets at the end of each year in qualified export assets (export inventories, receivables, and producer loans). The only escape valve built into the asset requirement was the ability to count loans to producers—which could include the parent—and investments in the Export-Import Bank, and the like.

The 1976 Revenue Act limited the amount of DISC income that could be deferred to 50 percent of that income in excess of 67 percent of its base-period income (the previous four years). This revision hurt established DISCs, since they could continue to benefit only if they continuously expanded operations, and then only on one-third of the growth in profits. Those DISCs beginning in 1976 or later were given a four-year breathing spell, in effect, before the base period became a threat to their status and deferral privilege.[16]

Western Hemisphere Trade
Corporation (WHTC)

The Western Hemisphere Trade Corporation was established under Section 921; it afforded a special deduction from taxable income by Section 922.

A U.S. corporation could form a WHTC as a sales arm if all of its business was done in the Western Hemisphere (excluding Bermuda and Falkland Islands); if 95 percent of its gross income was from such sources outside the United States; and if 90 percent of its gross income was active (as opposed to passive, generally).

The WHTC could operate from anywhere in the Western Hemisphere, including the United States; however, title had to pass on 95 percent of sales in a qualified Western Hemisphere country other than the United States. The final destination of the goods was irrelevant. Purchases of all but incidentals (up to 5 percent, usually) had to be from within the Western Hemisphere but could have been manufactured anywhere.

Prior to 1976, a qualified WHTC enjoyed a special deduction from taxable income (not a direct reduction in tax rate) of

$$\frac{14\%}{\text{normal + surtax rate}}$$

Based upon the standard U.S. corporate tax structure prior to 1975 (normal tax of 22 percent on the first $25,000 plus a surtax of 26 percent on any excess, or a total of 48 percent), the effective tax rate was slightly less than 16 percent on WHTC taxable incomes up to $35,000 and 34 percent on the excess.

The 1976 Revenue Act phased out the WHTC deduction by reducing the 14 percent numerator in the foregoing fraction as follows: 1976 to 11 percent; 1977 to 8 percent; 1978 to 5 percent; 1979 to 2 percent; and 1980 to no benefit.

During the phase-out period, parents of WHTCs have three options for reorganization: as a foreign corporation, as a DISC, or, possibly, as a possessions corporation. Since such reorganizations are subject to Section 367, toll charges on asset transfers can be offset more effectively early in the phase-out period, while the WHTC deduction is largest.

Possessions Corporations

To encourage U.S. investment in its possessions and dependent states, special U.S. tax incentives were enacted for possessions in general (Section 931) and Puerto Rico in particular (Section 933).

Domestic U.S. corporations with gross incomes of which at least 80 percent were derived within a possession, and at least 50 percent were earned in an active business, were not subject to U.S. tax until the income was received in the United States. Upon receipt in the United States, incomes were taxed the same as any other foreign income.

U.S. corporations operating in Puerto Rico, for example, generally benefited from Puerto Rican tax holidays of up to 30 years. Consequently, earnings accumulated in Puerto Rico usually remained there or were reinvested in other foreign operations.

To encourage repatriation of profits accumulated in possessions, the 1976 Act indirectly permitted the earnings to be sent to the U.S. parents free of any U.S. tax (Puerto Rican tax of 7 percent would be levied on repatriations made prior to the expiration time of the firm's tax holiday). The new act merely taxed the repatriations as foreign income and provided for a simultaneous tax-sparing credit of the same amount.

Many clouds threaten the Puerto Rican tax sanctuary, even though possessions corporations were the only foreign operations to benefit from the 1976 Act. In June 1978, Puerto Rico replaced its 100 percent tax exemption for new industries and products with a schedule calling for graduated reductions to 50 percent over time and graduated increases in effective corporate taxes from 2.2 percent to 22.5 percent. The U.S. government is still smarting over the earnings accumulated in Puerto Rico—estimated from $3 billion to $6 billion. Finally, the IRS is challenging the fairness of transfer prices used by Puerto Rican affiliates of many large U.S. pharmaceutical firms.[17]

Foreign Income, Earnings, and Profits

Concepts of income, earnings, and profits are far more complicated in the area of international taxation than they are in domestic taxation.

Major concerns relate to matters of definition, classification, remission, location, and generation.

Definition of foreign income is critical. Income as defined for taxation in foreign countries rarely agrees with U.S. tax laws. Foreign income must be recast to conform with U.S. tax-accounting standards, and, in the process, the statutory foreign tax rate becomes meaningless. The effective foreign tax rate (foreign tax liability divided by income as defined by the United States) will indicate whether or not a potential tax liability exists.

The *classification* or nature of the income, in whole or in part, will determine whether or not it will be subject to deferral or concurrent taxation by the United States.

The *remission* or payment of foreign-source income to the U.S. parent subjects the transaction to taxation by the United States, less any foreign tax credits or other relief provisions that might apply.

Location (or source) and *generation* (or time frame) of foreign incomes affect the calculations of earnings and profits as well as accumulated profits—both of which are terms peculiar to tax jargon. *Retained earnings* is an accounting term. *Earnings and profits* is a tax term, often used but never defined in the Internal Revenue Code, and is similar to retained earnings except that earnings and profits must be calculated each year for each foreign location and assembled in a LIFO layer-cake fashion. Accumulated profits are maintained in a similar manner and represent earnings and profits, less amounts taxed currently in the United States (such as Subpart F income).

Foreign tax liabilities and dividend distributions must be related to a specific year's earnings and profits in order to compute foreign tax credits and other potential benefits.

The foregoing comments stress the need for mutual understanding and cooperation between the accounting and tax departments of corporations. For instance, the tax department cannot use consolidated financial statements; it needs detailed reports for each foreign operation. Also, foreign tax receipts and copies of foreign tax returns (translated into English) are essential and may be difficult to obtain from other than controlled foreign entities. (These latter needs should be included in all written agreements covering operating arrangements with less-than-controlled foreign firms.)

Tax Planning

Any consideration of international tax planning should always be made subject to two cardinal rules:

1. Tax considerations are important, but under no circumstances should they act to relegate business strategy to a minor role.
2. Change, in frequency and magnitude, will severely restrict the potential benefits of international tax planning.

Those who ignore or reject these rules tread where angels fear to go. Those who recognize and appreciate the warnings often choose not to plan at all; they walk the same path as the first group, but a few steps to the rear. Each leaves the future to chance—the first unwittingly, the second by choice.

International tax planning lies on the middle ground; it has potential benefits as well as limitations. The United States must share most of the blame, since its tax philosophy and system are the most complicated and other nations are tending to emulate it.

International tax planning is the process in which all relevant known and projected business factors, both tax and nontax, are considered in order to determine whether, how, where, and with whom to enter into and conduct business operations so that the total tax burden may be kept as low as possible while attaining the desired business objectives.

Given this definition, the planning of new international ventures has a slight edge over that for ongoing operations.

Tax planning for new ventures[18] affords wider choice of country and form of taxable entity, at least insofar as the possible tax costs associated with changes in these choices are concerned. International tax planning for proposed new operations should include the following measures:

1. Obtain as much information as possible regarding the existing business and tax climates in the locations under consideration.
2. Evaluate the business and tax aspects of each location and form of organization.
3. Select the most favorable location and entity form based upon business objectives (present and future), the lowest total current tax burden, and the ability to cope with changes in the future.
4. Obtain the review and opinions of experts on the locations considered. (Public accounting firms and their foreign affiliate networks are excellent sources of counsel.)
5. Manage change by monitoring the business and tax climates in the foreign locations and in the United States.

Some may not consider the last step as a part of planning. However, to the extent that planning produces a destination and a roadmap, planners are well advised to monitor detours that may occur along the road to assure that the destination is not lost along the way.

Managing change, or coping with uncertainties, is the most demanding and tedious step, as will be evident from the following examples of planning for or adjusting ongoing operations.

Essential components of the tax planning of ongoing operations are specialists in the field of international taxation, responsive accounting and other information systems, continuous interchange of communication between headquarters and foreign management, and close (formal and informal) association between local management and tax authorities in the foreign countries. (Some argue that computerized models are essential, but, in the author's opinion, humans can adjust much more rapidly to change than can computer programs.)

On second thought, tax planning for ongoing international operations should more properly be called tax supervision. For United States-based parents, three major problems must be coped with: (1) how to minimize foreign taxes; (2) how to minimize U.S. taxes; and (3) how to do both in the event of change.

Foreign taxes can by minimized best by knowing the rules in the particular countries and by not being too greedy. Foreign governments are not the problem—most merely want some tax. Apparent greed in a foreign domicile poses the threat of loss of deferral privileges in the United States, particularly under Subpart F or Section 482 (transfer pricing). The effective tax rates in foreign countries (based upon income as defined by the United States) must be analyzed. Foreign nonincome levies (such as VAT) must be taken into account, in amount and in character (noncreditable against U.S. income taxes). Withholding rates on dividends and other remittances must be reckoned with. In some countries, such as Iran, repatriations may be taxed at four or five times the income-tax rate. Also, in the case of multiple overseas operations, dividends may be routed through an affiliate location, having a favorable tax treaty with the country of origin and the United States.

There is also little question that foreign income taxes may be minimized in tax-haven or tax-holiday countries. Here again, the best caution is to know the local conditions and the rules of the game. Eventually, specious uses of such tax sanctuaries may prove to be costly. Firms operating in such locations are at once suspect by the IRS. Unless the sanctuary is closely related with the United States (such as Puerto Rico), requests for tax relief when local shelters are removed or expire can fall upon a virtually deaf IRS. Given an uncertain future, operations in tax sanctuaries should be undertaken with the realization that subsequent events may result in some costs of immediate taxation in the United States or charges upon reorganization and transfer of assets. The time value of the money saved on taxes deferred should be appreciated—and the wounds should be licked and forgotten.

Finally, the economic effect of foreign taxes can be minimized by determining whether to pay them from foreign or U.S. assets. Naturally, the currency with the lowest purchasing power should be selected.

Guidelines for the minimization of U.S. taxes are more dependable but also more complicated.

The very nature of the foreign tax credit mandates use of a flexible or pay-as-you-see-fit dividend policy on foreign earnings. A simplified example is shown in table 14-1. Wherever possible, the time value of money dictates that unused credits should be avoided. In this respect, elimination of the per-country method in favor of the overall method has removed some of the effects of uncertain future foreign tax rates. On the other hand, repeal of the per-country

Table 14-1
Timing of Dividends and the Foreign Tax Credit
(in thousands)

Facts: U.S. parent wishes to distribute *equivalent* of $250,000 per year. Foreign operations are as follows:

			Year		
	1	*2*	*3*	*4*	*Total*
Total profits	$1000	$1000	$1000	$1000	$4000
Foreign taxes paid	300	500	300	500	1600
Net profits	$ 700	$ 500	$ 700	$ 500	$2400

Option 1: Distribute $250,000 from each year's profits:

	1	*2*	*3*	*4*	
Dividend	$250	$250	$250	$250	
U.S. tax before credit	$171	$240	$171	$240	
Foreign tax credit	(107)[a]	(250)[b]	(107)[a]	(250)[b]	
U.S. tax after credit	$ 64	$ -0-	$ 64	$ -0-	$128

Total U.S. tax on dividends = $128,000

Option 2: Distribute $500,000 from each of years 2 and 4:

	1	*2*	*3*	*4*	
Dividend	$ -0-	$500	$ -0-	$500	
U.S. tax before credit	$ -0-	$480	$ -0-	$480	
Foreign tax credit	0	(500)[c]	0	(500)[c]	
U.S. tax after credit	$ -0-	$ -0-	$ -0-	$ -0-	$ -0-

No U.S. tax on dividends

[a]300 × (250/700) = 107.
[b]500 × (250/500) = 250.
[c]500 × (500/500) = 500.

method can substantially reduce the credit of an affiliated group filing a consolidated U.S. return.

Tax treaties, existing and pending, should be examined for potential savings. In many cases, the advantages of newly approved treaties may have to be weighed against possible future charges upon reorganization and transfer of assets.

Appropriate U.S. tax incentives should be examined. Some, such as the DISC, should be recognized for what they really are—temporary but valuable deferral options that should be evaluated on the basis of the time value of money. Possessions corporations may represent convenient repositories for tax-free local and passive foreign earnings; may sometimes be used as sources of financing for overseas expansion; but also may tempt abuse of transfer prices in transactions with the U.S. parent.

Last, but not least, much of the foregoing effort may be offset (or accentuated) by fluctuations in the prices of monies reflected in the required translations.[19]

The third planning factor—minimizing taxes in the event of change—is a reactive mechanism. In most cases, some form of international restructuring or reorganization will be called for. The tax aspects of international reorganizations are affected by a veritable maze of U.S. Code sections. Many conflicting alternatives will exist and must be weighed in light of current and projected levels of international operations.

Summary

International taxation is a highly specialized field involving ongoing analysis of trade-offs that are themselves in a state of flux. Examination at any point in time represents but a still picture of a moving scene.

For some, tax aspects have replaced international business acumen in importance. Others concentrate upon the creation of income wherever opportunities exist and consider taxation to be an unmanageable cost of doing business. Still others—and these are the large majority—tread the middle ground, attending to both the lawful creation and retention of income. The latter group tends to recognize international tax planning as a maze of variables, the inherent benefit of which is not to be found in taxes saved—for who keeps a record of the opportunity costs? The true value of international tax planning lies in the better understanding created of the complex organism known as the multinational enterprise.

A very small minority of corporations (and individuals) will find lawful means of paying no taxes at all, at least for a period of time. Lawful or otherwise, few societies look with favor upon those who, by position or purse, find means to avoid paying their fair shares of taxes, which, after all, are the costs of civilization.

Notes

1. The value-added tax has perennially been considered in the United States. A review by the AICPA concluded that a better choice would be a comprehensive sales tax, revised to exempt exports, and administered by the federal government. *Statement of Tax Policy No. 2*, "Value-Added Tax" (New York: AICPA, 1976).

2. See Frederic K. Howard, "Overview of International Taxation," *Columbia Journal of World Business*, Summer 1975, pp. 6-8; Charles E. McLure, Jr., and Stanley S. Surrey, "Integration of Income Taxes: Issues for Debate," *Harvard Business Review*, September-October 1977, pp. 169-181; and Ernest S. Christian, Jr., *Integrating the Corporate Tax: Methods, Motivations, and Effects*, Reprint No. 80 (Washington, D.C.: Center for Tax Policy Studies, American Enterprise Institute, 1977), p. 40.

3. Ernst & Ernst, *Foreign and U.S. Corporate Income and Withholding Tax Rates*, January 1978, Retrieval No. 48388.

4. Elliot G. Steinberg and Sheldon M. Sisson, "Foreign Tax Credit: How Taxpayers are Affected by New Rules Under TRA 1976," *Journal of Taxation*, April 1977, pp. 250-254.

5. Gulf Oil reportedly saved $20 million in U.S. taxes in 1976 by filing separate returns as required by the Tax Reform Act of 1976. "Many Happy Returns," *Wall Street Journal*, November 23, 1977, p. 1.

6. "Treasury Bars Tax Credits to Oil Firms for Certain Payments to Saudis, Libyans," *Wall Street Journal*, January 17, 1978, p. 16.

7. The source-of-income rules for U.S. firms and citizens are contained in Sections 861-864 of the Internal Revenue Code; those governing foreign corporations appear in Sections 881-884.

8. *Taxation and Finance*, No. 74 (Washington, D.C.: Bureau of National Affairs, Inc., 1976), Section J, p. 6. Details on U.S. treaties may be obtained from the local offices of the large national CPA firms, or from Tax Management, Inc., a division of the Bureau of National Affairs, Inc., Washington, D.C. 20037.

9. Ronald Drier, "U.S. Income Tax Treaties," *Columbia Journal of World Business*, Summer 1975, pp. 21-28.

10. *Double Taxation of Income and Capital* (Paris: OECD, 1974).

11. Peggy B. Musgrave, "The OECD Model Tax Treaty: Problems and Prospects," *Columbia Journal of World Business*, Summer 1975, pp. 29-39.

12. Barry Newman and Jeffery Kadet, "United States Taxation of Foreign Flag Shipping," *Columbia Journal of World Business*, Spring 1977, pp. 103-111.

13. *Price Waterhouse Information Guide*, "Doing Business in the Republic of Ireland" (New York: Price Waterhouse & Co., September 1977) and the *Tax Supplement*, "Tax Planning for Irish Operations," October 1977.

14. Richard H. Kalish and John P. Casey, "The Dilemma of the International Tax Executive," *Columbia Journal of World Business*, Summer 1975, pp. 66-68.

15. See George C. Watt, Richard M. Hammer, and Marianne Burge, *Accounting for the Multinational Corporation* (New York: Financial Executives Research Foundation, 1977), chapters 27, 31, 32, and 33.

16. Harry G. Gourevitch, "DISC's Ability to Defer Tax on Income Restricted by Tax Reform Act of 1976," *Journal of Taxation*, January 1977, pp. 9-13.

17. "Closing in on Puerto Rico's Tax Haven," *Business Week*, May 22, 1978, pp. 154, 156.

18. Three excellent cases are presented in Kalish and Casey, "The Dilemma of the International Tax Executive," pp. 62-73.

19. Michael L. Moore and Ronald N. Bagley, *Studies in Federal Taxation No. 6*, "U.S. Tax Aspects of Doing Business Abroad," (New York: AICPA, 1978), pp. 345-360.

15

Internationalism: Accounting Full-Circle

The future represents uncertainty. Because of this, the future is a safer place for writers.

The opinions sprinkled liberally throughout this book will be disagreed with by some and challenged by others. That is precisely the purpose for expressing considered opinions. We often learn what we really think by questioning others. Some of us have even learned to change our opinions.

At the risk of belaboring the topic of opinions, some comments should be directed to students of accounting. Early on in introductory courses, accounting students struggle to master *the* way accounting is supposedly performed. As they progress, these same students learn that, more often than not, many ways of accounting may be applied to a given situation; the method selected will depend upon their opinions of what is best. The makings of opinions regarding materiality and fairness permeate the whole of accounting without ever being defined other than by convention.

Accounting, then, becomes recognized as a process in which considered opinions are reflected through organized ways of doing things, or conventions. Opinions are of the higher order of importance. The process of developing considered opinions is learned behavior. The best way to learn is to question, not to the point of being repugnant or of doing nothing, but by reasoned examinations of issues, familiar and unfamiliar.

Evolution and Revolution

To the extent that accountancy is a profession having a public interest and, consequently, a public responsibility, accountants must learn to recognize when the results of their considered opinions conflict with economic sense—and must learn to reconsider. On the other hand, it will be just as important, if not more so, that accountants learn that it is best to lose clients whose actions affront the considered opinions of economic and ethical sense of society as a whole. Both must evolve if accountancy is to retain its status as an independent profession in the United States.

The multinational enterprise will also continue to adapt to change. The next most likely stage in its evolution appears to be the transnational network (TNN) suggested by Perlmutter (see chapter 1). Not all MNEs will grow in this manner. Many will and have divested themselves of operations abroad for a variety of reasons. The MNEs or TNNs that remain will continue to be agents of change.

265

To the industrial countries, including the United States, the multinationals will continue to bring increased competition and consumer choice. Some domestic industries that have become complacent and fossilized will seek out the government, first as protector, next as a partner. Many will not survive. All will change.

To emerging and developing nations (those young and not so young), the multinationals will bring change in the form of evolution and revolution. Social change will occur by both means, although the effect of the multinationals will involve the tedious and often painful process of socioeconomic evolution—improvement in the standards of living for peoples as a whole. Various economic frameworks will be tried, but, for the large majority of nations, some degree of private enterprise will be found to work better than controlled isolation. Coping with "to each, according to his need" presents little problem; obtaining "from each, according to his ability" is quite another matter. The revolution brought by the multinationals to most emerging nations will be the industrial or technological one that passed them by two centuries ago. The MNEs will bring the promises and the problems of industrialization.

The major contribution of the evolving multinational will probably be indirect and will involve a growing appreciation of interdependency among all nations.

International Reporting

Accounting is apolitical and transcends national boundaries. As such, it can assist the recognition of interdependency among nations. It can help improve the management of companies and countries, as well as the flow and allocation of resources—natural, human, financial, and technological.

All the foregoing are contingent upon the ability of accountants (1) to earn and maintain the essential public and governmental confidence in financial reports, and (2) to make their services and language as international as the publics they serve.

The first task only requires some fence-mending in the United States and most other industrial nations. In some other countries, accounting is tolerated, yet suspect, much the same as is business in general. In still others, the role of accounting will initially involve helping emerging governments to manage resources, since industry does not exist to any meaningful degree.

The second job will take some doing; it has already begun, and it is helping accomplish the first goal as well.

Much has already been accomplished by the large accounting firms, which were forced to become as international in scope as their client firms. Kubin[1] has reported that, as of 1975, at least ten U.S. accounting firms had become multinational practitioners—each operating member-offices in 25 or more foreign countries. (Kubin also stated that data were not available for another six American accounting firms that might well have qualified for inclusion.[2]) In total, the ten firms maintained nearly twice as many offices abroad as in the United States (1,294 versus 722),[3] and only one firm reported fewer foreign than domestic offices. Kubin also noted that the global nature of accounting firms was an "Anglo-American phenomenon."[4] Firms based in other countries tended to be regional in that foreign offices were limited to one or a few spheres having certain commonalities.

Just as foreign business operations outgrew their stepchild roles, there are signs that foreign affiliate offices of multinational accounting firms have evolved into full-fledged partnerships. Most large U.S. accounting firms expanded overseas by associating with qualified local firms in the foreign countries selected. Over time, the local practitioners became partners in the international segment but not in the worldwide organization, since one did not exist. Initially, a one-firm concept seemed implausible because of the differences in national laws and regulations. Today, there are movements toward a one-firm, worldwide organization in which the foreign partners are full-fledged members. Examples are Coopers & Lybrand, Arthur Andersen & Co. (October 1977), and Peat Marwick (July 1978).

Concurrent growth in two directions—national and international—presented many dilemmas, internal and external.

A single-firm concept requires reasonably integrated auditing standards, which must be developed and maintained. The most successful approach thus far has been based upon the construction of modular segments that can be selected and applied as conditions warrant anywhere in the world.

External problems have yet to be put to rest. Reorganizations and one-firm concepts result in larger entities that fly in the face of urgings (such as those in Moss and Metcalfe reports) for dismemberment of the so-called "Big-Eight" firms and more direct surveillance by the SEC. The profession's success will depend upon its willingness to surrender authority for peer review to an effective public oversight board or, alternatively, to the SEC. Events could cause the pendulum to swing in either direction.

The accounting profession in the United States is certainly old enough in years to police itself. Whether it is mature enough to recognize that retention of its status as a self-governing profession depends upon its actions in the public interest—rather than in its own self-interest—remains to be demonstrated.

International Accounting

A moment's reflection indicates that the genesis of accounting represents an international birthright. Accounting is a synthesis of the contributions of many peoples and nations.

The Babylonians contributed the concepts of private property, insurance, and silver as a store of value. The Greeks refined the use of money as a common denominator, developed the tabular account, and formalized the rudimentary practices of auditing. The Roman empires created a wide variety of complex legal, political, social, and religious organizations that paved the way for commerce and trade, while the needs of the feudal estates prompted the concept of duality in accounts. The Turks, by seizing the Holy Land, united the nations of Christendom and amassed their resources in one locale. The Italians synergized these resources into productive capital, created vast banking networks, developed the use of credit monies, organized large business *compagnie*, and devised an efficient method of recording their interests and profits. A German, Johann Gutenberg, perfected the use of movable printing type, and a Franciscan monk described the double-entry methodology in print for use by the rest of the world.

The exodus of bookkeeping methods and the development of accounting that followed resulted in the crystallization of national practices. Today there is American accounting, British accounting, French accounting, and so on. Differences in national laws and the various degrees of involvement in (and respect for) business were primarily responsible. Also, the language of business was not as apolitical as that of mathematics or the natural sciences and did not travel as well. The net result is a business language having a number of dialects.

Two forms of reconciliation are often suggested: harmonization and uniformity.

Harmonization in accounting is comparable to that in music. Various practices (or tones) exist and are blended or combined (as with chords) into an orderly structure with synergistic results—the whole being greater in value or usefulness than the sum of its parts. Such an arrangement enables accounting to serve particular needs within a local environment while maintaining an accord with the needs of the larger regional or international communities.

Uniformity, on the other hand, represents more of an unvarying sameness, with consequent rigidities in structure, application, and purpose. Uniform accounting could hardly serve varying needs. In truth, the needs of the users of accounting information would have to become nearly identical in order for uniform accounting to accommodate them.

On balance, there is much more reason to believe that accounting and reporting practices will adapt to evolving needs than to expect the needs of a diverse world community to converge into a rather narrow band. Historically, accounting has survived and prospered because of its affinity to adaptation. There is little cause to renounce the belief that accounting practices will be modified to serve the needs of the international community.

It should be remembered that, in today's terms, the international community is a composite of nations that, at least in the economic sense, represents a study more of contrasts than of similarities. Since the needs for accounting information of industrial nations differ from those of the simpler, agrarian economies, the various states of the accounting art also differ. Time will be required for metamorphosis.

In the poorest, lesser-developed countries, time will be necessary to permit the growth of industry and business. As the language of business, accounting should also grow and benefit. As their self-confidence grows, these countries will tend to join various spheres of accounting influence determined by historical, geographical, or ideological relationships. Within each sphere, one or two progressive nations will serve as the flux for internal harmonization of accounting practices. Further harmonization among spheres will occur later. How much later will depend upon how soon the fledgling nations feel comfortable with the business environments, internal and international.

A significant harmonization of accounting and disclosure practices of industrial nations will be accomplished in the next decade. The IASC and the EEC will play the major roles. The impetus will come more from the demands of business than from the desires of accountants.

Accounting Full-Circle

Accounting enjoyed an international birthright. In the past, accounting traveled and prospered in the wake of international trade. In the future, international accounting will develop in response to the demands of international business— and will come full-circle.

Mutual awareness of the need for international accounting is the essential step. This awareness will develop as more and more nations move along the continuum from dependency, to nationalism, to interdependency, and, ultimately, to internationalism.

Notes

1. Konrad W. Kubin, "The International Profession of Accountancy," *Collected Papers of the American Accounting Association's Annual Meeting*, August 18-20, 1975, Tucson, Arizona (Sarasota, Fla.: AAA, 1975), pp. 123-135.

2. Ibid., p. 125.

3. Ibid., table 2, p. 126.

4. Ibid., p. 127.

Glossary

AAA. American Accounting Association. An organization founded in 1916, composed primarily of accounting educators. Its major journal, *The Accounting Review,* has regressed from conceptual discussions to abstract symbolism.

AIA. American Institute of Accountants. Forerunner of the present official organization of the accounting profession in the United States—the American Institute of Certified Public Accountants.

AICPA. American Institute of Certified Public Accountants. The "Institute," as it is often called, is the professional society of American CPAs. The official publication, *Journal of Accountancy,* addresses conceptual and practical issues as well as reviews official pronouncements in the United States and elsewhere.

AISG. Accountants International Study Group. A cooperative effort begun in 1966 by the professional institutes of Great Britain, Ireland, Canada, and the United States. The group of approximately a dozen individuals issued occasional reports of comparative studies of accounting practices in the countries represented before it was disbanded in late 1977.

APB. Accounting Principles Board. The standard-setting body of the American accounting profession from Sept. 1, 1959 to May 31, 1973.

APBO. Accounting Principles Board Opinions. Authoritative pronouncements (31 in total) of the APB, issued after research and study.

APBS. Accounting Principles Board Statements. Preliminary expositions (four in number) issued by the APB in advance of research and study, to enhance understanding of issues.

ASC. Accounting Standards Committee. The standard-setting body of the British accounting profession with representation by all six major accounting groups. Succeeded the ASSC (change in name only) following issuance of the Sandilands report in 1976.

ASR. Accounting Series Release. Issued by the Securities and Exchange Commission. Compliance is mandatory in reports to the Commission by registered companies.

ASSC. Accounting Standards Steering Committee. Predecessor of the ASC in the United Kingdom. The word "steering" was deleted in 1976.

BEA. Bureau of Economic Analysis of the U.S. Department of Commerce. Requires data inputs to implement Public Law 94-472, the International Investment Survey Act.

CASB. Cost Accounting Standards Board. A five-member body responsible to the U.S. Congress under Public Law 91-379, charged with the pronouncement of uniform cost accounting standards applicable to negotiated defense contracts.

CCA. Current cost accounting. A method of price-level accounting (popularized by the Sandilands report) with the objective of protecting the current cost or value of a firm's assets. A derivative of replacement value theory.

CFC. Controlled foreign corporation. A U.S. tax term referring to a non-U.S. corporation with 50 percent or more of its voting stock owned by a U.S. parent firm.

CICA. Canadian Institute of Chartered Accountants. The professional accountants' society of Canada, with the authority to establish accounting and reporting standards in the private sector.

CPP. Current purchasing power. A method of accounting for changes in *general* price-levels proposed by the Accounting Standards Steering Committee of the United Kingdom (in its Statement of Standard Accounting Practice No. 7), patterned after the general-purchasing-power proposal in the United States except that the U.K. committee preferred use of the Consumer Price Index.

CRVA. Current replacement value accounting. A collection of various, although similar, methods of accounting for changes in prices of *specific* assets to protect either the productive capacity or the current value of a firm's assets.

DISC. Domestic international sales corporation. An organizational vehicle of the U.S. Internal Revenue Code to encourage U.S. exports by deferral of corporate income taxes on half of qualified net income.

ECOSOC. Economic and Social Council of the United Nations. A primary objective is the socioeconomic development of the less-developed member nations.

EEC. European Economic Community or the European Common Market.

FASB. Financial Accounting Standards Board. Organized on June 1, 1973 (as successor to the Accounting Principles Board) to promulgate financial accounting practices in the private sector of the U.S. economy.

FTC. Federal Trade Commission. In concert with the Justice Department, it is charged with implementing the antitrust provisions of the Sherman and Clayton Acts.

GATT. General Agreement on Tariffs and Trade. A contractual document or agreement (not a legal organization) aimed at minimizing restrictive discrimination in international trade. Created in 1947, the agreement represents a contractual arrangement among the nations which become signatories.

GPLFS. General-price-level financial statements. A term applied to financial reports expressed in terms of the general purchasing power of a currency (such as the dollar) as of a given date rather than in numbers of units of the currency.

GPP. General purchasing power. The command over domestic goods and services of a currency (such as the dollar) at a given date. Various price indexes (such as the Gross National Product Implicit Price Deflator) are available and denote changes in general price levels of various market baskets of goods and services over time.

IASC. International Accounting Standards Committee. Formed in June 1973 by the professional bodies in the United States and nine other countries to publish international accounting standards. Member societies pledge their "best efforts" to gain national acceptance of published standards. Membership now exceeds 53 societies in 42 nations.

IBOP. International balance of payments.

IBRD. International Bank for Reconstruction and Development. An agency of the United Nations organized in 1947 and commonly known as the "World Bank."

ICA. International Congress of Accountants. Meetings of members of professional societies in interested countries every five years since 1904 have involved fraternal exchanges of ideas.

ICCAP. International Coordination Committee for the Accountancy Profession. Organized by the Tenth International Congress of Accountants in 1972 to pursue a "coordinated worldwide accounting profession with uniform standards."

IDA. International Development Association. A subunit of the International Monetary Fund. Provides long-term loans to the world's poorest nations at low (usually less than one percent) service charges.

IFAC. International Federation of Accountants. Established in October 1977 by the Eleventh International Congress of Accountants to issue guidelines for upgrading educational, ethical, and auditing standards.

IFC. International Finance Corporation. A World Bank affiliate which provides nonguaranteed loans to private companies in developing countries.

IMF. International Monetary Fund. The clearing house and overseer of the worldwide money system established by the Bretton Woods agreement in 1945.

IRS. Internal Revenue Service. The familiar tax-collecting arm of the U.S. Treasury Department.

LDC. Less-developed country. Often referred to as a developing country or "have-not" nation. Collectively, LDCs are often referred to as the "third world" (an incorrect political connotation) or the "fourth world" (a socioeconomic term).

MNC. Multinational corporation. Loosely defined as a corporation with business operations in several countries.

MNE. Multinational enterprise. A business organization, not necessarily a corporation nor privately owned, with business operations in several countries.

NAA. National Association of Accountants. A U.S. organization (formerly known as the National Association of Cost Accountants) whose members are predominantly accountants in industry. The published journal, *Management Accounting,* covers conceptual and practical topics.

OECD. Organization for Economic Cooperation and Development. An association organized by 24 member countries, primarily industrialized nations, to encourage and expand trade in the free world.

OPEC. Organization of Petroleum Exporting Countries. Composed of Algeria, Ecuador, Gabon, Indonesia, Iran, Iraq, Kuwait, Libya, Nigeria, Qatar, Saudi Arabia, United Arab Emirates (seven small sheikdoms), and Venezuela.

OPIC. Overseas Private Investment Corporation. A U.S institution with a joint private-public directorship, created by the Foreign Assistance Act of 1969 to provide coverage against political and commercial risks of private American investments in less-developed countries.

SEC. Securities and Exchange Commission. Authorized by the U.S. Securities Acts of 1933 and 1934 to oversee the offering and trading of public securities and to establish the accounting and reporting standards of registered firms.

SSAP. Statement of Standard Accounting Practice. The vehicle used by the British accounting profession to promulgate official accounting standards for the private sector in the United Kingdom. Equivalent to statements of the current Financial Accounting Standards Board in the United States.

TNN. Transnational network. A form of future multinational enterprise envisioned by Professor Howard Perlmutter, having various "stakeholders"— governments, unions, banks, and employees, as well as private investors.

UNCTAD. United Nations Conference on Trade and Development. The U.N. organization composed of the less-developed countries. Obtained U.N. acceptance of a "New International Economic Order" as a goal in 1975.

VAT. Value-added tax. A form of sales tax peculiar to the European Economic Community levied upon the incremental increases in the values of goods produced as opposed to the consumption stage common to the United States.

WHTC. Western hemisphere trade corporation. A firm under U.S. tax laws that purchased and transferred title to the majority (95 percent) of its goods within the Western hemisphere. A special deduction from taxable income allowed to qualifying corporations will be phased out by 1980.

Selected Bibliography

American Accounting Association. Committee Reports. *The Accounting Review, Supplement to Volume 48*, 1973, pp. 120-167.

_____. *Supplement to Volume 49*, 1974, pp. 250-269.

_____. *Supplement to Volume 51*, 1976, pp. 198-212.

_____. *Supplement to Volume 52*, 1977, pp.65-132.

Arthur Andersen & Co. *Accounting and Reporting Problems of the Accounting Profession*. 5th ed. Chicago: August 1976.

_____. *Client Inflation Clinic*. A report on Inflation and Accounting for Inflation in Europe. Chicago: September 1975.

Anthony, Robert N. "A Case for Historical Costs." *Harvard Business Review*, November-December 1976, pp. 69-79.

_____. *Planning and Control Systems: A Framework for Analysis*. Boston: Harvard Business School Division of Research, 1965.

Apter, David E., and Goodman, Louis Wolf (eds.). *The Multinational Corporation and Social Change*. New York: Praeger Publishers, 1976.

Barrett, M. Edgar. "Case of the Tangled Transfer Price." *Harvard Business Review*, May-June 1977, pp. 20-22, 26, 28, 32, 36, 176, 178.

Carmichael, D.R. "The Report of Tentative Conclusions of the Commission on Auditors' Responsibilities: What Does It Say?" *Journal of Accountancy*, August 1977, pp. 55-60.

Chamberlain, Neil W. *The Limits of Corporate Responsibility*. New York: Basic Books, 1973.

Choi, Frederick D.S., and Mueller, Gerhard G. *An Introduction to Multinational Accounting*. Englewood Cliffs, N.J.: Prentice-Hall, Inc., 1978.

Christian, Ernest S., Jr. *Integrating the Corporate Tax: Methods, Motivations, and Effects*. Reprint No. 80. Washington, D.C.: Center for Tax Policy Studies, American Enterprise Institute, 1977.

Churchman, C. West. *The Systems Approach*. New York: Dell Publishing Co., 1968.

Columbia Journal of World Business. Focus: International Taxation. Summer 1975.

Conference on Currency Translation in Business Operation. *Proceedings*. Miami, Fla.: School of Business and Organizational Sciences, Florida International University, March 18-19, 1977.

Davis, Gordon B. *Management Information Systems: Conceptual Foundations, Structure, and Development*. New York: McGraw-Hill Book Co., 1974.

Dearden, John. "The Case Against ROI Control." *Harvard Business Review*, May-June 1969, pp. 124-135.

Ernst & Ernst. *Accounting Under Inflationary Conditions*, 1976. Retrieval No. 38474.

Financial Accounting Standards Board. *Financial Reporting in Units of General Purchasing Power*. Exposure Draft. Stamford, Conn.: FASB, 1974.

_____. *Statement of Financial Accounting Standards No. 8*. "Accounting for the Translation of Foreign Currency Transactions and Foreign Currency Financial Statements," October 1975.

_____. *Statement of Financial Accounting Standards No. 14*. "Financial Reporting for Segments of a Business Enterprise," December 1976.

_____. *Statement of Financial Accounting Standards No. 21*. "Suspension of the Reporting of Earnings per Share and Segment Information by Non-public Enterprises," 1968.

Friedman, Milton. "Monetary Correction." *Essays on Inflation and Indexation*. Washington, D.C.: American Enterprise Institute for Public Policy Research, 1974.

Gilpin, Robert. *U.S. Power and the Multinational Corporation*. New York: Basic Books, 1975.

Hansen, Roger D., et al. *The U.S. and World Development: Agenda for Action*. New York: Praeger Publishers for the Overseas Development Council, 1976.

Inflation Accounting: Report of the Inflation Accounting Committee. F.E.P. Sandilands, chairman. London: Her Majesty's Stationery Office, September 1975.

Journal of Contemporary Business. Boundaries and Big Business: The Regulation of Multinational Corporations. Vol. 6, No. 4, Autumn 1977.

Kolde, Endel J. *International Business Enterprise*, 2nd ed. Englewood Cliffs, N.J.: Prentice-Hall, Inc., 1973.

Kugel, Yerachmiel, and Gruenberg, Gladys W. *International Payoffs*. Lexington, Mass.: Lexington Books, D.C. Heath and Co., 1977.

Leontief, Wassily. "What an Economic Planning Board Should Do." *Challenge*, July-August 1974, pp. 35-40.

_____. *National Economic Planning*. Second Annual Distinguished Guest Lecture Program. Saint Louis: Saint Louis University School of Business and Administration, April 23, 1976.

Metcalf, Senator Lee. "The Accounting Establishment: A Staff Study." Subcommittee on Reports, Accounting and Management of the Committee on Government Operations, United States Senate, 94th Congress, 2d Session, December 1976.

Moore, Michael L., and Bagley, Ronald N. *Studies in Federal Taxation No. 6:* "U.S. Tax Aspects of Doing Business Abroad." New York: American Institute of Certified Public Accountants, 1978.

Nader, Ralph; Green, Mark; and Seligman, Joel. *Taming the Giant Corporation*. New York: W.W. Norton & Co., 1976.

National Association of Accountants. *Management Accounting for Multinational Corporations*, Vols. I and II. New York: 1974.

Negandhi, Anant R., and Prasad, S. Benjamin. *The Frightening Angels: A Study of U.S. Multinationals in Developing Nations.* Kent, Ohio: Kent State University Press, 1975.

Perlmutter, Howard V. "The Tortuous Evolution of the Multinational Corporation." *Columbia Journal of World Business,* January-February 1969, pp. 9-18.

Pyhrr, Peter A. "Zero-Base Budgeting." *Harvard Business Review,* November-December 1970, pp. 111-121.

Price Waterhouse International. *A Survey in 46 Countries: Accounting Principles and Reporting Practices.* Canada, 1975.

_____. *Information Guides.* Series, "Doing Business in . . . " (all major foreign countries).

Robbins, Sidney M., and Stobaugh, Robert B. "The Bent Measuring Stick for Foreign Subsidiaries." *Harvard Business Review,* September-October 1973, pp. 80-88.

Savoie, Leonard M. "Price Level Accounting, Practical Politics, and Tax Relief." *Management Accounting,* January 1977, pp. 15-18.

Schiff, Michael. "Depreciation Short Fall: Fact or Fiction?" *Journal of Accountancy,* March 1977, pp. 40-42.

Touche Ross & Co. *Economic Reality in Financial Reporting.* New York, 1976.

Vernon, Raymond. *Sovereignty At Bay.* New York: Basic Books, 1971.

Vancil, Richard F. "What Kind of Management Control Do You Need?" *Harvard Business Review,* March-April 1973, pp. 75-86.

Watt, George C.; Hammer, Richard H.; and Burge, Marianne. *Accounting for the Multinational Corporation.* New York: Financial Executives Research Foundation, 1977.

Wilkins, Mira. *The Emergence of Multinational Enterprise.* Cambridge, Mass.: Harvard University Press, 1970.

Zimmerman, V.K. (ed.). *The Multinational Corporation: Accounting and Social Implications.* Urbana, Ill.: Center for International Education and Research in Accounting, Department of Accountancy, University of Illinois, 1977.

Index

accountancy, profession of, 71, 265; peer reviews of, 74-75

Accountants International Study Group (AISG), 219-220

accounting, constraints of, 99-100; genesis of, 267-268; as language of business, 99

accounting information system, 200-201, 204

Accounting Principles Board (AICPA), *Opinion No. 6*, 150, 161n; *Opinion No. 10*, 215, 225n; *Opinion No. 16*, 225n; *Opinion No. 18*, 215, 225n; *Statement No. 3*, 104, 107, 121n, 162

Accounti Research Bulletins (AICPA), *No. 33*, 102; *No. 43*, 103, 161n, 214, 225n; *No. 51*, 214-215, 219, 225n

Accounting Research Studies (AICPA), *No. 6*, 103-104, 121n, 162; *No. 12*, 161n

Accounting Series Releases (SEC), *No. 190*, 114, 119, 122n; *No. 236*, 232; *No. 244*, 239. *See also* Securities and Exchange Commission

Accounting Standards Committee (UK), inflation accounting recommendations of, 107

Accounting Standards Steering Committee (UK), composition of, 107; *Exposure Draft No. 8*, 107; *Exposure Draft No. 18*, 107; *Provisional Statement of Standard Accounting Practice No. 7*, 107

accounting systems: normative, 99, 101, 108, 120, 148, 159; orientations of, 13-15; situational, 99, 148, 159, 163; transnational networks, 17

Adela Investment Company, 53

affiliates, foreign: disclosure of, 221; 236; spawning of, 9, 10, 213. *See also* multinational enterprises

agent commissions: concealment of, 65; criteria of, 65, 70; disclosure of, 66, 70. *See also* bribes; illegal payments

Ameiss, Albert P., 225n

American Accounting Association, committee reports of, 9, 54-55, 57n, 102, 141n, 163-164, 190, 197n, 210n

American Institute of Accountants, 102

American Institute of Certified Public Accountants (AICPA), 11, 67, 72, 75, 102-104

Andersen, Arthur, and Company, 121n, 122n, 163, 267; and concern for individual, 98n

Anthony, Robert N., planning and control

systems, 205, 210n; steady-state company, 118, 122n

anti-planners, 204. *See also* systems

anti-trust legislation, 212; in the European Economic Community, 38, 40n; and foreign investment, 213; inadequacies of, 32; trivial fines of, 67. *See also* Sherman Anti-Trust Act

Arabian-American Oil Company, 3

Argentina, inflation accounting, 105

arm's-length criteria, 28, 169-171; definition of, 178n. *See also* transfer prices

Arrow, Kenneth, 96, 98n

assets, measurement bases, 109

audit costs, and inflation accounting, 113

Australia, inflation accounting, 105

bank transfers, 136-137

Barrett, M. Edgar, 178n

Biegler, John C. (Price Waterhouse & Co.), 74

bills of exchange, 136

Black, Eli M. (United Fruit), 25, 61

black market, in currencies, 135, 138

Boeing Aircraft Company, 65

border taxes, 27, 243; and transfer prices, 175, 244; and value-added taxes, 244

Brazil, indexation methods, 105; inflation accounting, 105

Bretton Woods Agreement. *See* International Monetary Fund

bribes, and agent commissions, 65, 69; concealment of, 75; definition of, 59, 63; illegality of, 69-71; materiality of, 76; taxation of, 252; U.S. multinational enterprises, 27, 37. *See also* extortion

Brown, Richard, 141n, 143, 161n

budgets, and standard costs, 192; as flexible evaluators, 192-193; computerization of, 202; tailored, 191. *See also* performance evaluations

Bureau of Economic Analysis, 236

business cominbations, 211-212

business cycles, 89

business information system, 204-205. *See also* information systems

business segment, 227, 230; dominant, 235. *See also* segmented reporting

Canada, consolidation practices, 219-220, 224; inflation accounting, 105

capital: concepts of, 44; "crunch," 35; definition of, 44; dynamic cycle of, 44

About the Author

Elwood L. Miller is a CPA and associate professor of accounting at Saint Louis University. His previous academic background includes positions as college dean and director, as well as chairman of a department of business administration. His business experience involved more than a decade of management in international operations, built upon a similar period of experience as a corporate officer and in public and commercial accounting.